PRAISE

The Kitchen Whisperers

"Kalins digs deep into memories and sessions with internationally known chefs (e.g., the late Marcella Hazan) to uncover the answers to 'what, exactly, are the secrets of great kitchen work?' . . . Beautifully written, thoughtful content that mirrors our current mindfulness movement."

—*Booklist* (starred review)

"Kalins . . . reflects on the cooks and chefs whose 'generous lessons' enriched her love of food in this meditative memoir. . . . While each memory is a pleasure to savor, what resonates most is the how these stories will inspire readers to take stock and appreciate their own whisperers. Food lovers will want to devour this one slowly."

—*Publishers Weekly*

"Well-written. . . . Kalins has written a timeless culinary memoir that allows readers to experience her life in food. Recommended for foodies and cooks of all ages."

—*Library Journal*

"[Kalins] organizes eloquent chapters around the kitchen lessons she's learned from family members, chefs, gardeners, and cookbook luminaries such as the late Marcella Hazan. . . . [Her] wisdom-sharing meets her aims: a quarter of the way into the book I'm suddenly staring into my kitchen, thinking about which dishes I can make from muscle memory . . . and from whom I want to learn next."

—Bill Addison, *Los Angeles Times*

"I don't remember a book that has left me feeling quite so moved and warm and just cheerful and optimistic about the human condition. . . . There is so much richness in this book. . . . [It's] brought me so much joy."

—Liel Leibovitz, Tablet Magazine, *Unorthodox* podcast

"Dorothy Kalins—a well-known figure in the publishing world, particularly on the subject of food—has made it her life's work to help writers connect with deeper truths."

—John Kessler, *Atlanta Journal-Constitution*

"*The Kitchen Whisperers* is a personal chronicle of culinary wisdom collected over a lifetime of eating, cooking, and making friends over food. Dorothy's voice is both evocative and intimate; the stories extraordinary; the lessons they teach us are ones any home cook might put to use. This book reminds us what food lovers already know—that food memories are the most powerful memories."

—Claire Saffitz, author, *Dessert Person*

"Reading *The Kitchen Whisperers*, one can't escape Dorothy Kalins's profoundly intimate love of food. All Kalins's memories are smelled and tasted. Were we all lucky enough to have such richly scented scenes in our personal pasts, we would never be alone."

—Tamar Adler, author, *An Everlasting Meal*

"We'd kill to have such voices in our heads!"

—Sylvie Bigar, author, *Cassoulet Confessions*

THE KITCHEN WHISPERERS

*Cooking with the
Wisdom of Our Friends*

DOROTHY KALINS

wm

WILLIAM MORROW
An Imprint of HarperCollins*Publishers*

A hardcover edition of this book was published in 2021 by William Morrow, an imprint of HarperCollins Publishers.

FIRST WILLIAM MORROW PAPERBACK EDITION PUBLISHED 2022.

DESIGNED BY BONNI LEON-BERMAN

Library of Congress Cataloging-in-Publication Data

Names: Kalins, Dorothy, author.
Title: The kitchen whisperers : cooking with the wisdom of our friends / Dorothy Kalins.
Description: First edition. | New York, NY : William Morrow, [2021] | Includes bibliographical references. | Summary: "A beautifully written tribute to the people who teach us to cook and guide our hands in the kitchen, by the founding editor of *Saveur*" —Provided by publisher.
Identifiers: LCCN 2021012939 | ISBN 9780063001640 | ISBN 9780063001664 (ebook)
Subjects: LCSH: Cooking. | LCGFT: Cookbooks.
Classification: LCC TX714 .K3553 2021 | DDC 641.3—dc2 3
LC record available at https://lccn.loc.gov/2021012939

ISBN 978-0-06-300165-7

22 23 24 25 26 LSC 10 9 8 7 6 5 4 3 2 1

For Roger,

— ❧ —

who sees it all

CONTENTS

———— ❧ ————

FOREWORD

———— ❧ ————

FOR ME, FOOD—AND COOKING FOR OTHERS—is almost indistinguishable from love. Like Dorothy, I have many cherished voices in my head when I cook, each one coaxing me to cook so many different things in so many different ways. And like her, I have almost *no* voice that's telling me how to bake a cake. (I'm fortunate to have a wife and a daughter who are so good at dessert, they've given me a hall pass from confronting my own reluctance to cook with exactitude.) So, while I'm not obsessing about exactitude, I do think a lot about how to pinpoint flavor. There are so many voices. I'll try to name a bunch of them.

I grew up cooking with my dad quite a bit, on the outside grill, and at the stove, too. From early on—I was five, six, seven—the love of cooking was a bond between us. The first thing he taught me to make was ratatouille; we named our miniature French poodle after that dish. On weekends, we'd make Eggs Saturday: scrambled eggs with crispy crumbled bacon on top. Or we'd make Swiss Eggs: cook bacon, drain off almost all the fat, put the bacon back in the pan, crack a bunch of eggs on top, season with salt and pepper, blanket it with Swiss cheese and paprika, and put the lid on just until the cheese melts and the yolks are still soft and runny. The food wasn't always great, but it was fun. And it was always more about who I was with than what we were making.

Without question, my dad is in my head, still.

As soon as I got my driver's license, I'd drive to the house of our cherished housekeeper, Mary Smith, for Saturday afternoon lessons in the fried chicken, macaroni and cheese, and collard greens she'd grown up with in Mississippi. As a junior in high school, I was the only male in home ec class. I loved the girl-boy ratio for sure, but I really loved the teacher, Mrs. Holecamp. I brought home and cooked every recipe she taught us, like pizza and tacos from scratch.

Eventually I wanted to turn my love of cooking into doing it the right way. In college, thanks to my dad's travel business, airfare was incredibly cheap, so I could go to Italy for a long weekend. I went every chance I got and learned from every meal I had.

When I moved to New York at age twenty-two, I wanted to keep this cooking thing going. I signed up for cooking classes from an amazing woman, an Egyptian-born Jew named Andrée Abramoff. She had a sweet little restaurant called Andrée's Mediterranean in a town house on East 74th Street. I learned to make kibbe her way, and bouillabaisse, too. And to this day, I almost always make Andrée's turkey for Thanksgiving. She didn't brine it; she'd layer a pound of bacon strips on top of the bird. The bacon-draped bird goes into a really hot oven (450°F to 500°F) for half an hour. I remove the bacon strips (setting them aside for tomorrow's turkey sandwiches) and lower the temperature to 375°F. The bacon creates a tasty sear, sealing in the juices. Meanwhile, every 15 minutes I baste the bird with the bacon drippings. It's antithetical to conventional turkey methods and takes a lot less time. And it's so good.

My love of barbecue led me to cook with some of America's best pitmasters, whose voices I still have my head. Low and slow, with plenty of stories while cooking. I have Roman cooks in my head. I have Joyce Goldstein, the San Francisco chef and cookbook author in my head, I have the French chefs I worked with in Bordeaux in my head. And Ruthie Rogers from London's River Café speaks to me constantly. I've come to realize that everybody who cooks with other people has their own Kitchen Whisperers.

From the very early 1990s to about 2010, I was keenly interested in experiencing as many Michelin-starred restaurants as I could. It's kind of where the puck was for fine dining during that era. But since then, my taste in restaurants and my taste in cooking has just gotten simpler and simpler. There's a sensibility among people who are at home in a great trattoria, in a great bistro. A large part of my inspiration for Gramercy Tavern, which opened in 1994, were the two-star restaurants in the French and Italian countryside, not the urban three-star restaurants. These places weren't trying to be fancy. They were warm. Their food was way better than average.

I was never interested in choosing between eight kinds of bottled water or five kinds of butter. But then I stopped being interested in *all of that*. For the last ten or twelve years, I've found that I just want to have a great bowl of pasta, or a great roadside version of something really good—burger, ribs, pulled pork, or breakfast tacos. My wife, Audrey, and I went to Santa Fe in 1991 when David Tanis was cooking at Café Escalera and liked it so much we went back for more the very next night. We never do that when traveling! What David's food has (and Dorothy's, too) is the confidence to season pristine ingredients and leave everything else off the plate.

Daniel Humm, of Eleven Madison Park, is as a talented a chef as any I've ever had the privilege of working with, but

I do not have his voice in my head when I cook. I don't even know how he pulls off his technique. I love experiencing his food, but his fried chicken is the only thing I can imagine cooking. It's going-out food, and when I cook, I want you to feel like you are coming home.

I've never cooked a meal where I tried to impress anybody. Two Kitchen Whisperers who really are in my head are Michael Romano, the defining chef of my first restaurant, Union Square Cafe, and Michael Anthony of Gramercy Tavern. Michael Romano has perfect pitch as a taster and chef, and Mike Anthony taught me all about layering flavors. His cooking does not require tweezers or showing off. It one hundred percent succeeds at blurring the lines between going out and coming home.

The minute I walk into Dorothy's kitchen for one of the many dinners we've shared over the years, I know the amount of effort that went into what she's prepared; yet she doesn't let us see any of that. Not only have I had the privilege of sitting down at her table, but I believe I could probably remember every single dish I've ever had there. It starts with comfort and love. What she lets us see and feel is her joy of preparing a meal for us.

I know there's going to be a salad, and I know it is going to be great for what's *not* in it. She makes sure that every ingredient on the plate is so good that you wouldn't *want* to add more. She cares about each lettuce leaf, judiciously dressed, and a beautiful presentation. Her salad takes me to Chez Panisse and to Chez L'Ami Louis in Paris. It's just a bowl of salad, but it is damned good!

What she lets us see and feel is the experience; whatever she happens to be interested in at the time: Morocco in one meal. France, California, Spain. The through line besides the generosity and love that went into it, is that ineffable thing that I love so much: "I went out and I came home." Dorothy is one of my Kitchen Whisperers, and I'm moved by how much we still keep learning from each other.

—Danny Meyer

INTRODUCTION

———— ✦ ————

Flour, Butter, Salt & Words

ALONE IN THE KITCHEN? IMPOSSIBLE! My kitchen is noisy with chatter. Swirling around me in that room are voices from other kitchens, other lives, nudging me, reminding me, making me smile. It's how I became a cook, how most of us do— hearing the words of a mama or a grandpa, a wise writer or a savvy friend, remembering their wisdom, and repeating their moves. These messages from the past help make us the cooks we become.

People who do not cook, or who are uneasy doing it, assume that good cooks go into the kitchen and just whip something up. They become anxious when this kind of magical transformation of disparate ingredients into a meal does not happen for them automatically in their own kitchens. What they do not know is how far ahead the cooking process begins in your mind. How constantly it's recalibrated with every decision. And how much you just make up as you go along, trying to sniff out the next move, sense where each ingredient wants to go. I wake up worrying where my next meal is coming from. My first thought: "Is this a market day?" (Union Square Greenmarket: small on Mondays, progressively larger on

Wednesdays, Fridays, and Saturdays. Wednesday means I get to walk to the market opposite the United Nations, nearby.) I picture what's in the refrigerator: In my mind I smell the cantaloupe I bought yesterday. Ripe enough? Prepping in my head, I slice its cool orange flesh, rind on, with a wedge of lime (do we have limes?) and a branch of mint (if I'm lucky). Any good salad greens lurking in the veg bins? A nubbin of fresh ginger? Are those shiitakes I bought last week still good? Anything to work with from dinner last night? Or the night before? What stock's in the freezer? Such is my version of a morning practice; as a routine, it is hardly meditation. It's neither calming nor enlightening. Only necessary.

Where, then, do our cooking ideas even come from? From those crazy-fast videos where the ingredients are preprepped and premeasured into glass bowls and propelled together at warp speed by two disembodied hands? I seriously do not think so, although some magazine test kitchens are producing video cooking lessons that hit home more effectively than their pages do. Enterprising internet chefs (and cooks) are reaching folks once reluctant to enter a kitchen. I've produced dozens of cookbooks—good ones, award winners—and I know we can learn some lasting kitchen moves from books like these, propelled by the riveting stories they tell us and the secrets they share.

But we really learn from vivid experiences of actually cooking that we somehow internalize and eventually come to own. We learn by memory. And by mimicry. We learn by doing. I love reading the user comments about online recipes, say on the NYT Cooking site, that show the gradual process of ownership: "Well, I didn't have the X, so I substituted Y, and then I ran out of Z, but the dish came out great. I'd make it again."

Cooking works when we can see the whole arc of a dish in our heads. When we don't get hung up on the details. As Marcella Hazan, dragging on a Marlboro Light, once told me: "When you start to cook, you have to know where you are going!"

It's different with baking. Baking is scary. Baking is laboratory stuff. Chemistry. I would never attempt to bake *anything* without a recipe. And quite honestly, I would far rather roast a goat than make a pie. Can a person learn baking? I am trying. But I am secretly convinced that I'm lacking some mystical quality—pastry hands?—that keeps me from the perfect piecrust. From any piecrust. Last night, I made a strawberry shortcake, really just a very big biscuit, halved, with piles of fragrant berries for filling and topping, and lots of hand-whipped cream. The dough, my recipe told me, should come together in the bowl "until it looks like coarse meal." And I'm worrying: *Is it coarse meal yet?* I clearly worked the damned thing too much before turning it out on the pan to bake. So instead of a light, crumbly biscuit, I had an unevenly dense, crusty mound. Then I heard Sally Schmitt in my head, warning: "Don't overhandle the dough." She's talking to me from her kitchen at the Apple Farm in the lush Anderson Valley in Philo, California. Sally has pastry hands. I sure wish I'd listened sooner.

Into the same shallow cobalt-blue Clay City Pottery bowl she always uses to make apple clafouti (essentially, fruit in a pancake-like batter), Sally cuts heirloom Pink Pearls, rosy inside, gathered from the organic orchards that roll over the gentle hills just out the door of her sunny kitchen. Sally, who with her late husband, Don, decades before, owned the original French Laundry in Yountville (yes, those signature herb gardens in front were the Schmitts'), slices each small apple in half, then in quarters, and tucks one of those quarters into her palm. She picks up a well-worn paring knife and in one stroke, removes the peel from a pointy end. Then she flips the quarter around and deftly peels it from the other end. "This is the way my mother peeled apples," she says. "I never do it any other way." Nor do I, now.

I GRAB A LEMON TO juice it (to make baba ghanoush) and feel its weight in my hand, solid as a lump of earth. As I roll it on the counter with the gentle pressure of my palm, I realize that I'm unconsciously copying what I've seen Christopher Hirsheimer do a hundred times while panfrying fish or dressing a salad—freeing the juices from the pulp; easing the juice flow. Christopher is my culinary North Star; cooking with her, and watching her, is better than any cooking school.

I learned something different observing Christopher's business partner, Melissa Hamilton, the other half of Canal House (cooks and writers who make books and cook inspired meals at Canal House Station, a renovated nineteenth-century stone train station on the Delaware River in Milford, New Jersey). Melissa is a far better cook than I'll ever be. But it is the soapy exuberance of her after-dinner moves that I recall when I'm staring down a sink full of dirty dishes. Melissa shows me how to take a breath and will myself to enjoy this afterglow of cooking, remembering to lovingly wash the *bottoms* of those pots, because they, too, should look shiny with promise as they hang overhead, as they slide onto the stovetop, ready for their next act. What cookware—and the kitchens it lives in—looks like matters as much as what it cooks.

CAMILLE LEHMAN FOLLOWS ME INTO the cleverly engineered kitchen of her Manhattan high-rise apartment. We've just had dinner in her dining room, which is painted the kind of confident red only her kind of top interior designer can pull off, and I'm in search of milk for my coffee. She opens a carton and *oof!* It smells awful. It's gone bad. For years after that, she'd leave this message on my answering machine: "Come for dinner. We have fresh milk!"

Camille was my parents' friend, and perhaps from the time she gave me a hug and whispered that my hair needed washing (I was nine), I instinctively knew I had much to learn from her. At ten, I was making collages at her instruction, pasting up the various materials she used to design each project. Assembling these swatches of paint and fabric and wallpaper, this carpet square, this sample of furniture finish, and gluing them all to a scrapbook page was my earliest experience of making a magazine page. "Sofa," she'd declare in her delightfully dramatic New York voice. "Never couch!" "Draperies," she'd insist. "Not drapes!" And for the decade-plus that I edited the design magazine *Metropolitan Home*, the words *couch* and *drapes* never darkened our copy.

From Camille I learned that the way food looks is every bit as important as how it tastes. She would serve chubby red strawberries lined up in rows on a white ironstone platter, their jaunty stems and spiky green hats all marching in the same direction, like preschoolers in strawberry costumes on their way to the class play. She gave me one of my kitchen's essential tools: a round apple cutter that, when its blades are pressed on top of the fruit, and you press on its two curvy handles, yields a lotus blossom—eight impeccable slices that fall into a perfect flower, their core intact. Everything makes a picture. Once, she took me to see an apartment she'd designed for clients in a building on Fifth Avenue opposite the Metropolitan Museum of Art. It had an oval dining room. I never pass that building without looking up.

Her chicken salad was always enlivened by fresh grapes; her letters to the grown-up me, on saucy white-rimmed tangerine-colored stationery, are full of cooking:

"I always resented disposing of the carrots I use for poaching chicken," she once wrote. "Don't mind wasting the onions or celery, but those carrots—gorgeous things that they are—look disapprovingly at me as I take them to their final resting place. Sooo, I rescued three large carrots, put them in a blender with a bit of the broth and enough pepper (preferably white so it won't discolor the final gorgeousness), then two large tablespoons of lovely sour cream, and let it rip. Voilà! Puree à la Camille." She would fold a couple of blank sheets of that tangerine paper into her letters, so I could answer her quickly.

Camille taught me, without ever saying it, that it matters, too, how food looks when it's sleeping in the refrigerator. Open hers and there'd be rectangular ribbed-glass containers in architectural stacks: olives and pickles and all manner of leftovers, not only showing beautifully but looking good enough to go right to the table. Cabinets should never be deep enough to get lost in, she believed, designing her shelves narrow so cans and jars could be intentionally displayed, labels facing out. Knife drawers were built shallow for the same reason: you don't want to be fumbling around in a deep drawer full of sharp blades. Camille was never fussy as she connected food with design; she knew instinctively that food tastes better when it looks better, which made the two inseparable for me. Her down-to-earth self invented a way to deal with unruly kitchen-appliance cords by stuffing them in cardboard toilet paper rolls she'd cover with (tasteful) Con-Tact paper. She called them "hoo-has."

KITCHEN TOOLS MATTER, TOO. Not those dopey Instagram gadgets for foodie tricks nobody needs to perform, but ingenious ones, like my treasured plastic pastry scraper from a Paris kitchenware shop, its name and address worn but still visible: *E. DEHILLERIN, 18 rue Coquillière.* I use it every day, never for pastry but as a shovel to gather up every bit of minced onion, diced celery—chopped anything, really—and deliver it to a pan. My son, Lincoln, who was folding origami orchids at age eight and assembling his own IKEA bed at eleven and is now in his twenties, walked into the kitchen as I was finding my way around a new bright-yellow metal lemon squeezer. "Mom, I think you've got the lemon half in wrong. It just looks like it goes pointy side down 'cause that's the way the sieve is shaped. But really you have to turn it the opposite way, cut side down, so that the juice has somewhere to go." Though I doubt this would charm him in any way, Lincoln's somehow in my head when I squeeze a lemon.

Each time I boil fresh corn, I think of Miles Chapin, descended from an impossibly long line of Pilgrims, whose family used a special device—it looks like a horned church

key—to puncture the kernels of an ear of corn just after
it's boiled, all the better to get the butter inside the kernels.
Rather decadent for those Pilgrims, I think, but after hearing
Miles describe eating corn as a child, I always wish I had one
of those scrapers.

Roger, my husband, makes me coffee most mornings.
Though he does not touch the stuff (he's a tea drinker, and
claims the very taste of coffee turns him off), he performs the
moves flawlessly, using venerable kitchen objects—an Aldo
Rossi stainless-steel espresso pot tall as a young medieval castle, which I bought decades ago from the original Alessi store
in Milan, and an old Nissan manual milk frother—that add
layers of meaning to that drink. It is delivered in an oversize
blue-and-cream-striped T.G. Green Cornishware cup and sau-
cer, a gift from the original Habitat store in London. Roger
makes coffee way better than I do, though I think we both
suspect a case of learned helplessness on my part.

When his mom, my beloved mother-in-law, Ray Sherman, left us, there was a gentle scramble to apportion the
belongings from her old Scarsdale house. What I wanted
most were some funky banana leaf–shaped platters and her
worn kitchen utensils, especially a big slotted spoon with a
paint-chipped handle—mint green giving way to buttercup
yellow—that spoke of its use, perhaps in kitchens older than
hers. "The things we cook with matter," I think each time I
reach for that spoon. "History is in my hands." Ray cooked
less in her later years; we would bring our food to her dining table. I do not know if I was wise enough then to realize
what I know now: Beware of thinking these things are solid
and unchangeable. She was the center of a family that was
never the same without her, I reflect as I stir my soup with

her spoon. (Roger made me a photograph of that spoon handle: it's three feet long and hangs in my office.)

SOMETIMES, WHEN PEOPLE ASK WHAT I'm working on, and I tell them what this book is about, I can actually observe their eyes soften with understanding as they immediately connect to their own memories. Sometimes those memories live in our minds, uncooked. Over lunch, my editor, Cassie Jones, immediately fixed on her grandmother's apple pie: "But I never learned to make it from her," she told me. "She did it all by memory, and I didn't write it down. But it was perfect—the crust was always flaky and the apples the exact right amount of doneness (not saucy but not too firm). Always a lattice top, perfectly browned. I miss it!"

Last night at dinner, after I explained this book to my tablemate, she shared a cutting-board moment. "Oh yes!" she said. "I can't stand my ex-brother-in-law, but every time I slice a garlic clove in my kitchen, I remember how he showed me how to smash it, not peel it."

My own cutting board is the locus of received wisdom that swarms like so many thought bubbles overhead: Wait! I stop slicing a fresh garlic clove in midair: Am I supposed to remove the bright-green germ from the center of the clove before I use it or am I expressly *not*? I'm paralyzed, remembering a moment in time when we were all obsessed with green garlic germs, but I lose the punch line. I stop and try to conjure the source of that information. Faintly, I hear the voice of Patricia Wells. But what, exactly, is that journalist and cookbook writer trying to tell me? Somehow, I make the leap to the book she wrote with Joël Robuchon, because *there* was one demanding chef, very likely to obsess over such things as green garlic germs. I find *Simply French* on my bookshelves, and on page 120, under "To Degerm or Not to Degerm," is my answer. When you're using garlic raw, cut out the germ lest it ferment a dish, thus making it indigestible, Wells counsels. In cooking, however, it's fine to leave it in. "When the germ is removed," she elaborates, "it also helps to preserve foods that you might want to keep for several days, such as a tomato sauce, or ratatouille." Well. Good to know!

THIS IS NOT A COOKBOOK; rather, it is a book about cooking, about what—and who—we think about as we cook. I believe that the recipes we remember best, and the moves we make, seemingly automatically, are those that tell familiar stories. Take brisket. I never make brisket without the soundtrack to my clever friend Stevie Pierson's *The Brisket Book* playing in my head. She asks the essential questions: "Whose heart wouldn't melt a little hearing about Aunt Irene's New England brisket recipe, which was passed down to her niece Alice, who gave it to her friend Ellen, who shared it with her nephew John, who let his girlfriend—who had never even eaten a brisket—copy it for her mother so she could help her cook it?"

I often cook the coffee-braised brisket that was a specialty of the chef Mike Solomonov's extraordinary mother, Evelyn. As Mike said in his cookbook *Zahav*: "My grandmother made her brisket with carrots, potatoes, and Heinz Chili Sauce, which gave it a traditional sweet-and-sour flavor. My mother added the coffee—she doesn't remember why, but it's pretty brilliant, actually. Unlike stock, coffee is a braising liquid ready in minutes, and its deep, roasted flavors work really well with beef." The result is unforgettable. I once sustained a not-insignificant brisket-related injury carrying Evelyn's brisket down a steep flight of stairs. As I stumbled, the gravy flew. The ankle turned. The brisket was saved. But when I imagine the ur-brisket, it's no surprise that it's my aunt Gillie's I crave. Her notes, scribbled on lined yellow paper and pasted into my recipe book, actually include the phrase, odd from a golf-playing Long Island lady, "Schmootzie some ketchup on each side." And I do.

Neither my mother nor any of her five sisters was ever called by her given name. Gillie's real name was Esther. (Can you blame her?) Their family name was Gillery. Hence my mother's nickname, Gil, for Gertrude, itself another story. Aunt Gillie always made her exemplary chicken soup and matzo balls, she confided to me, with leeks, never onions, which kept the broth clearer. Once, she took me into her kitchen, opened a cabinet, and, believing she was passing along the secret to a long-held family mystery, pressed into my hand a cylinder of some kind of chicken soup flavor helper I wish I had never seen.

I did not come equipped with the grandmothers-who-cooked that you might expect to find sentimentalized in a book like this. But I have always been lucky enough to find plenty of other grandmothers. And grandfathers. I vividly remember watching a venerable old lady (probably younger than I am now) in Corsica spread out her husband's catch of small sea bream, whole (yes, scaled and gutted), on a large baking pan. Over the fish, she scattered branches of fresh rosemary and thyme, then lemon and orange slices. A high sprinkle of coarse salt. Bay leaves. Many of them. Garlic cloves. Then she poured a gentle stream of olive oil right from a tin over the pan and slid it into the oven. You could just *do* that? I marveled. Without a recipe! This was nonchalance. This was mastery. This was cooking. I may not remember that woman's name, but I'll never forget her fish.

I'm hunched over a sink in a tiny French kitchen in the otherwise undistinguished but oddly rhyming town of Tignieu-Jameyzieu, on the outskirts of the outskirts of Lyon, in a house you enter through the vegetable garden. As she watches me wash the greens she's just picked, Émilienne Vignon, my step-daughter Sandrine's grandmother Mamie Mimi, shyly advises: "Il faut laver la salade à trois eaux," making sure I know that those leaves must be rinsed three times to rid them of dirt. Yes, I think of Mamie Mimi when I wash my greens. Nor have I forgotten the way she would brown chicken livers, then press them through a strainer to enhance her salad dressing—mixing them right into her Dijon mustard vinaigrette with a little red wine vinegar and a bit of chopped shallot.

LEARNING BY WATCHING OTHER PEOPLE cook can sometimes be more effective than words. When I walked into the kitchen of the brilliant color field painter Hector Leonardi—one of the most elegant cooks I've known, but nowhere near the fussiest—and found him boiling just-shucked pea pods in water for what would be the broth for his fresh green pea risotto, I was so excited. *Of course* you would use those pods that way. Anything for a bit more pea flavor. Just like the exquisite paintings Hector makes in his studio in a converted potato barn in Bridgehampton (he uses "light as subject matter, color as the thinking agent," a critic once wrote), Hector's food manages to be vividly flavorful and sensitively presented at the same time.

For a few seasons, I tried growing peas in my Long Island garden, remembering to order the seeds—a satisfyingly heavy half-pound packet of Maxigolts, the very definition of hope— early from Johnny's in Albion, Maine. A still-vivid memory has three-year-old Lincoln, in a bright-yellow slicker and little rubber boots, poking those peas into the ground, then running out to check on them every fifteen minutes—expecting them to grow to full size by the next day. But although peas like cool weather, the early spring in my garden is often too cool and too wet. So I planted the seeds and watched them . . . do nothing. When June comes, and for the one week I can find fresh peas at the farmers' market, I always make risotto the way Hector does, using the pea pod–infused water to fatten the rice.

Shakshuka is made of stories. The first time I had that now-ubiquitous Israeli breakfast dish (so dead simple—eggs poached in a pan of veggies—it's hard to believe it once seemed so "other") was an early morning in Joan Nathan's kitchen in Washington, DC. I'd spent the night at her house after we'd taken a long walk around the Mall, past the Lincoln and Vietnam Memorials, around the newly installed pink-granite Mountain of Despair to confront the startlingly rough-hewn Stone of Hope from which the memorial sculpture of Martin Luther King Jr. is forever in the process of emerging. How Dr. King connects with the woman known as the doyenne of Jewish cooking, and thus my revealer of North African–born shakshuka, escapes me, but such incongruous connections make vivid food memories. My surprise was to watch Joan produce shakshuka by opening a 28-ounce can of whole stewed tomatoes and dumping them, along with half a dozen roasted peppers and onions and a shower of cumin and sweet paprika, into the largest frying pan she had and cooking them up on the stovetop. Then she cracked maybe eight eggs, separately, right into that pan and shoved the whole thing into the oven. "So *that's* all there is to the famous shakshuka," I thought.

It is curious the way we process new information and incorporate it into our lives; transforming it from something other to something owned. I love to observe the way a new dish or an unfamiliar ingredient enters our cooking mind, settles, and makes a place for itself, until it seems, eventually, as if it has always lived there. It's a distinct process you can trace. Tagging along at the tail end of Roger's film shoot for his documentary *In Search of Israeli Cuisine*, I watched the great chef/showman Erez Komarovsky (who, himself, pretty much brought exceptional bread to Israel) in his beautifully crafted house in the Upper Galilee, just eight hundred meters from the Lebanese border. His cooking is pure theater, all gestures—chopping up hot green peppers and gleefully listening for their sizzle in a deep pan of olive oil; quartering lots and lots of impossibly ripe red tomatoes; explaining that while the origins of the dish may be North African, shakshuka has become an Israeli breakfast staple: "Crude, hot, and lots of olive oil."

In his Philadelphia restaurant, I watch Mike Solomonov break sixteen large eggs into a welcoming bed of peppers and tomatoes scattered with paprika, cumin, and coriander in an enormous Lodge cast-iron skillet for a photo shoot for *Zahav*.

He brings that skillet to the table for his business partner, Steven Cook, and their families—I can still picture Steve and Shira's twins then so little they had to be spoon-fed on their parents' laps, Mike and his son David in a jubilant high five. Once the idea of shakshuka takes hold, I discover that you can poach eggs in almost anything. The Tel Aviv–based American cook Adeena Sussman has an admirable recipe for green shakshuka in her book *Sababa*. She turns a panful of spinach, kale, and other leaves creamy by adding a little half-and-half and dropping eggs into that soft greenness. In their book *Shuk*, the dynamic duo of the New York–based chef Einat Admony and the Israeli food writer Janna Gur call their shakshuka "Cinderella in a Skillet," poaching one version of the eggs in charred eggplant, another in . . . preserved lemon and coconut.

Back at my home stove, I make shakshuka in my biggest cast-iron skillet, sometimes with chard and sometimes with fresh tomatoes (or canned whole outta season) or roasted red peppers, the panful of eggs sprinkled with flakes of sun-dried tomato and red pepper I've been hoarding from an ancient Israeli spice shop. Dishes as iconic as these evoke a rich chorus of voices. But you always remember your first time.

WEEKS BEFORE IT'S MY TURN to cook the annual dinner that rotates among four couples—a holiday tradition we've celebrated for decades—the restaurateur Danny Meyer is in my head as I shop. I've never known anyone as sensitive to or enthusiastic about ingredients as he is, so I always try extra hard (without looking like I've tried hard, of course) to surprise and amuse him. Seeing his eyes light up is its own delicious reward. He'll hover over the green olives I've marinated with rosemary and orange peels, running through a list of varieties. ("Cerignola? Castelvetrano?" "Nope. Old-fashioned jarred Manzanillas work best.") He'll marvel over the fat white beans I serve with steamed clams. ("Gigantes?" "Close. Fabadas from Asturias.") He'll ask to see the actual jar of the amba—the pickled mango preserve—I spoon over grilled eggplant. He just can't help it. Danny was born that way. He told me this: "As a boy, I was embarrassed that I knew my friends' families by the brand of ketchup they used: Heinz, Hunt's, Brooks. Same for mayo (Hellmann's vs Miracle Whip)."

SOMETIMES, ALONE IN MY KITCHEN, I can conjure the bubbly, slightly naughty, always laughing voice of my girlhood friend Sheila Lukins, half of the cooking/writing duo, with Julee Rosso, that was the Silver Palate. And I can promise you that chicken Marbella was the farthest thing from Sheila's mind in high school in Westport, Connecticut; that girl was more likely hell-bent on figuring out how to scramble out her bedroom window after dark to meet some cute boy at Compo Beach. We sat next to each other in art class, where she perfected the charming drawing style that would enliven the pages of millions of copies of Silver Palate cookbooks.

Once, years later, when I was to introduce her as a speaker at a magazine industry dinner, we both showed up in the same dress. And it was not just any dress. This was a Calvin Klein number, navy-blue silk patterned with unfortunate big pink peonies. (What were we thinking?) Since I'm more than two heads taller than Sheila, when we stood next to each other, we looked like a really bad sight gag. I tried to save it by telling the audience that the last time Sheila and I wore the same clothes was as cheerleaders at Long Lots Junior High School. Except, as our great friend Betsey Buddy reminded me, for the year that we three made matching lavender-and-white gingham aprons in home ec and learned how to stuff green peppers with canned corn.

When Sheila cooked a spectacular dinner as a guest chef to celebrate the tenth anniversary of An American Place, Larry Forgione's esteemed New York restaurant, I went back to the kitchen to ask her about the velvety sorrel soup she'd just served. "Darling," she said, looking up at me with those mischievously sparkling eyes, "there's nothing you can't make better with a ton of butter, plenty of parsley, and loads of salt!" Proving her point, the original recipe for sorrel soup in *The Silver Palate Cookbook* called for one stick of butter, but in the 25th Anniversary Edition, the recipe calls for two sticks!

POACHING A CHICKEN, FAT AND ORGANIC, in a generous pot of water loaded with aromatics and vegetables—carrots and parsnips, leeks, celery leaves—plus bay leaves, parsley (stems, too), and whatever other herbs I can get my hands on, letting the broth barely burble for hours, watching the drama build . . . that's my kind of kitchen movie, slow and sweet-smelling. Slicing the chicken, still warm and silky from its bath, is the only time I like white meat.

Chicken sends me back to Helen Feingold, the first (and only) food stylist I ever worked with. That lovely lady taught a whole staff of design editors at *Metropolitan Home* about food and gave us permission to ask about what we did not know, helping our curiosity drive the food coverage for a whole generation of new cooks. Once, after a long day's shoot involving chicken, I asked Helen to name her favorite part to eat. She immediately dove into the remains of that roasted bird and came up with the plastic-like cartilage on the breastbone. "It's called the keel," she said. After that, I always search out the keel, too. I find it reassuring.

GUMBO, THE FOOD HISTORIAN Jessica B. Harris tells us, is the product of a "Creole . . . cuisine that is recognizable even when its origin is not." But I can easily trace the origins of my gumbo. That defining soupy stew of southern Louisiana was patiently taught to me over many years by a gifted chef with whom I've produced four books but whose star has fallen so far that I cannot even print his name. Gumbo is, for me, now a saddened dish, but in this way it is perhaps not so far from the experience of the many generations of Creoles and Cajuns who have cooked it—sometimes in celebration, sometimes in sorrow, but sometimes, too, as bare sustenance. That onetime sunshine man taught me how to make a roux with the reverence he always showed his forebears, starting by rendering chicken or duck fat in a deep pot, then whisking in the flour constantly ("for about as long as it takes to finish two-long neck beers," the Louisiana cook Marcelle Bienvenu once put it to me). Not until the roux has achieved a deep chocolate color can the chopped onions be added, their bubbling glossiness as they caramelize an ebullient reward for the cook's patience and a visible link to the past. Then come

the other ingredients—bell peppers, andouille sausage, tomatoes, celery, garlic—and duck or chicken or shrimp (or just
greens, as in gumbo z'herbes), and sometimes the excellent
smoked pork andouille sausage I still order from Jacob's in La-
Place, Louisiana. After that, quite late in the cooking, comes
the okra (and only the smallest pods, I've been taught), and a
shot of Worcestershire sauce. Filé (powdered sassafras leaves)
is sprinkled on only at the table, and only if there's no okra. I
can still hear the emotion in his voice as that chef explained,
"We make gumbo with what we have. With the tomatoes we
put up, with the peppers we grow, with the ducks we shoot at
daybreak on the bayou, the quail from the cornfields, the fish
from the gulf, or the shrimp our neighbors catch." Only then
do the layers of growing and hunting and fishing and curing
come together in one pot. We can learn, I realize, from people
we no longer want to think about. I find gumbo irresistible
and make it still, its flavors bittersweet.

ONE MORNING AFTER A PROFESSIONAL cook had made a dinner
in my kitchen, I found a jar of Better Than Bouillon in my
fridge. I certainly had not put it there! I wouldn't even *think
about* not making my stock from scratch—an hours' long process of boiling the bones (sometimes roasting them first); then
adding the veg; then painstakingly ladling the contents into
a strainer balanced over a plastic quart container; then flinging away the spent fuel, inevitably dribbling a path across the
kitchen floor; then lugging out the resulting wet bag of garbage. Could this jarred stuff be any good? I wondered. And is
it even okay to use it? *Well, she uses it, and she's a really good*

cook! I thought. Similarly, once, as I stashed some white wine in the fridge of a friend who's an accomplished Italian cook, I came upon a plastic container of grated Parmigiano cheese. At first shocked, then curious, I again reasoned: If *he* uses pre-grated Parm, I guess I can, too.

Such thinking led me to invent the Theory of Implied Endorsement. It goes like this: If a known good cook takes a shortcut—well, not a shortcut, exactly, because that's too much like cheating and pretty soon you're mainlining instant ramen, so let's call it a workaround, an easier way to get to the same place—then I can do it, too.

No theory works without proven examples from unimpeachable sources. As a writer for *New York* magazine, I would breathlessly race the hand-typed pages of my latest story up four flights of stairs to the magazine's offices on the top floor of the brownstone where the great graphic designer and *New York* cofounder Milton Glaser would years later paint "Art Is Work" over the front door. If I was lucky, I'd get to go to lunch with Milton, a man of admirable culinary sensibility (he'd created The Underground Gourmet, a column reviewing the kind of inexpensive local restaurants that make New York New York). I once asked Milton what he cooked for dinner on a typical weekday night. Without hesitation, he answered, "Pasta with Rao's tomato sauce," citing the sauce bottled by the tiny, impossible-to-get-into East Harlem red sauce restaurant. And from that moment on, Rao's sauces found a permanent place in my pantry.

Maya Kaimal was a trusted photography editor at *Saveur.* She'd written two Indian cookbooks before we sent her back to Tamil Nadu, at the tip of South India, where her father's family still lived, to write a memorable story. Small wonder then that in her post-magazine career, Maya launched a line of jarred Indian sauces so flavorful as to become staples in the best cooks' kitchens. So, when I make Indian-inspired vegetables and rice, sometimes I start the sauce with the *pop pop pop* of whole coriander and mustard and cumin seeds in hot oil. But probably more often, I'll open a jar of one of Maya's Simmer Sauces, like Tikka Masala or Spicy Vindaloo, and spoon some into a pan of sautéed vegetables and rice. No guilt.

I remember Floyd Cardoz sliding into my booth downstairs at Tabla, his warm, puppy-brown eyes amused at my squeals over his chaat, a crunchy appetizer of crisp diced apples and green chickpeas (maybe there were peanuts) topped with a sprinkle of the toasty bits called sev—wiry fried chickpea noodles. "*Chaat* is the Indian word for street snacks," he explained excitedly. "The name comes from *chaatna*, which means 'to lick.' Chaat is as common as hot dogs, but the ingredients are way more interesting. Anything can be a chaat, as long as it's chopped and it's crunchy. Chaat masala, a mix of Indian spices including amchoor—the mango powder—black salt, cumin, cloves, and coriander," Floyd confided, "is the only premade spice mix I ever use." High bar, I think, recalling the display of exotic fragrances that required an entire room upstairs at Tabla. *Chaat masala.* I hold on to those words as keys to Indian flavor. With chaat masala, I discover, anything can be a salad, heaven to a salty/crunchy girl. When I don't find Floyd's favorite MDH brand, I use Kalustyan's house-made chaat masala mix, soaking and boiling up dried green chickpeas, stirring in diced apples and tamarind chutney, and scattering a snowfall of sev (which comes in a bag like potato chips) on top. Chaat masala is only the first of the many things I miss about Floyd Cardoz, a shocking early COVID victim.

I discovered as I wrote this that Floyd's wife, Barkha, has developed a trio of Floyd's favorite spice mixes with Burlap & Barrel. Of course I ordered them: the everyday goan masala; Floyd's secret garam masala, his favorite to bloom with ghee; and Kashmiri masala, a northern mix Floyd perfected. Just looking at those three spice jars on my shelf is comforting.

SYLVIE BIGAR, A SWISS FRENCH journalist and cook (she cowrote Daniel Boulud's lush *Daniel* and is now at work on a memoir called *Cassoulet Confessions*), invited Roger and me into her big open New York kitchen for . . . cassoulet. Now, this was exciting. But when we arrived and she excitedly told us, "I made this from D'Artagnan's cassoulet kit," I had a momentary pang. Our quintessential *Saveur* story was to go to the place where the food was born; in the case of cassoulet, it was Castelnaudary, to learn the roots of that venerable southwestern French stew. I thought of our friend Michael, who would revel in shooting the very ducks and stuffing his own sausage for the cassoulet he would make for us.

But then I conjured the radiant French face of Ariane Daguin, cofounder of D'Artagnan. Who would not want this daughter of André Daguin, the most famous chef in Gascony, and herself an extraordinarily exigent food purveyor, to confit your duck legs, to perfume your artisanal sausage with Armagnac, to prepare your ventrèche (pork belly), to cook down your duck and veal demi-glace, and to send along a bag of just the right Tarbais beans: flat, white, and local. "Cassoulet," Ariane says, "is less a recipe than a way to argue between villages." Genius, that Sylvie, I decided. Can't wait to make it myself.

TO FURTHER TEST MY Theory of Implied Endorsement, I reached out to some of my trusty journo/cook friends who'd served with me for years on the James Beard Journalism Committee. The restaurant critic and writer John Kessler immediately responded: "I've found so many uses for Philadelphia cream cheese. It's so good in pan sauces—*monter au* cream cheese—particularly with pork chops. It's also the key ingredient in my pressure-cooker mac and cheese, stirred into the penne and cooking water with grated cheddar. These days my favorite, albeit most obscure, shortcut is buying awase miso, which has the dashi already in it. Dilute, garnish, and you have miso soup. Also the little shaker of MSG by the side of the range . . ."

Francis Lam, the writer, radio personality, and book editor, told me: "Stock—chicken, veal, and fish—was the first thing they taught me to make in culinary school (always eight pounds of bones per gallon of water, plus one pound of mirepoix, if you want to know the kind of thing that gets hammered into your head and doesn't leave twenty years later).

"So I know the power and beauty and craft of well-made, perfectly skimmed, grease-free, infinitely versatile stock. And I pretty much never make it! In my home, cooking is not about clarity and subtlety. It's about flavor, wherever you can find it, and getting it on the table at a reasonable time. And so I save all the liquid from cooking beans—it's a terrific broth and adds plenty of background flavor to whatever you want to make. I save liquid from boiling grains. Same deal. I have even been tempted to save *pasta water*, but I guess I just feel too goofy pouring three quarts of pasta water into Tupperware. But I will end up doing it one day. I'm also not shy about just shaking a few dashes of fish sauce or soy sauce into water and calling that a stock. Bouillon cubes? It's happened. (Just go easy.)"

The cookbook author and journalist Kim O'Donnel hits the stock note, too. "Unless I'm making risotto or paella, I do not worry if I've got stock on hand. Water and spices like cinnamon bark or whole ginger infuse a pot of rice or lentils, and it's how I like to teach, too. I find that if aspiring cooks believe they must have stock to make a dish, they might not make it. Cottage cheese," she confides, "when whizzed in the food processor, gets nice and smooth, and works like a thin sour cream. Silken tofu is my go-to secret weapon for dips and spreads and puddings. In the food processor, it gets good and creamy, and because of its neutral flavor, it is a chameleon— and undetectable."

GIFTS FROM MY KITCHEN WHISPERERS may not be homemade cookies in fancy tins, or jars of fruit preserves tricked out in gingham headscarves, but they are greater gifts by far: the generous lessons I have learned from the kitchens—and the lives—of the wonderful cooks and chefs I have been lucky to know and work with. Each time I roll a lemon, or make a biscuit, or throw together a salad, or stuff a chicken, or stir a risotto, or slice an apple, or sniff a carton of milk for freshness, I hear their voices, and they comfort me, warm as a hug.

— ⁊ —

MOTHERS & DAUGHTERS

IN THE UNCANNY WAY OF archives—which, in this case, are lodged in boxes and boxes of unexamined life sitting on my office floor—I happen upon this letter, written to the adult me on pale-blue stationery in the loopy, feminine script of my mother, Gil Kalins:

Darlingest,

Please don't think I'm foolish or stupid—neither of which I am.

Sorry I had to break in with what you should eat during your business day, but there's never the right time.

Have to tell you because I have had problems and helped myself and studied nutrition <u>and it does do some good.</u>

Stay away from <u>white bread.</u> Wonderfully delicious, sure, but not good. <u>Sugar. Rice desserts.</u>

Butterfat. Try margarine—you'll get used to it like most of us have had to.

Eat carrots. Broccoli. Cabbage.

Drink water.

Eat fruits, apples, papaya, etc.

So there you have it—all of which you know.

Love you,
Mother

PS I do cheat sometimes.

Reconstructing the circumstances of that letter, she'd obviously tried calling me in my office without satisfaction (I was already an editor in chief, overworked but not overweight) with my eating habits on her mind. None of the above was news to me. I'd heard it all before. But *rice desserts?* Where did *that* come from? That was so specific. I must have made rice pudding when she'd come for dinner last. So now the quintessential comfort dessert of my own childhood was to be ripped out of my life? The favorite pudding of that very poky little puppy in my favorite childhood book! For what did that errant little doggie devour when he returned home ("roly-poly, pell-mell, tumble-bumble") too late for dinner? I heard the answer every night of my toddler life: "He ate up the rice pudding and crawled into bed as happy as a lark." Just when had rice pudding become evil?

IT HAS BEEN SO MANY years—decades, even—since I stood with my mother in a kitchen, it is difficult to summon the kind of images that for other people come as easy as Instagram.

I can almost feel her hands on my four-year-old arms guiding a wooden spoon around a bowl of chocolate chip cookie dough. But I do not trust that memory. It seems too stock photo; like I'm conjuring someone else's mother. I cannot hear my mother's voice patiently explaining to me how to stir the walnuts into the brownie mix, though make brownies I surely did. From a box. But I have no difficulty recalling her admonishing me about what *not* to eat (*see* rice pudding), or regularly sending me envelopes of newspaper clippings touting the benefits of vitamin D. Or cardio exercise. Or non-saturated fats. This memory makes me cringe every time I'm about to press "Forward" to Lincoln on some unassailably relevant article on, say, the amazing biodiversity of squid, or to Sandrine on anything related to New York City politics.

I think of the time after my father's first heart attack when the anti-cholesterol demons invaded my girlhood refrigerator and everything became ersatz overnight: There was skim milk, low-fat cottage cheese, and margarine where butter and cheddar and sour cream once happily lived. There was yogurt, so long before its time that we had to go to a health food store to buy it. Or, we'd make it in an electrified egg poacher–like device where five little glass cups of milk warmed their bottoms in heated water overnight.

You would never catch Gil Kalins in a frilly apron. Cozy up, and her scent was more Miss Dior than fresh-baked bread; her slim, expressive hands with their red-polished fingertips were rarely flour-dusted. Hers were painter's hands, sculptor's hands, hands that were nonetheless cool and welcome on a daughter's fevered forehead. Yet those hands made dinner for us every single night of my childhood. And it never, not even once, occurred to me from my later smug and liberated feminist distance to marvel at how she managed to do that with such grace and ease. In my mother's day, cooking was what you did, not who you were.

Gil Kalins would never allow a milk carton—or any box, bottle, or package—on the dining table, which means that on the off chance a container of something or other winds up on our table, Roger will look up and say, "Sorry, Gil." In my kitchen, she was forever hovering behind me, putting away the butter before its time, the cleaning up more important than the cooking. For me, piles of breads, cabbages, and peaches mean warmth. For my mother, they meant ants, fruit flies, and varmints. "Your mother was a good cook," my high school friends recall. I believe that to be true, but if I remember the tune, I've forgotten most of the notes.

HER PAINTINGS ARE BEAUTIFUL: Generous sweeps of color. Her sculpture is expressive and full of life. I keep a small bronze on my desk—a woman holding a young child above her head, their faces turned toward each other in sweet connection. Such a free, exuberant gesture. Between the woman's outstretched arms and the child's body is a generous O of negative space—an act of communication I never readily felt. That's it, I understand, looking at the mother and child. That's the way she showed emotion.

Another letter surfaces. This one's dated. I'm twenty. She wrote, evidently, to thank me for a dinner I'd made on a weekend home: "The dish was delicious. Everyone enjoyed it. We had it again tonight. What a wonderful little cook you could turn out to be." 'Nuff said.

You know how in homecoming novels the Mom is always making the Kid's favorite dinner? I honestly do not know what in the world mine would be. It never came up. I have few memories of cooking with my mother, of lessons patiently taught. Yet the table was always lovingly set. My mother knew to make dinner a ritual—a gathering time for the whole family at the end of the day, the food always beautifully presented, always healthy (we later learned the truth about margarine). No TV, and mercifully, no cell phones yet. I feel those intense gathering impulses, too. Almost every night.

Marjorie, my younger sister, and I marked our childhood dinners by peeling off paper-doily place mats to set the table with. I can still hear the snap as each white perforated sheet left the pad, can still see the white flurry of paper bits that inevitably fell from their punched-out snowflake patterns. Sometimes rectangular, sometimes round—were those paper doilies my mother's nod to propriety? Surely real lace tablecloths were too old-fashioned for her. Perhaps forever doily-spooked, and never much a fan of the clunky sixties earth-mother woven numbers that followed, I find place mats way too fussy. I like my plates on a bare table of warm wood. My mother's old pine table, in fact.

WHAT WAS IN OUR MID-CENTURY pantry? Strawberry Jell-O for sure, and raspberry and orange and lime, and chocolate pudding. In boxes. And tapioca. There was Campbell's cream of mushroom soup, used, in a pinch, as a white sauce for creamed chicken. And the Hellmann's mayonnaise and Heinz ketchup I depend on still. There were Toll House cookies made with

Nestlé's chocolate chips from the same yellow bag they come in today. Thomas' English muffins, which you'd pull apart with your fingertips. Never Pop-Tarts. There was Crisco. And Bisquick. And for dessert, tins of canned peaches, and pears, and mixed fruit cups with maraschino cherries, so sweet and gummy they freaked me out. Canned corn, canned petits pois, sometimes succotash, though that was usually in the form of a Bird's Eye frozen block, with the limas always stuck to the corn. In the freezer, too, was the chicken potpie we'd shove in the oven when the parents went out, and Minute Maid concentrated orange juice. Hardly ever TV dinners. In the fridge, deli-sliced bologna with the plastic still on the slices, foil-wrapped cheese triangles called La Vache Qui Rit, and silver blocks of Philadelphia cream cheese.

My father made the typical dad-style pancakes and waffles, he grilled outdoors, and would routinely leave a carrot and two lumps of sugar on the seat of our family exercise bike (a horse joke), but he didn't cook much. He would sing: "Mashed potatoes and gravy. That's what we had in the navy," (he was never in the navy) to describe his favorite lunch as young man on Wall Street—an entire plate of soft mashed potatoes with ladlefuls of thick brown gravy—made that forever my comfort food. Though I've carried on a conversation with my father in my head for more than half my life, it is never about food.

IN THE MELANCHOLY PROCESS OF clearing out my mother's last apartment, my hand fell on her recipe box. This was news! I never even knew she'd kept one. I grabbed the box and stuck it in a closet in my office, where it stayed, unopened, for years—

until I began writing this book, in fact. Suddenly, that white plastic box became an exciting thing. What did I hope to find inside? Secrets? Clues to what cooking meant to her? Hints of what she loved? Opening it, I saw that the recipes were carefully organized: Each food category was typed, then painstakingly scissored and glued onto tabs of four-by-six-inch manila index card dividers. Starting with Appetizers & Dips, on through Poultry & Stuffings, Soups & Stews, Eggs & Cheese, Cakes, Pies, Cookies. These category headings seem suspicious to me, like they were part of a kit. Or somebody else's best intentions. I do not think my mother had a Dewey decimal system approach to food.

The recipes in that box come from everywhere. One for baked chicken breasts is scribbled on the back of a price sheet from a Los Angeles machinery company; when she took over my father's machine tool distribution business after he died at age sixty, her mind was still on dinner. "As a woman," she told *Metalworking News* at the time, "I know I have got to prove myself in what is generally considered to be a man's world." And later in the article: "'I did sell my first machine, a K.O. Lee surface grinder,' she reported happily."

The box only appears to be well organized; the recipes in each section are twenty kinds of random. This is one unlikely cabinet of curiosities: cuttings from the *New York Times* are easiest to recognize, browned now, and stuck to index cards with the kind of red-rubber-tipped-dispenser glue that inevitably shows through. Recipes seem haphazard, scribbled, unintentional. Hastily written on the back of a bank deposit slip: "For steak: Marinate in bourbon, lime juice & brown sugar." On the back of an envelope with an engraved address for the Sherry-Netherland hotel is a complete recipe for beef à la provençal, in teeny ballpoint script: "For a 3-pound slab of chuck: ¼ tsp pepper, 1½ tsp thyme, ½ tsp allspice. Cook for 4 hours." Oh my!

Hoping for a lost culinary legend, I find, instead, jotted on a subscription solicitation from *BusinessWeek,* a recipe for Veal Birds—pounded scaloppine rolled around a stuffing of mushrooms. There's a recipe for molded liver pâté based on canned bouillon, handwritten on a folded sheet of that pale-blue stationery. Carefully taped to a card, a clipping of my friend Jonathan Waxman's bouillabaisse recipe, from some magazine (mine?). On a torn sheet of loose-leaf paper floats a single idea: "orange slices + apricot gelatin." In Appetizers & Dips, there's at last a dish I recognize: Shrimp or Lobster Mold, heavy on the mayonnaise, requiring one whole package of Philly cream cheese, a can of Campbell's tomato soup, and a packet of gelatin. There's Veal Chop with Red and Green Peppers from the *Times.* I discover veal marengo and smile to find its requisite orange peel. There are any number of recipes for pot roasts and, of course, chicken breasts, one with "mango, mint, ginger & avocado." And mushroom caps stuffed with onions, sour cream, and sherry. On the back of an envelope: "Striped bass stuffed w/spinach: Put in broiler—turn, not near flame. Or bake." And on the flip side of a Xeroxed list of winter classes at Beverly East Bridge Club, hurried ideas for a buffet menu featuring "sliced tenderloin (marinated and packaged in double tinfoil, bake for 25 minutes)."

There is a world in my mother's recipe box, but it is ultimately unrewarding. I find mid-century classics like Swedish meatballs, but no confirmation that she ever made them. In fact, there is no evidence on any of the cards in that white plastic box, as deliberate as they appear, that she ever cooked *any* of these dishes. Nothing is annotated. It's enough to drive an archivist wild. Did she ever cook that pot-au-feu on a recipe card from *Elle* magazine? Did she ever act on the scribbled note-to-self on a sheet of lined, three-holed-punched notebook paper involving a slab of beef with a sauce of coriander and yogurt? Stuffed cabbage, sure. And stuffed peppers, often. But why is there a card for stuffing that called for cans of French-fried onion rings and stale bread crumbs? "Perish the thought," as she would say.

In that box, I find no recipes for the things I loved that she *did* cook, like a full-on Thanksgiving dinner. Just what does this archive represent? Her best intentions? Food fantasies? Or did she, in fact, make these recipes for dinners that happened after her daughters left home? What was she up to with that recipe box? Was it wishful cooking? I sure wish I had asked her. These memories are like water through your cupped fingers—you think you have it, then it all drips away. Kinda breaks your heart.

YOU CAN SEE WHERE Gil Kalins entered the cooking game: my mother didn't have a tuna-noodle-casserole bone in her body. When we were kids, there was every-night food, and there was dinner-party food. Company meant full-on anxiety. Days ahead, everyone in the household was nervous. Even the furniture was nervous. So much cleaning. So much getting ready. You could cut the tension with her grape shears. The boiled shrimp had to be picked up from the fish store and, just before the guests arrived, put into a white porcelain serving dish surmounted by a perky life-size bright-red ceramic lobster clutching a bowl for the Russian dressing in one claw and marinated artichoke hearts (from a jar) in the other. Such serving pieces (bowls, platters, pitchers) were as important as sculpture to my mother, and I loved that lobster serving dish long before I learned its lesson: It's a clever organizing vessel for all the hors d'oeuvres you ever need—just three things. My mother never messed with trays of little toasts bearing mincy morsels of undetermined origin.

Dinner parties meant Marjorie and I were pressed into service, and my father's inevitable quip: "We have two in help." Two daughters, that is! We were combed and curled, on edge and on our best behavior, dashing back and forth between the dining room and the kitchen. Mother's main dish was often a particularly velvety veal scaloppine that I loved, served over wide noodles. (A recipe *not* in her recipe box—maybe she knew it by heart?) Or shrimp Creole (in which case, the cold shrimp app would be replaced by herring in cream sauce from a jar). Which reminds me of what my friend John Kessler wrote in the *Atlanta Journal-Constitution*: As a kid, he understood his mother's standard dinner party dish to be "cocoa van."

MY MOTHER WOULD MAKE BEEF tongue with a sauce of gingersnaps and raisins, a dish whose tangy flavor I fondly recall without being remotely moved to cook it. I found the recipe she used in *The Settlement Cook Book*, originally published in Milwaukee in 1901, with the mission of connecting Jewish Americans with their immigrant roots. On the white cover of my mother's well-worn copy, dozens and dozens of line-drawn little-girl chefettes, wearing prettily bow-tied aprons over puffy floor-length dresses, their squishy chef's hats pulled down over their Dutch bobs, are intently reading the book while marching two by two smack-dab into an outsize heart shape, surprinted with the phrase "The way to a man's heart." Don't even get me started.

Another favorite of my mother's was tomato aspic, a ring of jellied tomato juice with chopped vegetables, chilled and turned out on a plate. This was a fifties standard—the up-scale version of a Jell-O mold—a cold jellied salad much loved by ladies who'd serve it at luncheons, though that was hardly Mom's style. The closest recipe I can find is in the last book Marion Cunningham wrote, a charming little volume called *Lost Recipes*, whose intent was to revive home cooking classics. Marion, the person to trust on American cooking—she loved a good iceberg lettuce wedge—worked with James Beard for years and revised the classic *Fannie Farmer Cookbook*. Marion was a great fan of *Saveur*. Once, in the early days of the magazine, she turned up in the doorway of our cramped little office with a cheery "I just wanted to see what you all are up to!" We made her a contributing editor.

There was no aspic in my mother's recipe box, but I did find a clipping from the *Times* of Pierre Franey's Kitchen Equipment column on Savarin molds, illustrated by a photo of the very same aluminum ring my mother used to make her tomato aspic. The Savarin pan's highest calling was the rum-soaked cake named for the great nineteenth-century food philosopher Jean Anthelme Brillat-Savarin. Franey recommended filling the cake's capacious center with whipped cream. Growing up, Savarin meant the brand of the big red coffee can my mother kept her paintbrushes in, not the author of *The Physiology of Taste*, famously translated by M. F. K. Fisher, or the oozy Burgundian triple-crème cheese, both of which I later learned to devour. This Savarin is the mold my mother used to make her tomato aspic, and I have it still.

Trying to recapture this cooking memory, I decide to attempt the aspic. A certain rigor drives me to blend my own pickling spice from mustard and coriander seeds, ground allspice, ginger, celery seeds, red pepper flakes, whole peppercorns, bay leaves, and a cinnamon stick—something that would not have occurred to my mother. Deciding against the canned V8 juice she likely used, I cook down tomato juice (organic, bottled. We are all caricatures of ourselves) with celery leaves, sliced onion, sugar, salt, and the ground pickling spices, strain it, then stir in the softened gelatin, thrilled to see it dissolve, Jell-O-like, into the warm liquid. I pour half the mixture into the Savarin mold, spread the finely chopped veg—celery, cucumber, and zucchini, mixed with lemon juice—on top around the ring, and pour in the rest of the seasoned tomato juice. Especially familiar are the scary moments, hours later, when I remove the chilled aspic from the refrigerator, dip the outside of the mold really quickly in warm water, turn the mold upside down on a lettuce leaf–lined platter, and hold my breath as the aspic slithers out, intact. Gil Kalins would have recognized it.

ONLY A VERY BAD CHILD would not remember her mother's meat loaf. My mother's was yummy: loose and juicy and tomatoey. It was soft, unlike those thick school cafeteria slabs made dense with too many bread crumbs and too little finesse. It certainly did not contain, as Roger remembers his mom's version did, an entire package of Lipton's onion soup mix. But *which* meat loaf recipe is it? I flip through her recipe box to the section marked "Meats." And now I'm stuck. Did she make a *New York Times* recipe pasted on its own card: Meat Loaf with Peppers and Mushrooms? Or Meat Loaf with Tofu? (Ewwww.) Did she make Craig Claiborne's Italian Meat Loaf from a yellowed page torn from a *New York Times Sunday Magazine* piece entitled "Hamburger—Above and Beyond"? Did she agree with what Craig told his readers? "Filet mignon may be fancier, and chateaubriand more chic, but nothing appeals to the American appetite like ground beef." His recipe does not seem familiar. Even as it calls for a few spoonfuls of grated Parmesan cheese, and I can see the umami advantage, it doesn't play right in my taste memory.

What *did* my mother do? I'm guessing that, unlike me, she didn't overthink it and just made the damn meat loaf: three pounds of ground meat, seasoned with whatever dried herbs she had on hand, sautéed onions, canned stewed tomatoes. I picture her soaking a couple of handfuls of torn bread in milk first. But did she know she was making panade—the suave French thickener? Was she aware of how key that addition of panade was to making her meat loaf lovely? I don't think so. Her graceful fingers would shape the meat into a loaf, plop it into a rectangular pan, and pour on canned tomato sauce. And on top of that? Most certainly ketchup. Heinz. From a bottle. What I had to go on was a recollection of taste and texture. Mind pictures. Recipe forensics.

I recall a trek to a meat-processing warehouse in North Bergen, New Jersey, where I went hoping to tease out secrets from the famous meat impresario Pat LaFrieda for *Shake Shack*, the cookbook I produced for that spirited enterprise. "The Shack secret blend dies with me," Pat warns me; he does, however, share some advice. "Always get the butcher to grind your meat," he declares, unsmiling. "You never know how many days the pre-ground stuff has sat in the butcher case." And, he continues, "Forget economy cuts. The flavor's in the whole muscles." The legendary ShackBurger (I might as well share with you) should be a twice-ground mixture of either brisket and chuck for a light blend or short rib and chuck for a rich blend. I do recall the makeup of my mother's meat loaf: one-third beef, one-third pork, one-third veal. But my politically correct organic butcher does not even carry veal.

In their charming book *A Meatloaf in Every Oven*, the *New York Times* writers Frank Bruni and Jennifer Steinhauer laugh in the face of veal:

Frank: There's a place for veal in a meatloaf, but it is limited . . . there's altogether too much veal in meatloaf . . .

Jenn: Let's get right out there and say it: Veal is sort of the truffle oil of meats.

Which definitively convinces me not to use veal in my effort to re-create my mother's meat loaf—or as close to it as I can come. I go with a mix of 1¼ pounds chuck (the muscle meat) and ¾ pound pork, freshly ground together (as my butcher suggests) before my eyes. In a bowl, I tear up four slices of good bread, crusts removed (and later sautéed in olive oil for salad croutons), and soak the bread in a cup of milk until soft. I add two beaten eggs and ½ cup chopped parsley, mix it up, then stir that mixture into the ground meat that's waiting in a bigger bowl. I chop and lightly sauté two medium onions in olive oil, then add them to the bowl. Then comes salt, pepper, and ½ teaspoon each of fennel seeds, grated nutmeg, and pimentón (a spice my mother of course had never heard of, but necessary to me now). But *no funny stuff*: no olives, or cheese, or bacon, or pancetta, or beans, or mushrooms, or anchovies, or hot sauce. I mix the meat well with my hands (a childhood pleasure I do recall), then pat it into a loose mound in a rectangular baking dish (a loaf pan is too confining—and drying). I pour a cup of good tomato sauce over the top and slide the dish into a pre-heated 375°F oven. About 20 minutes in, and in homage to my mom (*and* because it tastes like childhood), I squirt ketchup (from a plastic squeeze bottle she never dreamed of) over the top, scatter dried oregano on top, and baste the meat loaf with its pan juices. At about 45 minutes total, I take the meat loaf's temp (it should be 150°F). And that's it. It's a little bit country and a little bit rock 'n' roll.

MEAT LOAF PROPELS ME FURTHER into the food of my childhood. Which propels me to the supermarket, and I immediately realize I need to find a store that does not pride itself on politically correct food. Since it took four tries (forget Whole Foods) to find plain gelatin for the tomato aspic, I knew I had to head to the heartland (suburban Long Island) to find such venerable brands as Jell-O and Reddi-Wip. The hunt for consommé madrilène, a hot-weather delicacy my mother always elegantly served as a first-course soup—chilled and jellied, right from the can, with a squeeze of lime juice—was a bust. I find the only hint that the soup ever existed in old recipes for the Madrid-born original that begin with cooking down two pounds of veal knuckles.

Campbell's cream of mushroom soup was the favorite from my childhood kitchen. When I was sick in bed, its creamy texture calmed me more than chicken soup. As I hold the can in my hand, its Warhol-esque iconography seems unchanged (the red and white colors taken from Cornell University's football uniform of 1898), except now there's an unfurled blue ribbon that wraps the can with the seal from the Paris International Exposition in 1900 (where the soup received a medal, *mon Dieu!*), plus the words "Great for Cooking," reminding folks of its stature as the OG American white sauce.

But this celebrated can is now tattooed with consumerist messages, with warnings and disclaimers. Graffitied around the new ring-pull pop-top are three aggressive black arrows with the words "Recyclable" and "Non-BPA Lining," repeated twice. There are nutrition facts ("100 calories per serving") with the recommended servings: "about 2.5." From a 10½-ounce can? Are you kidding? (The can Warhol glorified in 1962 held 11.53 ounces.) There are the usual suspects— cholesterol and carb content (0% and 3%, respectively)—and an ugly list of provenances: "The ingredients from canola, corn and soy in this product came from genetically modified crops." A chauvinistic flag-like seal boasts: "Cooked with Care in the USA." And there's more! Printed in red is the entire recipe for Beef and Mushroom Lasagna, with a long list of ingredients, featuring, besides said soup, two cups of Prego Fresh Mushroom Italian Sauce. Just reading this can takes days. There are instructions for mixing the contents with 1 can of water (though I remember using milk) and heating the soup either in the microwave or on the stovetop. There's the requisite cover-your-ass consumer protection warnings: "Metal edges are sharp . . ." There's a number to call, and a website to visit with questions or comments. ("Excuse me, sir, but why does this soup now have overtones of cardboard, and the rare mushroom bits the texture of squid?")

Though you might think it a stretch to consider cream of mushroom soup a palate shaper, I can draw a straight line from that can to the beloved sauce velouté in Julia Child's blanquette de veau recipe from *Mastering*, Volume 1. And from there to Sam Sifton's recipe for the Best Clam Chowder that I make every summer with local cherrystones and heavy cream, and on to my favorite thing I ate last year: Lee Hanson and Riad Nasr's blanquette de lapin at their SoHo restaurant, Frenchette.

When I dump the results of my nostalgic supermarket shopping trip on the kitchen counter, my Chipotle-obsessed son remarks: "What's all this? Has our kitchen been invaded by aliens?" Those boxes sit there for weeks, unopened and unloved. I've bought two Jell-O chocolate puddings. On their flimsy cardboard cartons, cheaper and sadder than when I knew them, and printed with paler colors, the "Cook and Serve" is marked "chocolate flavor" and the "Instant," "chocolate artificial flavor." It has been two months now, and I somehow cannot bring myself to make what I now dread: a gooey-sweet imitation of the original. More boxes of Jell-O— raspberry, strawberry, and even lime, so exciting when it first came out—remain untouched. The can of Reddi-Wip sits, even now, in the back of the refrigerator, unsquirted. I guess you can go home again, but sometimes you just don't want to.

INDEED, CHILDHOOD FOOD MEMORIES so indelibly mark us that we run eagerly toward or defiantly away from them. An unfortunate experience with a pressure cooker at an early age has made me skittish around and admittedly nutty about all kitchen appliances. The food processor sends out negative vibes only I can hear; give me a good mortar and pestle, except for, like, hot creamed soups. For those, I'm currently circling around an immersion blender we just bought, dreading its rogue power. I'm afraid it'll run wild on the stovetop, scalding the kitchen with flying bits of leek and potato soup.

Which is precisely what happened just before my first-grade teacher, Miss Grant, was expected for dinner. As if that event itself were not terrifying enough (how could my mother have invited her?), we were near the stove when we heard an alarming bang. The valve had sprung off the top of one of those old pressure cookers and lodged itself in our kitchen ceiling. Then the lid disengaged, and quickly the pot's contents flew out—an explosion of green beans, bits of which were still to be found on cabinet doors and walls long after I left elementary school.

Yes, I know these appliances have been improved (they no longer have valves), but the memory still haunts me. When a chef I worked with convinced Roger there was nothing better for cooking dried beans, he gave me one of those new pressure contraptions with a dial to release the steam. That new cooker stayed in the box it came in for a few years before I pressed it, unused, into the hands of a friend. As for the electric Instant Pot, so fetishized by my son's generation, well, except for cooking rice, I don't want to know.

I make an exception for the industrial design wonder of all appliances, the KitchenAid stand mixer, designed by one Herbert Johnston in about 1918, and updated in 1930 into such a majestic kitchen icon that the company has been smart enough not to change it much since then. But as much as I loved its look, I never actually owned a KitchenAid (like moving a jet engine into your kitchen) until we were producing the *Federal Donuts* book and needed to show how to make donut batter at home. And even then we were careful to add the caveat: "You can certainly use a hand mixer or even a sturdy whisk." As much as I admire the KitchenAid's streamlined aeronautical brilliance, I am always happier to let someone else drive.

ON THE OTHER HAND, I've been easy with cooking fish since one lucky fishing trip when I was a kid. My father and uncle Jack happened to catch a mighty striped bass, trolling an articulated wooden lure (that was, to my ten-year-old eyes, cuter than any fish) from a small motorboat in the waters of Buzzards Bay off Pocasset on Cape Cod, waters that rarely yielded anything much larger than the scup (aka porgy) we loved to catch.

My ladylike mother, in the kitchen with her oldest sister, fairly giggled at the huge fish. Shedding her usual self-consciousness, she lightened up. Laughed! She and Aunt Sally stuffed and roasted that bass, an act that modeled for me fearless whole-fish wrangling. Was it the reassuring presence of her big sister? Aunt Sally was the walking opposite of neurotic; her smile lit up the whole family. Was it the sandy sunniness of Aunt Sally's summer house on Spur Road, where all the "shoulds" and "what-will-they-thinks?" were left in a tangle at the screen door with our sandals? Were we on vacation from doing the right thing?

The heroic tales of landing that bass became instant family lore. I no longer remember its weight and have likely handled bigger animals since (wrapping gleaming whole bluefish in fig leaves and stuffing them with rosemary branches and lemons), but there was so much joy in welcoming the striper into that simple kitchen; such slicing of onions and tomatoes and tearing up of white bread and (since this was before fresh herbs were common) chopping of parsley for stuffing. Inhibitions rolled away. Yes! The striper would fit in the oven's roasting pan if you angled it just right. I remember the way the setting sun slanted into the old-fashioned screened porch; how splendid that roasted fish looked as it went from the oven to the center of an oak dining table. How we kids filled extra-big glasses of milk to drink before bedtime. Taking tiny sips, we were allowed to stay up as late as the milk lasted.

GROWING UP AMID THE SWIRL of anxiety my mother had around entertaining has made me an easy hostess (members of my immediate family should feel free to disagree here). Thanksgiving won out over her usual entertaining angst, though, and even she grew more lighthearted as the excitement built. Extra energy filled the house. Thanksgiving morning was always sunny, Harry Belafonte and the Kingston Trio on the stereo. Sometimes there were strangers among us. Lone soldiers in their pressed khakis would show up for dinner like little lost puppies; Marjorie and I giggled and thought them romantic. Where my mother found soldiers in uniform in Westport, Connecticut, it never occurred to me to ask.

Thanksgiving is my holiday, and I'm never happier than when Aaron Copland's *Appalachian Spring* fills the kitchen and I'm messing around with some big turkey. (It's a total extravagance, FedExed in from Kansas, ordered months ahead from Heritage Foods every year; by now it seems as if Frank Reese, the Kansas farmer who raises the organic heirloom Bourbon Red at Good Shepherd Poultry Ranch, should be coming to dinner, too.) I'm a "bring it on" Thanksgiving host, and it always gets me in the gut when people admit they have nowhere to go. Some years I have to order two turkeys.

My mother always did Thanksgiving, too, and her wide-planked Early American pine table held as many folks as she could fit. Her Thanksgivings brought so much high-spirited chaos that everyone almost forgot to worry. My dinner begins with that same table, to which two or sometimes three more tables are added—end to end—to make one long, splendid surface. (Roger adjusts the tables' heights, slipping squares of one-by-fours under uneven legs.) The tables are always draped with the heavy persimmon-colored cloths I had made years ago from material I found at a French fabric store on Lexington Avenue that was going out of business. (Now, in 2021, half the shops on that same block are empty.)

My mother would, as she'd appreciatively say of others, "set a beautiful table." Stars of our Thanksgiving table are the deep green majolica plates she saved "for company." I smile to recall how, as executive editor at *Newsweek*, awaiting copy for our weekly close around midnight on Friday nights, sometimes even later, while the boys down the hall were in a huddle over politics, or, more likely, watching basketball, I'd be hunched over my computer, prowling eBay, searching out those 1940s Dick Knox California majolica plates with the raised geranium pattern, so I could invite even more people to Thanksgiving dinner.

Over the years, Marjorie raised the cornucopia centerpiece to an art form. Weeks ahead, she'd collect brilliantly colored fall leaves from Central Park and carefully press them flat. Then she'd lay them down the middle of the tables like a forest floor, a leafy ground for the fall fruits and vegetables and votive candles that spill out on top of them. At the Greenmarket, I forage for kabocha and honeynut squashes and dazzling yellow-and-orange-splotched acorns, tiny pumpkins, fat red onions with their greens in the air, Brussels sprouts on the stalk, miniature cauliflowers in three colors, little brown Seckel pears, and rose-tinged Lady apples, all destined to sit on those fall leaves—a modern medieval river of abundance.

I have come to believe that no matter who's at your Thanksgiving table any given year, everyone who has ever left their mark on your ritual meal is right there, too. My mother's whole gleaming roast turkey takes pride of place. That turkey is so gloriously browned you'd swear that, like Keith Haring's Radiant Baby, it generates light. I cannot believe that just because a flattened, spatchcocked sheet-pan bird may cook more evenly and be easier to carve, some cooks would actually sacrifice the iconic impact of the whole bird to slicing convenience. I do not want my turkey spatchcocked; it kills the look. I do not want my turkey brined; it kills the gravy. And although my mother's turkey was most likely a frozen Butterball (with that pop-up timer) from A&P, it was always regal on her old white ironstone platter and carved by my father with high good humor, and with much heckling from Uncle Frank.

You tell me how you cook your turkey, and I'll tell you who you are. Every fall, I defend myself against books full of opinions, and food sites that light up with a frenzy of seasoning ideas (jalapeños? kimchi?), trying not to second-guess what I know works. I still remember those days—actually two days—when you had to defrost a frozen bird in the refrigerator before you could start the real anxiety: to stuff or not to stuff? High heat or low? Tenting? Basting?

Always-succulent heritage birds are easy: As soon as the turkey arrives on Tuesday, rub it all over with cut tangerines and salt generously. Leave it uncovered in the fridge until Thursday morning, then stuff more sliced tangerines and fresh herbs (rosemary, sage, thyme) into the cavities. The dressing, at least two pans of it, bakes separately.

I set the turkey on a rack over a roasting pan filled with cut apples and onions and carrots and celery and a cup or so of water. I rub the bird with soft butter and slow-roast it at 325°F, basting after an hour and then every 15 minutes. If the pan juices seem scant, I'll do a late baste with tawny port, or pour ½ cup of Madeira over the bird. Couldn't hurt the gravy.

The pan juices, with the fat poured off and stored in a jar in the refrigerator, are the fond of Mother's clear and dark mushroom gravy (made glossy with cornstarch, never flour), with a whole lotta white mushrooms I've sautéed ahead in butter and thyme.

Then, my aunt Gillie's sweet potatoes, pureed with orange juice (for decades, she brought them—silky smooth and bright orange—in a shallow bright-red Dansk pan, with those two iconic handles, covering the top with tiny marshmallows and sliding it under the broiler just before serving). One day I got to wondering where the nutty idea of marshmallows on sweet potatoes (total sacrilege to people who've not grown up with it) even came from, betting it was from some women's magazine recipe that went the equivalent of viral. Bingo! A bit of research led to a 1929 issue of *Ladies' Home Journal*, the recipe developed, of course, by the Campfire Marshmallow Company. Women's magazines were so crazy about that recipe (and the advertising it brought) that they were still running it as late as the seventies.

After four decades, my brother-in-law, Jack Taylor, is no longer at our Thanksgiving table, but his mashed potatoes outlast him. Years ago, Jack became so fed up with those roasted-marshmallow sweet potatoes that for Christmas he presented me with a heavy metal potato ricer. The device, he announced, was so I could make the mashed white potatoes of his WASP childhood. That potato ricer does its magic on peeled and boiled Yukon Golds and I am committed to Jack's mashed potatoes.

Our mother's recipe for cranberry sauce involved opening a chilled can of Ocean Spray from both ends, using the bottom to push the jelled cylinder out whole, onto a (charming) dish, and slicing it into rounds. My sister makes two kinds of cranberry sauce—in one, the berries are blended; in the other, left whole. When Lincoln was ten, I took him to a Thanksgiving cooking class for kids that our friend Kerry Heffernan, the original chef at Eleven Madison Park, gave in EMP's upstairs kitchen. Lincoln, apron-wrapped and eager, learned that cranberry sauce comes from fresh berries, not a can, and how to gently cook the berries down with orange juice and orange zest and not much sugar. I make a version of Kerry's sauce still. Now that I've learned what a scary chemical cocktail cranberry-growing requires, we buy organic berries and cook a pound of them down in the juice of two oranges, their zest, and only ½ cup of sugar. Just as when making berry preserves,

I gently boil the cranberries and wait for the foam to subside. Once the berries pop open and the mixture thickens and turns glossy, I stir in a bit of water. Then I spoon the hot cranberry sauce into my mother's pressed-glass footed dish (presentation is all) and slip the whole thing into the refrigerator. Accomplishing this as early as a week ahead helps defuse preparation anxiety.

The question of stuffing is *soooo* loaded. Inside the turkey or out? Bread, or rice? Pistachios? Red peppers? Sausage or bacon? Deep in my past, I learned to make the corn bread I always use for stuffing in a cast-iron skillet, Mississippi-style, from Sam Gore, a total original and a born cook. When he explained that true corn bread depends on the chemical interaction buttermilk provokes, and warned me *never* to add sugar, I was forever hooked. Performing those corn-bread rituals regularly, every month or so, in my aged cast-iron skillet, is a close as I get to baking. (Sam also taught me how to make a killer lime pickle, a process that requires soaking 2 gallons of sliced cukes in 3 cups of pickling lime—calcium hydroxide—dissolved in 2 gallons of water, in a nonreactive container for 24 hours. Then, after changing the water every 4 hours to wash away the lime, you process the pickles in a brine of pickling spices. But that's another story.) Rituals matter, and I always order my organic stone-ground cornmeal (and grits, too) from a lovely man in Wilsonville, Alabama, named Frank McEwen, whom I met while reporting a story on that other Frank, the great Birmingham chef Frank Stitt, at Highlands Grill, who introduced me to Frank McEwen's cornmeal (mcewenandsons.com). And I'm sort of a purist with the corn-bread stuffing: hold that gochugaru pepper for a Korean dish. Just sage, lots of thyme, two large frying pans of sautéed onions and celery, whole bunches of chopped parsley. Salt and pepper. Sometimes I'll add chestnuts. And yes, there were years I roasted the buggers in their shells, making an X on their bottoms, so they'd be easier to peel. Except they were never easy to peel. Now I realize that the difference is minimal, so I buy the whole chestnuts in a jar, peeled and roasted.

Roger is a masterly carver (Mother called him "a handy gadget") and will do the deed while I am making that dark pan gravy from the turkey stock that I've begun the day before with extra wings and a leg roasted first in the oven with a carrot and an onion or two. Always, I remember the time that Aunt Gillie and I, lost in the frenzy of last-minute preparations (that may have been the year we served broiled oysters as a first course to commemorate the New York Native Americans, who, I learned on a school trip with Sandrine's class, formed the Palisades on the Hudson from their discarded oyster shells). I mistakenly grabbed baking soda instead of cornstarch to thicken the pan gravy, it was not good; but we said nothing. "I miss Gillie most at Thanksgiving," I hear myself telling her son, Herb. Roger especially misses the two batches of brownies she'd make: one for dessert and one slipped to him as she arrived, for our freezer. There is always plenty of room at our Thanksgiving table for the people who are no longer there.

ON THE MORNING AFTER THANKSGIVING, it's time to reconnect with the turkey, diving deep into the carcass to remove every bit of still-moist meat from the bones and transferring all the rest—carcass, skin, bones—into the biggest pot I have, all the better to make as much flavorful stock as that turkey will part with. (Rich frozen turkey stock is better than money in the bank.) On that morning, a passage from Jeannette Walls's remarkable memoir *The Glass Castle* always plays in my head. Walls, who lived then in a small town deep in the mountains of West Virginia, writes about visiting a neighbor, Ginnie Sue Pastor, who asked her: "You know how to pick a chicken clean?" Instantly, Walls was all over that chicken. With her bare hands. And her fingers. And her fingernails. She dug out every last bit of succulent hidden meat and tendon and jellied fat.

I think of Walls as I get equally *animal* about breaking down that once-iconic Thanksgiving turkey into stock. As if that golden broth would be a survival issue: all I'd have to get me through the winter. I pull off every bit of seasoned skin and the browned herbs that cling to it, and toss them into my largest pot, the jelly-making pot. I scrape up every last bit of the rich juices, now congealed on the platter, and into the pot. With the turkey meat it is always triage: weighing its turkey-sandwich potential—layered with dressing and cranberry sauce, sometimes with hot gravy (!)—against the stock-enriching flavor of odd-shaped morsels. I break the bones of the carcass—all the better to release their succulent marrow. Into the pot.

OUR BABY BOOM GENERATION'S PSYCHES were powered by the degree to which we were *not* like our parents. It makes me tired to remember how many of my own sociopolitical stances were motivated by defiance. Looking back, I can see how that resistance became the source of our energy. We were smart-asses, and we loved it. Now, as a parent to a kid from whose mouth I would not be surprised to hear a sardonic "Okay, boomer," I realize how insufferable I must have been at times to my parents, especially as a rebellious student spending her junior year in Paris, as every crumb of the very croissants I nibbled on was paid for by them.

I had as my coffee table for many years a very large, rough pine wine crate that I dragged home one night from the sidewalk outside a neighborhood liquor store. To me, it was street hip with its endearingly stenciled French words and the black umbrellas showing which side was up, itself concrete poetry. I'd gone to the Bowery to find the fat, techy black rubber wheels with shiny red metal centers it rolled around on. I loved that piece. And every time my mother said, "It drags the whole room down," she added another few years to that table's life.

And yet, I can still kind of feel my mother in the kitchen as I pull her dented metal colander down from its hook to drain my green beans, and when I brew tea in the blue-and-white Royal Crown Derby teapot she prized, and pile salad greens on her "good" gold-rimmed (no dishwasher!) Doulton green-flowered plates, or even as I reach for her aged aluminum measuring spoons to scoop out baking powder and make sure to level it on the straight side of the tin.

CHAPTER 2

BUTTERMILK BISCUITS & RED DIRT ROADS

WHEN SHE DIED AT AGE ninety-two, there was a heaping up of flowers on the coffin of Lola Mae Autry so startlingly magnificent that it seemed like one giant bouquet offered to the God she prayed to, sang to, played the organ for, and listened to thousands of thundering sermons (delivered by her Baptist minister husband, Ewart) about. Lola Mae was an unlikely friend to the tall brunette magazine editor from New York who became, for a decade, her daughter-in-law. But our relationship managed to survive the drama. We stayed in close touch. I just plain loved her.

She was born in Memphis and graduated with a degree in science and music from Memphis State, then fell madly for the charismatic minister at one of the largest Baptist churches in town, where she was a young organist. Only problem was, he was married with two young boys. When his divorce came through, in the early years of World War II, he and Lola married and got out of town. They headed due south, to a community called Hickory Flat in rural northern Mississippi that was still pretty much living in the last century. Their destination: Pine Grove Church, where Ewart's daddy had been preacher, too.

I understood the sense of dislocation Lola Mae later wrote about in her memoir, *Please, God, I'm a City Girl. What Am I Doing in the Country?* While I could be intermittently charmed and amazed by Benton County, Mississippi, Lola Mae had to learn to live—and thrive—and make a difference there. Those early years, what she called the "barely at the end of the Great Depression" era, were pure culture shock, moving from her family's comfortable home in Memphis into a long-abandoned country place the Mississippi musician Mose Allison, born not far away, would call a "One room country little shack a thousand miles from nowhere." All right, there were two rooms, but the windows had no glass, only wooden shutters that creaked. The house itself, deep in the woods, was ten miles from the nearest town. What it lacked in electricity and running water, it made up for in snakes, foxes, and skunks. Only over decades did a sturdy country dwelling take shape. With a bathroom. Shooting rabbits or squirrels for meat was sometimes the only shopping the Autrys could manage. Early on, they made this deal: He'd clean the animals with fur and feathers, and she'd handle the scales and fins. Dinner meant rolling the meat or fish in cornmeal and frying it up in a cast-iron skillet: maybe just-plucked quail from the morning's hunt or just-caught crappie from the creek below.

The men would pull huge catfish from the Little Tippah River at the bottom of their land, sticking their hands (their whole arms, really) deep into the water and grabbing the fish by its mouth—a kind of hand-fishing called grabbling. Visiting, I gradually connected to Mississippi. The Autrys knew their land. Not by street signs, of which there were few, but by its contours: every bottom and hollow and ridge had a nickname, like kinfolk. The earth's natural markers were the only ones the Autrys needed on those dusty county roads. They named their hollow in the woods Whippoorwill Valley. Nature—the thick woods outside their door, the fresh creek at the bottom of the hill, and the wild creatures that dwelled there—was a member of the family.

Once, Ewart came singing through those woods bearing a huge armload of branches and sat Lola Mae down on the ground to help her identify some forty species of trees by their leaves. "Sometimes," she told me, "Ewart might receive fresh sorghum molasses as part of the salary. Often it was chickens. Other times, only their eggs."

By the time I met her, Lola Mae had become not just totally at home but in charge, a Sunday school–teaching, piano lesson–giving church organist, photographer, musician, and writer, and every bit as beloved a pillar of their rural community as her husband the minister. The country ways of northern Mississippi never stopped astounding me: It seemed you could show up unannounced at the preacher's door, no matter what time of day. Or night. If they wanted to be married, couples would just drive down the dirt road to the house and, as long as the papers were in order, Ewart would do the job right there in front of their fireplace, with Lola Mae playing the Autoharp and singing "Oh Promise Me."

The Mississippi I discovered many decades later, when such

scarcity was part of their shared history, was captured in a passage of a poem written by her stepson Jim:

> It seemed all the food in the world
> fried chicken crisp and soggy
> country ham and sausage in biscuits
> deviled eggs and creamed corn
> and blackeyed peas and okra
> and green beans and sliced tomatoes
> and corn bread and spoon bread
> and all manner of pies and cakes
> stacked apple pies and Mississippi mud pies
> pound cakes sliced thick with strawberries and cream
> big wet banana cakes
> and coconut cakes you ate with a spoon.
> And the ladies would watch to see
> whose dishes got eaten first
> Miss Nora
> you just can't make enough
> of them old time buttermilk pies
> and smile and say how this wasn't near as good
> as they usually make.

—JAMES A. AUTRY, "ALL DAY SINGING WITH DINNER ON
THE GROUNDS" FROM *NIGHTS UNDER A TIN ROOF*

Almost every day, no sooner was everyone gathered around the kitchen table than there would be a knock at the door. Folks just showed up at mealtime. The New Yorker in me was secretly dismayed, the family totally unperturbed. Someone would get up and grab another chair or two to squeeze around the table; someone else would find plates and fill them with whatever happened to be left on the stove. And the lively chatter and the tall tales and the joyful laughter would continue without missing a beat. This instinctual hospitality, this pure impulse to share whatever you had, this inherent generosity of the table moved me. It was, I came to see, what really mattered about eating together.

THE AUTRYS WERE A WRITING FAMILY. Besides his weekly sermons, Ewart turned out books—including *Don't Look Back Mama*, about their early years—and articles about life in rural Mississippi for national magazines like *Reader's Digest* and *Field & Stream*. Lola Mae became so frustrated that his stories were so poorly illustrated that one day she just decided to learn photography. And she became good at that, too, jumping up from whatever she was doing when someone called her to come and record some animal—human or otherwise—up a tree, or a house struck by lightning. One time, two sheriffs showed up at her door at 2:00 a.m. asking Lola Mae to photograph an illegal whiskey still they'd just discovered. She simply threw on a sweater and followed them. Lola Mae wrote books, too, as did the Autry children. Storytelling came as easy as breathing to that family. "Faulkner didn't have to invent Yoknapatawpha," Lola Mae once told me with a twinkle. "He could have just come up here to Benton County and found his characters. I've met all of them!"

LOLA MAE HAD A STEEP learning curve when she first moved to Mississippi. She'd been a student and a scientist. Her husband taught her how to cook, and as with everything she applied herself to, she soon mastered it. But before there was an electric stove in that country house, before, even, there was a wood-fired cookstove, there was only the fireplace. "We'd put two large rocks about eighteen inches apart just inside the fireplace and set an old icebox rack on them," Ewart once explained. "On each corner of the rack, we'd have small rocks about five inches in diameter. On these, we'd place a sheet of tin. With hot coals between the big rocks under the icebox rack and more hot coals on top of the tin, we'd have a pretty good oven. Just slip whatever you want to cook on the rack and let it bake." And slip she did.

Lola Mae told me she reckoned she made biscuits pretty much three times a day for more than forty years. Sometimes, when biscuits were all there was for dinner, she'd make sawmill gravy—bacon drippings thickened with cornmeal and milk—so called because it was what the men who worked at the local sawmills would pour over their biscuits. She made biscuits when a distraught neighbor showed up at their door at 3:00 a.m. "Not everyone who asks for a biscuit is food hungry," she wrote. "He may need a listener-comforter even more. And after that, he may be like the birds and want a biscuit, too."

Once, when her son brought a bunch of friends home from college, she figured she made more than a hundred biscuits at that one breakfast. She'd scatter any leftover crumbs on the roof of their well house for the cardinals to finish. It's not hard to see why each time I make Lola Mae's biscuits, I am providing more than something to dip into a mess of collards; I'm reaching back, trying to connect with her entire way of life.

LOLA MAE WAS PIOUS AND PLAYFUL; by the time I met her, I understood that her intelligent blue eyes had seen it all. I was instantly at home in her kitchen, where the sunny morning light would slip through the dense piney woods and pour onto her windowsill. I close my eyes and I'm instantly back at her sink. Washing dishes meant looking out the window deep into the secrets of those knowing trees. Growing in those Mississippi woods among the wild roses and holly were the big sweet native muscadine grapes, sometimes called scuppernong, that we'd gather for jelly. Native huckleberries covered the red dirt roadsides; we'd pick them for pies and wild dandelion greens and poke salad, canning the leaves for greens and pickling the stems.

But biscuits are what I remember most about Lola Mae's kitchen. Turning them out by the dozens was as effortless as playing a keyboard for her. Same as breathing. Talking as she poured flour (she used that soft, cakelike, Southern self-rising White Lily or Martha White, so low in protein and therefore gluten that her biscuits were soft, too) into a big, chipped bowl. She'd work shortening (lard or Crisco) into the flour with two knives until it looked like coarse meal, testing the texture with her fingertips midsentence while commenting on the weather or checking on everyone's plans for the day.

Then, chattering away, her voice as musical as Southern birdsong, she'd add buttermilk to the flour: "Buttermilk," she'd say, "makes all the difference!" She'd work it in just until the dough came together. Without even looking at what she was doing, her movements so natural, she'd dust her hands with flour, then knead the dough just a few times, grab a rolling pin, and gently roll that dough out into a circle. She'd reach for a jelly glass from the shelf, or her old dented aluminum biscuit cutter, and she'd cut her biscuit rounds from the dough, forming each patty with her fine pianist's hands—the first knuckle of her index finger ever so slightly, arthritically, skewed (one of mine's getting like that now). Sometimes she'd bake her biscuits in a banged-up blackened baking pan, sometimes in a cast-iron skillet. In minutes, a plate of those biscuits would be on the table and she'd be on to the next batch.

For Christmas one year, she FedExed me a box of them.

I ASKED LOLA MAE'S DAUGHTER, Martha Lynn Crawford, a teacher of high school science and a writer, too, who lives in Blue Mountain, Mississippi, not far from where she grew up, what she remembered about her mama's biscuits, and this was her response:

Sweet Dorothy, we had a storm and were out of internet service yesterday. So, I am sending this info today about Mother's biscuits. When I was young, Mother's first thing to teach me to make were her biscuits. She never measured anything! The flour was put in a bowl, and solid shortening (approximately ¼ cup) was added. She would take a fork or the side of the big spoon and cut the shortening into pea-size pieces in the flour. She would pick up some of the pea-size shortening in her hand to show me just the size that they should be—no bigger and no smaller!!! Mother would pour buttermilk into the shortening/flour mixture a little at a time. (One time, I remember, she didn't have any milk or buttermilk, and she added water. Those biscuits still came out perfect!)

There was no measuring of the buttermilk. It was added just a little at a time until when mixed, the dough was still a little sticky. The main thing she would always tell me was to not mix it very much and just add enough flour to be able to handle the dough. It was better to leave it a little sticky than to have it stiff, because the biscuits would be dense if the dough was too stiff.

Back in those days, she didn't have a cutting board, and I remember that she would spread some flour directly on the top of the counter, turn the bowl to its side, and let the sticky dough fall out on the floured counter. She would take her small hands and start sprinkling a little flour on the top of the dough, put her right hand on the floured spot on the dough, and give it a little flip. She would do that until she had a tiny amount of flour all over the ball of dough. A rolling pin would be floured, and she would just barely roll it over the top of the dough—not pressing down much at all. She told me that if the dough was pressed down, then the biscuits would be dense instead of light. (The rolling pin was used for so many years that the handles on each end wouldn't stay on anymore, so Mother just removed them and kept on using the rolling pin with no handles on it.)

Mother would always have a little pile of flour off to the side that she would dip her biscuit cutter in before cutting each biscuit and putting it in a greased pan. She never failed at making those famous Lola biscuits! They came out of the oven perfect. She always had a few little pieces of dough left after cutting out the biscuits and would let me roll them up in a tiny ball, and that would be my own personal little biscuit. Everyone was given stern notice from me that their fingers were not to touch that particular biscuit. I now have the cutter. The biscuit pan turned black and crusty on the bottom from being used over and over.

I asked her several years ago to type her biscuit recipe for me. I cherish it because it is personally signed. I make mother's biscuits by her recipe today, but mine never turn out as good. I don't roll mine out. I just press the dough out with my hands to the desired thickness. I cook mine in an old iron skillet rather than a pan. Often I use butter-flavored shortening. Of course, she didn't have flavored shortening years ago. If I happen to have any bacon grease, I'll melt it in my skillet, put the biscuits in the melted grease and then flip them so that it will be on both sides of the biscuits before cooking. Real healthy!!! I did see her do that a few times, also.

Here's the recipe Lola Mae sent to Martha Lynn:

BUTTERMILK BISCUITS

— ❧ —

2 cups self-rising flour, unsifted, plus ⅓ cup for
rolling and kneading

4 tablespoons (¼ cup) vegetable shortening

1 cup buttermilk

In a mixing bowl, put 2 cups of the flour. Add the shortening. Cut into the flour until about pea size. Add buttermilk. Mix. (This makes a very soft dough.) Dust the insides of your hands with flour and turn the "messy glob" onto a lightly floured board. (I use aluminum foil spread on a countertop. Place the foil on top of a dampened counter and it will not slip.)

Gently mold the dough into a soft manageable ball. Sprinkle flour on the foil as needed. Do not overdo this. Knead the ball no more than four or five times—very gently. With a flour-dusted rolling pin, roll the ball out until ¼ inch thick. Add a dusting of flour to the pin and dough as needed. *Never* have a stiff dough, just a workable one. Cut out the biscuits. Place into a seasoned iron skillet. (If the skillet is not seasoned, spray with cooking spray.)

Bake on the middle rack of a 425°F oven for 8 to 10 minutes. As tops of biscuits *begin* to show a tinge of browning, turn on the oven broiler unit and brown to desired color.

Two very important points: Do not over-knead the dough. Four or five turns of the dough are enough. *And*—do not overcook. These biscuits are at their best when the above instructions for cooking are followed.

WHEN I MAKE LOLA MAE'S biscuits at home these days, certain cultural differences arise. I've ordered her White Lily self-rising flour online (the shipping cost three times more than the flour). When I search for Crisco unsuccessfully on the shelves of my urban supermarkets, I am directed to Nutiva, a vegan shortening that bills itself as an "organic superfood" that will "nurture vitality." Reading the legends on the container—"A creamy blend of Red Palm and Coconut Oils" and "100% Less Cholesterol than Butter"—something not nice rises up in my throat. Here, then, is a cultural impasse: Crisco is made from (the dread) partially hydrogenated vegetable oil, namely cottonseed, a by-product of ginning cotton. It was invented as a substitute for the (formerly dread) pork fat–based lard. Crisco? Lard? What the hell, I think. I'll just make the biscuits with butter.

Just at this moment, Lincoln sails through the kitchen. "My pastry chef friends would use frozen butter," he opines, "and grate it right into the flour. They say it works better." Lincoln has taken a proprietary interest in all things Lola Mae ever since I brought him to visit her when he was twelve. She made him his first red velvet cake (it was three layers tall, and she deliberately forgot to mention that its color came from beets), and fed him his first meat-and-three at a local mom-and-pop restaurant, and they caught a box turtle and she painted his name on the shell and they went deep into the woods to release it. "I'm sure she would have used butter if she could have," he tells me, his confidence built by their years-long relationship of her reporting back to him on turtle sightings (none!).

I might have mentioned that baking is not my strong point. But tonight, thinking hard about Lola Mae, perhaps even channeling her, I make her biscuits again. Grating half a stick of frozen butter right into the soft flour does make the flour easy to work (and not overwork) and adds an agreeable salti-ness to the biscuits. I pay special attention to what Lola Mae was saying behind the words she wrote. My fingers are un-characteristically relaxed, my touch light. I actually feel the dough change as I bring it together in the bowl. I stop well short of worrying it. I'm beginning to get it. I'm beginning to make Lola Mae's biscuits her way: deliberately. Pausing to give every step its due seems like poetry. Like prayer.

I rip off a piece of aluminum foil as she suggests, and smoothing it on the counter, use that as a rolling surface, taking the time to flour it well, and to flour my hands, too. Then ("Lincoln!!!"), I can't find the @#%@ rolling pin, so (close your eyes, Lola Mae) I grab a corked, half-empty bottle of red, and that works fine. I find some saved bacon fat in a jar in the fridge and measure four tablespoons of it into my largest cast-iron pan. Grabbing a juice glass, I cut out the biscuits, careful to use every bit of dough, and gently lift them into the skillet and place the skillet in the oven. After 10 minutes, I take the step (sheepishly recalling that I'd never done it in the past) of turning on the broiler for half a minute, which admirably colors the biscuit tops.

Holding a warm biscuit, tasting it, I am thrilled. This is it! This time I have made Lola Mae's biscuits right: slim and crusty on the outside, cottony soft and warm inside. Serving them, I feel . . . in charge. A teeny bit powerful and a teeny bit proud. And in that moment, I come close to understanding the heady feeling of competence that making biscuits gave Lola Mae almost every day of her life.

OVER IN TIPPAH COUNTY, touching Benton County but really a world away, Ruth McKinstry, a relative, would set out an unforgettable lunch, never content until every square inch of her mahogany table, layered with her best white lace cloths, was covered with sparkling cut-glass serving dishes. What a picture it made! I loved the look of the pale-green cubes of watermelon-rind pickles, and clove-spiced peeled whole pears, sitting stems-up in a dish. There were slices of pickled green tomato and sweet, sticky fig preserves. There were bowls of creamy butter beans, slow-cooked okra and tomatoes, and potato salad with dill pickle and lots of celery. There was pale-pink baked ham with raisin sauce; soft, warm dinner rolls; and fruit salad (canned) with tiny marshmallows. By the time you sat down to dinner, there was hardly room for the plates.

And I remember how that same table looked when Miss Ruth passed: now heavy with macaroni casseroles, and fried chicken and rice, and sweet potato pies, and soft lemon pound cakes, and thick banana puddings, each made and carried over by a friend, each dish labeled with a name taped to the bottom so it could be returned to the right neighbor.

I think of Miss Ruth's table with a smile as I spread a lunch of platters over the entire surface of quite another table—this one on eastern Long Island, outdoors under a tree. Plain white ovals hold sliced tomatoes and peaches with tufts of thyme and a hit of sherry vinegar; my watermelon salad has feta and wrinkled oil-cured black olives and torn basil leaves; thinly sliced prosciutto is draped over cantaloupe slices with plenty of sliced limes and lots of mint; a pile of steamed whole green beans is sprinkled with sea salt and just a shot of olive oil; our bread-and-butter pickles and red pepper relish are served right from their Ball canning jars.

PRESERVING CAPTURES THE ESSENCE OF a place in a jar. I'd like to say that the pickle recipes I've made for years were born in Lola Mae's kitchen, but the truth is, I was inspired by a Southern cook I never knew. Freddie Bailey lived in a very different Mississippi, about three hundred miles southwest, in Natchez. Her house was an impressive Colonial Revival, with four turreted stories and white-painted porches. Freddie

Bailey was the aunt of Lee Bailey, a most stylish man and the author of dozens of cookbooks that influenced the effortless-seeming bountiful-platter entertaining style that appeared, for a while, at every New York dinner party. Lee Bailey had a small shop in a chic boutique department store, the late, lamented Henri Bendel on Fifth Avenue, that sold the simple and beautiful serving vessels that delivered those dinners. (In fact, the white oval metal platter with chipped enamel on the cover of Michael Anthony's *V is for Vegetables*—which shows Mike pouring olive oil over sashimi-thin slices of his beloved heirloom tomatoes—came from Lee's shop.) Everything about Lee Bailey was deliberately, and effectively, no nonsense. I remember a party at his East Side penthouse; there were full-size fruit trees in tubs fitted with permanent watering hoses on his wraparound terrace, and everyone was just wandering around the apartment, like family.

Lee sent me a copy of the little cookbook, *Aunt Freddie's Pantry*, he'd urged his aunt to write. It is a slyly deceptive book. Under a homey country-calico-patterned jacket, there's a foreword by Lee, and a word from his pal, the famous columnist Liz Smith. Looking further, you discover that the artfully moody black-and-white photographs—all that soft light spilling through curtained windows onto rows of jars and bottles, just so, and then onto great pots sitting on the white porcelain stovetop—were made by the renowned French portrait photographer Brigitte Lacombe. Lee was mad for his aunt's hot pepper jelly (which he also sold at Bendel's). That pepper jelly made Aunt Freddie a celebrity in Natchez; she turned it out by the hundreds of jars and even sold it by mail. But I never made her hot pepper jelly, probably snobbishly turned off by the Certo (bottled fruit pectin) and (optional) red or green food coloring her recipe called for. It was Aunt Freddie's bread-and-butter pickles that got me.

Around the time I discovered her book, our charming local Long Island farm stand, the family-owned Round Swamp, had ratcheted up their prices a few notches—considering its East Hampton clientele, it could. (We told its six-generation story of fishermen and farmers, "The Other East Hampton," in *Saveur.*) And as much as I admired the sisters, and their daughters and granddaughters, who ran the business, a single pint of their bread-and-butter pickles was costing about $10, which for me sort of missed the point of home canning. Admittedly sucked in by those arty photographs of her jelly kitchen—taking them for the real thing—I jumped on Aunt Freddie's pickle recipe. Roger and I would slice up a bushel of Kirby cukes (we liked their tight shape), fill two huge pots with them, salt them, layer them with white onions, and, as Aunt Freddie did, let them stand overnight.

Every year, I changed the recipe until we got it right. For the brine, I eliminated her green peppers and cinnamon, cut the sugar, upped the celery seeds and turmeric, and added mustard seed. Note to self on my recipe: "Cook about 20 minutes or until they look like pickles, which means the heat and turmeric have done their job." We filled a standing army of quart jars, but I didn't like what the pickles looked like after we boiled those jars for canning; those pickles stayed crisper and looked better refrigerated. Some years we'd make as many as twenty-four quarts. Friends looked forward to their pickle gifts; our recipe was published in a few cookbooks.

Then, strangely, we tired of bread-and-butter pickles—just no longer felt like making them. But it occurred to me that a version of that delicious pickle brine could be an excellent way to ensure that Long Island's August crop of bright-red bell peppers would last the year long. Now we mark the end of the summer season with our red pepper relish: using three-quarters of a bushel of red peppers, and two huge onions—about 32 cups, roughly chopped in the Cuisinart. This is tricky: that machine tends to get overexcited by the peppers and must be carefully tamed! The brine—2 quarts white vinegar, 7 cups sugar, 8 tablespoons salt, 5 tablespoons mustard seed, 4 tablespoons celery seed, 2 tablespoons turmeric, and 1 heaping tablespoon cloves tied in cheesecloth—is boiled first. Then the not-too-finely chopped peppers and onions are added and brought to a boil for just 10 minutes. Every year, I order cool French canning jars online, and after a 10-minute boil in my Granite Ware canner, those jars of red pepper relish are ready for us and our friends.

In the 2020 season of quarantine, as the summer wound down, making red pepper relish and resurrecting bread-and-butter pickles not only made good pantry sense but also suddenly seemed urgent: I found the process as reassuring as meeting up with an old friend and finding that we still had a whole lot to talk about. Roger and I turned a bushel of crisp Kirbys, their flesh made golden by the turmeric, their slices plumped by the brine, into a dozen quarts of pickles, a tender spray of fennel blossom from the Greenmarket slipped into each jar, arming us against the unknown winter to come.

BACK IN WHIPPOORWILL VALLEY, across the driveway from the house was Lola Mae's vegetable garden, carved from a red dirt clearing in the piney woods, rocky as a riverbed. What was most startling to me among what grew there were the greens: collard and mustard and turnip greens were a major food discovery for a girl reared on frozen spinach. Taking the greens home, I went full Southern, slicing up great armloads and cooking them in a big pot of water with smoked ham hocks. Dipping corn bread, hot from the cast-iron skillet, into the salty pot likker was a little bit of heaven. Then I hopped to my favorite Julia Child recipe for turnips, greens and all, called Potage Untel. It's a soup in which the turnips and their greens are cooked and pureed into a chicken broth. Sometimes I puree the greens and broth together, then dice the cooked turnips and serve them bobbing in the soup. I cook collards often, removing their center rib, then chopping them and softening them in a bit of oil, with other greens. Sometimes, I'll whisk in a few eggs, add some red pepper flakes, and run the pan under the broiler, and there's a collard frittata for lunch.

Once, after returning from a visit to Mississippi, I received this letter from Ewart: "We awoke again to rain this morning. Later I took a quick run out to the mustard patch. Despite the rain, the faint prints of your tracks were still there. I had a sudden siege of nostalgia at seeing those tracks with nobody in them. Don't wait too long to walk again in our mustard patch . . . The remembrance of your visit is as heartwarming as the sight of a man's face in an old maid's mirror."

"Y'all come back," Lola Mae would say when I visited. When I pointed out that I'd not even left yet, she'd reply: "Well then, we'll look for you when we see you coming."

THE RISOTTO LESSON
(& SO MUCH MORE)

BEGINNING WITH *THE CLASSIC ITALIAN COOK BOOK*, in 1973, Marcella Hazan brought real Italian cooking into the lives of American home cooks, and much later—and luckily, in person—she brought it into mine. I met her as an editor (we did Marcella stories in *Met Home* and *Saveur*); she left me as a friend. In a lesson for the ages—and our *Saveur* issue on Venice—she cooked one of the last meals she made in her kitchen tucked into the rooftop of a sixteenth-century palazzo before she and her husband, Victor, gave up their home there. Marcella taught me the defining dish of that watery city— risotto—how to make it creamy and wavy (*all'onda*), and why the shape of the rice grain matters as much as the shape of the pot. In that kitchen, she showed me how to cut punterelle, the spiky long-limbed Italian winter chicory, whose stems must be carefully split, then plunged into ice water (where they curl up playfully as they drink). Only then can the spiky chicory be dressed with a pungent anchovy vinaigrette and become the classic Roman salad that bears its name.

On Long Island, she showed me how bluefish can be better than striped bass, and made the odd, molded insalata russa, Russian salad, slyly pointing out that beets are the only thing Russian about it (otherwise, like most worthy things, it's Italian). I make fresh shell beans the way Victor's onetime Tuscan housekeeper did (with lots of sage, garlic, and olive oil and only a little water, in a heavy pot, its lid swathed in a dish towel); I learned to shape elegant little tortellini in the Bologna kitchen of Marcella's longtime assistants, the twins Valeria and Margherita Simili, themselves accomplished teachers. One Easter, I tracked down an Italian butcher in Queens to find the milk-fed lamb—abbacchio—she insisted was the way to celebrate that holiday properly. Marcella's vitello tonnato means summer to me. I learned from Marcella, too, that it's very okay to lose your patience sometimes, and especially when bad things happen to good ingredients.

Marcella was a world-class eye roller with a well-earned a reputation for being tetchy. My theory is that she was just far smarter than most people. (Smart as two universities, in fact, she held two doctoral degrees, one in natural science and one in biology, from the universities of Padua and Ferrara.) What I liked most about Marcella, besides her curiosity—her knowledge was deep and scholarly—was her no-BS manner. She was never a fussy entertainer and would only get visibly cross if people came to the table late. The food she cooked was to be eaten hot!

When you asked a direct question, when you needed the real take on something, a real answer is what you'd get. "Pesto," she famously said, "may have become more popular than is good for it." She would look you in the eye and speak truth, whether it was about how long to cook pasta ("Until it's done!") or a friend's cooking. "Is so-and-so a good cook? Well, he thinks he is!" she'd declare knowingly. But though she could be playful at times (she once described Maria, her longtime kitchen assistant, as "a cross between Mussolini and a tractor"), you quickly understood that Marcella did not suffer fools. Unfortunately, she met quite a few of them during the thirty years she taught classes in Bologna, Venice, and New York. Over the decades of teaching and publishing six books, with a growing public voice, Marcella still could not believe the kind of questions she'd get. "Students ask me if I cook every day," she once told me, incredulous. "They might as well ask me if I shower every day!" As our beloved mutual friend, the magazine editor Pamela Fiori, put it: "Marcella minces garlic; she does not mince words."

TO BE TRANSFORMED BY MARCELLA'S cooking—to really get it—you need a subtle shift of awareness. But it must be visceral. Her cooking does not mean mastering complicated techniques or even arcane ingredients. Hers is a totally engaged, all systems go, awake craft: What you see is what you cook. Marcella cooked every day, and every day, she was spellbound by the irresistible transformation of a few elemental ingredients—this chicken, these tomatoes, this fennel—into a meal. "In a recipe," she once told me, "it is the same importance what you keep out as what you put in."

Marcella had the rigor of a scientist and the wisdom of a nonna. The scientist in her never tired of the magic show of cooking: Just look at how *this* could become *that*, and then how *that* could become dinner. What drove Marcella was the bone-deep conviction that cooking was the everyday miracle. Ever the good Italian wife, she never tired of cooking for her demandingly exigent Italian-born American husband. Technically, I guess you could say Marcella was Italian American. But she was worlds away from those Italian American Sunday gravy cooks who immigrated to the United States primarily from Southern Italy, and whose red sauce involved four meats cooked down for five hours, would last all week, and was served over, under, and around everything.

Not that Marcella didn't love a good tomato sauce. Her own signature tomato sauce—positively austere by comparison, requiring only a can of tomatoes, butter, one onion, salt, and forty-five minutes—has become legendary. The recipe was demurely introduced as Tomato Sauce III in her first book. By the time *Essentials of Classic Italian Cooking* was published, it had become Tomato Sauce with Onion and Butter. Would that she and Victor had earned a dollar every time that sauce saved dinner in America.

IF I CLOSE MY EYES and concentrate, I can summon Marcella's distinctive voice: low, raspy, authoritative. When Marcella spoke English, it was like she was still speaking Italian, only you could understand her better. "DOOR-o-tee," she'd say to me, "I teach cooking. I do not teach recipes. I do not teach measuring. If I say three tablespoons and you end up with two tablespoons, in Italian cooking, it doesn't matter. Victor is so precise with the cookbooks, but sometimes I take the average of two measurements. If you chop more, you brown it more. If you chop less, you brown it less. Browning gives you flavor. Such things, they may not be in the recipe, but they are what cooking is."

Marcella spoke to me long before I met her, though I did not know early on that the elegant, formal English I was reading was all Victor's writing style. It's common knowledge that Marcella wrote every one of her six books in Italian—in longhand, on yellow legal pads. Then Victor—Harvard-educated, worldly, and robustly opinionated—took over, rigorously questioning her recipes and measurements, translating her thoughts, and adding considerable commentary of his own in lofty language that captured Marcella's intentions but not her voice. Victor's role in their partnership is much discussed, providing irresistible psychological material for food journalists, editors, and cooks around the world. Clearly, Marcella's marriage to Victor Hazan made her an international culinary star. I have my opinions, but I'll happily leave the psychodrama to others.

My first Marcella recipe was a roast chicken with two lemons, which appeared in her second book, *More Classic Italian Cooking*. I remember it coming first (as many good ideas do) from my friend Stevie Pierson, who had taken Marcella's classes in New York and Bologna. It was a revelation when I learned that I could pierce two small lemons with a fork, insert them into a whole chicken, close the opening with a skewer, rub the bird all over with salt and pepper, and roast it for an hour or so. That was all I needed! Dozens of chickens and twice as many lemons got our family through decades of dinners. And it was an auspicious place to start. "Were I to choose a dish to show how the simplest cooking can also be the most sublime, I would take this one," Marcella wrote about Pollo al Limone, Roast Chicken with Lemon, telling readers she'd traveled to Liguria, on the Italian Riviera, to discover the recipe. That fateful recipe, in fact, became the famous "Engagement Chicken" of *Glamour* magazine fame, passed along from editor to editor, each of whom, curiously, received a marriage proposal after stuffing her own chicken with two lemons and serving it to a grateful beau.

BECAUSE MARCELLA WAS ITALIAN, I just assumed that she always knew the food of her native country. All of it. Much later, sitting in on her class at the French Culinary Institute in New York, where she and Victor used two gigantic maps to illustrate their point, I understood more. "People do not know that Italy is not a nation. It is a collection of states. It may never be more than that. It may never be a nation," Victor lectured. "Italy," he declared dramatically, "is an unrelated collection of dishes!"

"People do not know," Marcella reiterated, "that Italy has such radically different geographic conditions. And it is those conditions that make the difference in their regional cuisines." So, as much as she felt in her bones the flavors of Emilia-Romagna—where she grew up in a small town on the Adriatic Sea—it took Marcella many years and living in markedly different Italian cities for her, ever the student, to master the ingredients and signature specialties of Italy's other regions. Just like the rest of us, I realized, Marcella had to teach herself the cosmopolitan ways of the Milanese, the earthy Roman dishes, the spectacular seafood of the Veneto, the spices and sun-baked flavors of the south.

In the early years of their marriage, after living in New York, Victor suddenly took a job in advertising in Milan. Marcella prowled that new city like the tourist she was. Cooking every day, she discovered markets and unfamiliar ingredients, developed new food rituals and recipes. There, she beheld with wonder the real Italian cooking she had been teaching in New York, "which," she wrote, "existed largely in my imagination. I had the confirmation I had longed for: My story was not a fairy tale." The Italian cooking she first taught in New York, Marcella told me, came straight from books by Italy's premier cook, Ada Boni. It wasn't until the 1960s in Milan that Marcella experienced firsthand the prepared dishes, like i ripieni, the aromatically stuffed vegetables, at the iconic market Peck, calling that extravaganza "a food lover's fantasy brought to life." Decades later, I was gobsmacked, too, by Peck and its sheer *abbondanza*—abundance and generosity of presentation. I trace the seeds of my passion for serving food on outsize platters to my first sight of Peck's voluptuous prepared salads on trays big as tabletops.

Several decades after Marcella explored Milan, a small group of editors from *Metropolitan Home* decided to cover furniture design the way fashion editors covered couture shows. We traveled to the annual Fiera Milano, where cutting-edge design from around the world makes its debut. Every day, we would trudge through the airline terminal–size buildings packed with chic chairs and shape-shifting sofas. And every night, we would get to taste dishes we'd only read about, like pappardelle with wild boar (cinghiale), and hare (lepre), and the irresistibly crispy pancake, riso al salto, the next-day incarnation of saffron-scented risotto alla milanese. We thrilled watching a waiter shave fresh truffle onto our pasta, and laughed when he refused our request for more. "Non sono i patate!" (These are not potatoes!) Writing about our first arugula salad, we had no idea even how to spell it: rucola? roquette?

But Peck, for us, was everything. I shared Marcella's awe as I beheld craggy mountains of Parmigiano, whole legs of prosciutto and other cured meats hanging from the ceiling, intricate displays of fresh seafood—creatures I'd never seen whose names I did not know—and rivers of olive oil. Peck was a delirium of food. Like Marcella, our little team could not believe our eyes. And like Marcella, we had our rituals. We would time our visit to Peck's bakery down the street, to coincide with the minute the focaccia, dimpled with green olives, rosemary, and flecks of sea salt, would come out of the oven. Then, the warm and fragrant flatbread in hand, we would proceed ceremonially to that other cathedral—the Duomo—to light a candle for our fledgling magazine.

I HAVE ALWAYS BEEN SEDUCED by the way real people cook real food (hence *Saveur*). The source of the recipe for Assunta's Beans is the housekeeper Victor employed in the small rooms he occupied in a once-grand Florentine villa among ancient olive trees. Victor, it must be acknowledged, has a flair for the perfect in his living arrangements (*see* the top floor of the Palazzo Ruspoli in Rome, approached by a hundred steps "hewn from a single magnificent block of marble";

see an apartment in a Venetian palazzo with two terraces and twenty-eight windows). "Assunta," as Marcella described her, "was a tall, hungry-looking, perpetually black-frocked woman with glowing, dark eyes and the largest feet I have ever seen on man or woman." Who could forget that image?

I make Assunta's beans with fresh shell beans like cannellini, or, most often, with gorgeous red-striped fresh cranberry beans: two cups of beans shelled into a heavy pot and covered with at least ⅓ cup of olive oil, a splash of water to start, three smashed garlic cloves, and a generous bunch of fresh sage leaves, the pot lid wrapped in a damp dish towel and tied up like a babushka to keep the moisture in. As with so much of cooking, the look is everything. The beans soften slowly; the dish towel absorbs the steam. The result? The creamiest, sageiest beans ever. The only thing about cranberry beans is that what cooking delivers in taste and texture, it takes away in color—the beans become dead beige in everything but their flavor.

That peculiar propensity of even the most colorful beans to turn drab with cooking reminds me of Burkhard Bilger's quote in his *New Yorker* story about the artisanal American bean grower Steve Sando: "Cooking beans is like going to see clowns and sword swallowers at a circus, only to find them all sitting inside the tent, playing canasta. It's God's little joke," Sando said. The clever grower, incidentally, struck up a friendship with Marcella when he noticed her ordering beans from his Rancho Gordo website. After he contacted her directly, she asked him why he didn't grow her favorite Italian bean, Sorana, calling it, "the most precious bean in Italy." Ever tenacious, Sando tracked down that bean and brought it to California, where he now grows the delicate, thin-skinned cannellini he calls (with her permission!) Marcella beans. And every year, I await Rancho Gordo's email alerting me that the tender long white beans are back in stock. Marcella beans are a favorite gift to friends.

THE FIRST TIME I WENT to visit Marcella and Victor in Venice, I wrote in my *Met Home* editor's page: "Over the years, I've learned lots of lessons from Marcella. ('You'll never be a good cook until you can close your eyes and imagine how something should taste.') I had seen photographs of the Hazans' bravura renovation of the top floor of a sixteenth-century palazzo and heard the war stories of the three years it took to complete. But nothing prepared me for the compact brilliance of Marcella's kitchen. Like all great cooks, she has far less equipment than many amateurs do. But it's all figured out—specially designed flip-out drawers and cupboards, high-function work surfaces—tucked into attic-like eaves. Marcella and Victor approached their renovation with scientific precision, but the result is anything but clinical." We assigned the Paris-based food writer Patricia Wells (author of the *Food Lover's Guides* to Paris, and France, and so on) the delightful task of following up on my visit with a story. In Patricia's piece, we featured such Marcella dishes as a simple tomato salad with garlic-steeped olive oil; a Venetian torte of Swiss chard, raisins, and pine nuts; and pappardelle with embogoné, a word, Marcella explains, that comes from a dialect name for snails—which, oddly, are not used in this dish—and may playfully refer to the cranberry beans' snail-like appearance as they cook down with pancetta, sage, and rosemary. In her article, Patricia wrote an appreciation that's uncannily prescient of this book:

"To this day, when I roll out my pasta, carefully stir my risotto, or peel a tomato with a swivel peeler, Marcella is at my side—challenging, correcting, her deep voice stern one moment, encouragingly soft the next. Her clear common sense—so characteristic of the food she has introduced to us all—has taken firm root in my own Paris kitchen. Marcella's is the voice of Italian cooking." Marcella was her Kitchen Whisperer, too.

YOU DID NOT WANT TO take the Hazans to dinner at just any good restaurant in New York; Marcella had little patience for most American chefs, and you'd cringe in anticipation of an encounter. "When I go to restaurants these days, I don't see food," she told me once. "I see ideas on a plate. And when I see plates like that, I say, 'That's beautiful. Give me a camera, I take a picture. And after, give me food!' It doesn't look cooked! People can make it beautiful because they are not interested in the taste. Or," she adds mischievously, "maybe they don't know how to make it taste better?"

And don't get her started on vegetable cookery. Heaven forbid you should choose a restaurant with a so-called farm-to-table chef. "American cooks," she'd say, "they don't cook vegetables. They just show them the water." Or, she'd complain, "I never like the way they use garlic in restaurants here," making me forever wary of overcooking it. "I use a lot of garlic in my cooking, but if you come to my house, you will never smell garlic burning! We use it, but we never make it dark. If it turns brown, it's already cooked too much."

When the Hazans came to town, you were much safer at a Chinatown restaurant like Oriental Garden on Elizabeth Street. Marcella loved Chinese cuisine; it was closer to its ingredients, to its traditions. It was always itself; it never tried too hard. At Oriental Garden, they would present her with a pan of live shrimp, still wiggling, and immediately cook them up in front of her plate. Those shrimp, she said, reminded her of schie, those tiny gray shrimp from the Venetian lagoon the Hazans knew so well. Schie, she would unfailingly remind you, are the only shrimp that remain gray with cooking.

SOMEHOW I GAINED MARCELLA'S TRUST, perhaps because I really wanted nothing more from her, and perhaps because, once, years ago, when she and Victor made their annual summer visit to eastern Long Island, where she was feted every night in yet another fancy Hamptons beach house with yet another fancy (catered?) dinner, Roger and I made them a simple meal served at a picnic table overlooking the harbor, surrounded by a few of our mutual friends.

Planning that dinner, I remembered that Craig Claiborne, whose house was just around Three Mile Harbor from ours, famously entertained big-time French chefs by going local, shopping only at neighborhood farm stands. Our farm stands! It was Claiborne, the famous food editor of the *New York Times*, who, fittingly, was the first to write about Marcella's cooking when she came to New York, a young Italian housewife cooking only the food she knew (from Ada Boni's books) for her elegant and demanding husband. Victor would come home for lunch every weekday. Marcella had enrolled in a Chinese cooking class, and accidentally became a teacher when theirs failed to show and fellow students coaxed her to teach them to make real Italian food instead. Craig had somehow heard about her classes. ("Six lessons for ninety dollars.") When he called and came to lunch, Marcella had no idea who he was. "Marcella doesn't read bylines." Victor recites the story and not for the fiftieth time. "Byline?" Marcella interrupts. "What is byline?" But they both remembered what Marcella cooked for that lunch: tortellini, carciofi alla romana, rollatini di vitello. And Claiborne knew the real thing when he tasted it. As our friend Tom McNamee wrote in his fine biography of Claiborne, *The Man Who Changed the Way We Eat*, "Marcella Hazan was but one paradigm of Craig's unprecedented innovations: the ennoblement of the home cook."

I was delighted to read in Claiborne's memoir, *A Feast Made for Laughter*, a story about making tête de veau, Calf's Head and Its Vinaigrette, with his writing partner/chef, Pierre Franey. Seems he'd had four calf's heads delivered to his East Hampton house not a half mile from ours, where he tested recipes and threw fabulous dinners with his chef friends. After several attempts to tame the heads (they arrived hairy, skin still on), the cooks just dumped them into the very body of water we shared—the water we beheld from our dinner table that night—for some fisherman to be shocked by days later.

For our Hazan dinner, we shopped local, stuffing beefsteak tomatoes with baby lima beans and serving platters of local corn on the cob; a salad of tatsoi, mizuna, and basil from our garden; and hot-smoked salmon over wood charcoal. And only American wines, and only red since Victor was writing a book called *The Color of Wine Is Red* (later published as *Italian Wine*). Marcella told me afterward that it was her favorite dinner of the summer. But maybe she said that to all the girls.

MARCELLA WAS SUSPICIOUS OF FOOD that looked too pretty, suspecting that the cook just might be guilty of prizing aesthetics over flavor. She made an exception, however, for the great painter and cook Hector Leonardi, a Yale-trained American with deep Italian family roots who had taken Marcella's course in Bologna and became a special friend to her—they'd speak (in Italian) on the phone almost every Sunday. When Marcella and Victor came to Long Island in the summer, they stayed with our old friends, Hector and the artist Karl Mann. There, Hector and Marcella often cooked together. Hector simply cannot help it if his platters of roasted red and orange and yellow peppers in olive oil looked like the sunset over Peconic Bay. He is built that way. Elemental. Never fussy. I learn so much from the way Hector handles food, his platters inadvertent canvases. Years earlier, Hector had made Marcella's lasagna— seven impossibly thin pasta layers of porcini mushrooms—for a dinner to celebrate Roger's and my wedding.

ONE OF THE CULINARY TREASURES of Marcella's home province, Emilia-Romagna, is balsamic vinegar, made from grape must—the pressings of grapes, long-aged in wooden barrels. Before America discovered Marcella, in fact, balsamico had been peacefully sleeping in kegs under the roofs of

Modena, sometimes for generations, used only occasionally and deliberately—as the flavor bomb it is—drop by precious drop. Marcella served it rarely, to heighten the essence of a fresh peach, for example. In *Marcella Says . . .* , she makes this categorical statement: "In a world of no compromises, when using balsamic vinegar, you would use only twenty-five-year-old or older Balsamico Tradizionale from Modena or Reggio Emilia. The younger Tradizionale . . . is an adequate alternative. If the only other choice available were the cheap supermarket balsamico, I would not even attempt to make the dish." Yet one of the unintended consequences of Marcella's high American profile has been the flagrant and mindless popularity of balsamic vinegar. In her memoir, Marcella recalls getting the first bottles of a commercial product, a five-year-old balsamico made by Fini, an old and trusted Modena family company, which she served to Craig Claiborne, who was, by that time, a real friend: "And he became the first person in America to taste it," predicting "this will be a sensation!" Neither of them could have imagined how right he was.

I promise you, Marcella never meant for commercial balsamic vinegar to be sitting in a squeeze bottle next to the canola oil on salad bars, offered in fast-food joints, and even used in routine vinaigrettes in pretty good restaurants across the country. Because of her, I hesitate every time I reach for it in the kitchen. Marcella did not like sweet vinegar, a fact she made plain in *Ingredienti: Marcella's Guide to the Market*, a lovely, little-known book which Victor wrote from her notes after she died and published three years later. She called the dissemination of balsamic vinegar "a calamity," wondering, "Why make a salad taste sweet?" "Someday," she wrote, "I hope to see good red wine vinegar restored to its long-honored place, alongside extra-virgin olive oil and sea salt as one of the three essential condiments of a salad." Just as for Victor the color of wine was red, for Marcella, so was the color of vinegar.

"RISOTTO HAS A REASON," she tells me in that unmistakable voice, paved by a lifetime of Marlboros and of speaking her mind. The risotto lesson she gives me for our *Saveur* issue on Venice, it turns out, is the last meal Marcella will cook in her Venetian kitchen. Venice was her dream city; she was in her dream home. When they first moved there, in the early eighties, Marcella would scamper up and down the steps to the four bridges she had to cross on her daily walk to the market, the last of which was the famed Rialto Bridge of travel posters. The Rialto market, looking like a sixteenth-century painting of itself, is where boats pull right up to the quays to unload their produce. It was where Marcella would shop for the chicories, natives of Veneto, grown on the market gardens on islands one could almost see from her terrace balcony. Chicories like the long red-tongued curls of radicchio tardivo brought from nearby Treviso, the voluptuous escaroles and fussy frisées, the pale-green Belgian endives that come in radicchio red here, too, and the spectacular cabbage-like Castelfrancos, their palest green leaves freckled with red.

Nearby is the Pesceria, an imposing neo-Gothic structure, home to a seafood marketplace of lagoon-dwelling creatures only Venice could invent. Marcella and Victor could call every one of them by name: squid and seppioline—baby cuttlefish, octopus in descending sizes, the miniature polpi, and clams: vongole veraci. Capesante—scallops nestled into their coral roe in suave flat shells big as a man's hand. Miniature shrimp (those schie), to be stirred into risotto, and the huge, quasi-monstrous creatures that jumped into vats of brodetto. And little silvery sardines, destined for the sweet-and-sour Venetian specialty sarde in saor, a recipe peculiar to this spice trade—perfumed city. And everything, every single ingredient that you find in the Rialto markets, would show up on the tables of Venice that night in both restaurants and homes. They'd swim in zuppa di pesce and flavor risottos and enliven pastas. They'd star in the lessons Marcella taught her students, who came to Venice to learn just this. At that time, she could easily navigate the narrow alleys lined with little shops that held such wonders as the dried porcini mushrooms she used in her refined, six-layered lasagnas—and the store where she could buy her beloved mostarda, a condiment of fruit preserved in mustard.

Almost twenty years later, she is planning to leave Venice. Her body is not working so well. Climbing those bridges has become more daunting than charming. She is unsteady on the public water buses—the vaporetti and traghetti that ply the canals. Victor, or sometimes her kitchen assistant, now does the daily shopping. It is not that the city had lost its charm. Far from it. It's that Marcella can no longer be an active participant. But she has agreed to meet with me before she leaves, for "The Risotto Lesson."

Marcella looks at me with her serious professor face. "You make risotto from carnaroli if you can find it. Look for carnaroli marked 'ai pestelli' on the package, which means it was hulled with a mechanical mortar and pestle. This leaves the rice covered with a powdery starch. You never wash the rice first, because you need that powdery starch to make it creamy.

Carnaroli doesn't go from undercooked to overcooked in a second; it has more finesse than arborio, which caught on in America simply because it was more available."

In a favorite photograph Roger made for the *Saveur* story, three kernels of carnaroli sit on Marcella's outstretched palm in such close-up that you can clearly see their two starches. The translucent exterior is amylopectin, the starch that dissolves by the very rubbing together of the grains, which is, of course, the long stirring movement that thickens the risotto. Inside is the whiter, interior protein, amylose, which swells and expands with broth and cooking to deliver a still-toothy body.

For that issue of *Saveur*, we were forced to credit the estimable Corti Brothers in Sacramento, California, as the *only* American source of carnaroli. Today carnaroli and Vialone Nano, like so many Italian products, are easily found at most good markets. "And never," Marcella continues darkly, "make risotto in a frying pan like those Italian American cooks do on TV. It goes too fast! You need a pot deep enough to keep stirring; one that will hold liquid long enough for the rice to absorb it."

With a bit of I-can-do-this-in-my-sleep swagger (after all, I did write "The Risotto Lesson"!), and even though I do not even *need* a recipe, I decide to make her risotto for dinner as I'm writing this, just to, you know, test my version of her recipe. I choose Risotto with Red, Yellow, and Green Peppers, from her last cookbook, *Marcella Says . . .* With reporting in mind, I follow her recipe exactly—not often my style, which tends to be more "Read it. Got it."

I remember that she does not ever wait until the pan is hot before sautéing onions, for example, but I am astonished to read that Marcella wants me not just to cook the peppers in the same pot with the onions and eventual rice but to cook them for half an hour *before* I add the rice. Fear of overcooking drives my usual risotto moves—cooking the other ingredients separately and adding them only at the end. Now, instead of casually filling one pot with some stock and dumping some rice in the other after sautéing the onion base, I rigorously follow Marcella's instructions. I'm startled to see that this recipe (like the recipes for most of Marcella's risottos) does not call for wine, the adding of which is typically my automatic next step after stirring the rice into the onion base. And the stock! How could I not have remembered that she distrusts my go-to chicken stock (the product of long hours of cooking down previously roasted chicken, or chicken parts, with vegetables, then dutifully straining and storing the broth in the freezer). She finds chicken stock "distractingly sharp," whereas I am always relieved to find it at all. And now I suddenly remember Victor's total distain for *anything* chicken (he will not touch the stuff!), and I wonder: Have generations of Americans made risotto with beef broth just because . . . *Victor hates chicken?*

And it gets worse. Reading on, I see that she prefers "6 cups fresh or frozen homemade beef broth." Oy, I groan. In my mind, I'm already off to the butcher for just the right combination of marrow bones and beef shank, which means at least a half day's prep, until I get to the reprieve: "or 1 beef bouillon cube dissolved in 6 cups simmering water." Whew. And I do get the rice right—carnaroli and I are old friends—but the cooking time wrong: for most of her risottos, instead of my usual 18 minutes, give or take (where did that come from?), Marcella says . . . about 25 minutes total stirring.

Then there's *mantecare*, which means "creamifying" the

cooked risotto at the end with butter and grated Parmigiano. And never adding more cheese at the table. I remember Marcella looking up from her stove and saying: "People, they ruin my dishes with too much cheese!" *Mantecare* is one Hazan rigor that, I admit, I often skip. Do we really need more butter? But when I actually follow the recipe to its creamy and flavorful result, I am convinced that *mantecare*—adding the butter and cheese right in the pot—makes all the difference. That, and not plopping each serving on a plate but smoothing it out into a flat round, which cools it a bit, and encourages nibbling from the edges in.

Newbies seem to delight in shortcuts like no-stir risottos. Sure, you can put all the rice and ingredients and broth together in a pan—or even, as I read on some cooking sites, in a microwave (or, *gasp*, an Instant Pot)—but doesn't that kinda miss the point? Where is the poetry? The contemplative time spent stirring the risotto is, as Victor would phrase it, the thing itself.

WHEN MARCELLA TURNED EIGHTY, in 2004, Victor and their son, Giuliano, decided to throw a big party for her at the Villa Giona, a wine estate in Valpolicella, near Verona, that dates to the fifteenth century and is now owned by the winemaking Allegrini family. There, Giuliano was carrying on the family tradition, teaching food and wine classes. By that time, I was executive editor of *Newsweek*, and though food was a tetchy subject for my hard news colleagues, I convinced them that Marcella at eighty was a cultural phenomenon worth covering. (Mark Whitaker, the editor, was easy—he's an accomplished and eager cook—but Jon Meacham, the managing editor, just hoped this piece would get food out of my system. His joke was that when he and Mark were out of town, leaving me in charge, I'd put cassoulet on the cover.)

Roger, Lincoln (then eleven), and I met the Hazans in Venice to accompany them to Verona on the train. Marcella is sitting next to me, and as our car passes through Padua, I'm surprised to look up and see a tear in her eye. When I take her hand, questioning, she tells me this train ride is so loaded with memories. Every day as a student, she would commute on this same train from her aunt's apartment in Venice to the university in Padua. "The past is always with us," she says, sighing.

The birthday celebration was extraordinary. "We asked almost everybody," Victor said, "and almost everybody said yes!" About a hundred friends from around the world gathered at the Villa Giona. Giuliano, as is his habit, had arranged everything quietly and flawlessly. Waiters in full-length aprons swept across the villa's green lawns bearing trays like presents: tiny fried sardines, asparagus-and-ricotta tarts, and the prized culatello di Zibello, Parma's most elegant preserved ham. Flutes of Prosecco, Soave, and Valpolicella Classico were offered under square white umbrellas. Once the guests were seated inside the villa, they were served platters of salume— like lardo stagionato, soppressata, and pancetta—and tiny goat cheeses in olive oil and chives. These were followed by two pastas: risotto with wild herbs and tagliolini with black truffles. The veal course, with its Amarone and almond sauce, was accompanied by an Allegrini Amarone, and everywhere, there was lively music from four men Marcella fondly called the "old-timers quartet," whom Victor had brought up from

Marcella's hometown of Cesenatico, playing a twelve-string guitar, mandolins, and a small accordion.

And in the library! In the library, shades of Peck—covering the surface of an ancient mahogany table that ran the length of the room was an opulent still life: plates bearing dozens and dozens of Italy's greatest cheeses set on pedestals of differing heights. There were little caprini—goat cheeses—and imposing quarter-wheels of Parmigiano-Reggiano, and the sheep's-milk Canestrato; there were taleggios and fontinas from the North, and runny robiolas, and whiffy Gorgonzolas (I could go on), punctuated by jars of homemade jams and preserves and honeys and mostardas. It was a knockout, even to the most jaded among us. Dessert was a creamy gelato of chestnuts cooked in honey. Suddenly summoned outside, we were dazzled to see the letters of Marcella's name ignite in fireworks on the lawn.

After my piece appeared in *Newsweek*, Victor wrote a typically courtly thank-you, mentioning two previous attempts by the magazine to cover Marcella, one of which, he remembered, was bumped by the Jonestown massacre, and the other by who knows what. "Your definition of Marcella's achievement, '[she] taught us to make dinner,' went straight to what Marcella and I regard as the most critical issue in cooking," he wrote. "It is critical because it looks to us as though 'making dinner' now comes close to the bottom on most people's lists. At least in the sense that Marcella and I attach to the act . . . It has been, up to the recent past, the central act of most people's daily lives, an act that had once the power to moor those lives to a feeling of contentment."

AND THEN IT WAS TIME to take the inevitable sentimental journey. Pamela Fiori and I knew Marcella was not doing well, and it had been a while since either of us had seen her. So, sometime in early 2013, we decided to make a pilgrimage to Longboat Key in Florida, where the Hazans had moved to a slick high-rise apartment right on the beach, to be near Giuliano and his family. Longboat Key is a thin sliver of land on the Gulf of Mexico, joined to the mainland by a bridge south to bustling Sarasota. Marcella herself had noted the obvious contrast between the forced hygiene of the shrink-wrapped vegetables at their local Publix supermarket and its distance both culturally and emotionally from the Rialto in Venice. It seemed a culinary joke too painful to make.

Pamela and I had visited the Hazans before—once, together—to participate with them in a panel at the Sarasota Library, though neither of us can remember the subject. I'd returned to produce a *Saveur* story with our pal, the *Atlantic* magazine editor Corby Kummer—a story on stone crabs, which are still fished from small boats in the Gulf of Mexico, virtually in front of the Hazans' apartment. (On the boat, we watch, amazed, as a trap is raised and crabs are carefully extracted. Then, only one claw—and that one only from the male crab—is expertly removed, and the crab is tossed back into the Gulf, where it will, hopefully, grow another.)

Pamela, my most elegant friend, whom I think of as the ampersand editor—she totally revamped and relaunched the magazines *Travel & Leisure* and *Town & Country*—surprises me by sliding behind the wheel of our rented SUV and powering it out of the Sarasota airport with muscular expertise. Well, she is a Jersey girl, I remember, checking my seat belt.

We find Marcella on oxygen (emphysema, smoking), a sight that clutches at our hearts. But she's up and chatty. Victor, too. Eager for news, grateful for company.

For dinner, Marcella had directed an assistant to make a familiar meal: tagliata di manzo, steak seared in a cast-iron skillet, then sliced and finished in another pan, where oil, garlic, and rosemary sprigs are waiting, scolding us, as always, to come to table while the steak was hot. At the table, she was still up to playing a mischievous trick: she loved cooking Swiss chard two ways, stripping the leaves from the stalks and quick boiling the greens, serving them with olive oil and lemon juice. But the stalks! Those, she cut from the leaves, diced, boiled in salted water for about 30 minutes, drained, then sautéed with olive oil and garlic until golden. Her great joke was to ask her dinner guests to name that white sautéed vegetable. But that was a trick she'd played with me before; this time I was ready for her.

MARCELLA DIED ON SEPTEMBER 29, 2013. The next week, I went to the French Culinary Center, by that time called the ICC, the International Culinary Center, to weep a bit with its founder, Dorothy Cann Hamilton, who had become as close as a daughter to Marcella. "We must do something extraordinary to remember her," she said. What she had in mind was nothing less than a National Marcella Day, on her birthday, April 15, where cooks all over the country—all over the world, even—would cook the same Marcella dish in celebration.

It was a wonderful idea, but dicey to pull off. Instead, we decided to establish a Marcella Hazan Scholarship that would send culinary students to Italy. To fund the scholarship, we'd have an evening celebration, followed by a lunch in her honor.

The evening memorial was hosted by Tony May, the Italian restaurant impresario (Palio, San Domenico) and a great admirer of Marcella's. Pamela's husband, Colt Givner, made a photographic presentation of wonderful Marcella moments we'd all shared. There were moving tributes, and of course, there were tears. The lunch to raise money for the scholarship was held the following year, on her birthday. Paul Bertolli sent Fra' Mani handcrafted salume from Berkeley. Giuliano Hazan made pasta alla busara, spaghetti with fresh lobster and tomatoes (a recipe that was, indeed, circulated around the world; some restaurateurs and home cooks did, in fact, make it to celebrate Marcella's birthday). Mark Ladner, then the executive chef at Del Posto, made Marcella's vitello tonnato. Dessert, a flat and delicate Bolognese rice cake, was served by the pastry chef of Tony May's restaurant SD26.

MARCELLA'S HOMETOWN OF CESENATICO, on the Adriatic Sea, was a place of abundant seafood. Among all that bounty, she remembered and loved best the little, local saraghine "larger than an anchovy, smaller than a sardine, but with similarly dark and unctuous flesh." She described eating the succulent little saraghine, cooked right on the beach where the fishermen, after tying up their boats, would set up small grills and share their fish with her: "I had quickly learned to eat them as they do. Holding the small fish by the tail and the head, I brought it to my mouth, pulled back my lips, and used my teeth to lift the entire tiny fillet off the bone and suck it into my mouth. Then I turned the fish around and sucked away the fillet from the other side. Oh, the succulence of it! '*Si mangiano col bacio*,' the fishermen say: You eat them with a kiss." Federico Fellini, who grew up on the Adriatic in a town not far south of Cesenatico, named the voluptuous beach-dwelling rhumba dancer in his film *8½*, Saraghina, for those luscious little fish.

Bluefish are much bigger than saraghine, but they have the same succulent dark flesh and nonglamorous image on eastern Long Island, where they are disdained by the locals in favor of the far flashier, costlier (and, we all think, far less flavorful) striped bass. (The joke is that you bake bluefish under a layer of mayonnaise on tinfoil, then throw away the fish and lick the foil.) Marcella didn't know from bluefish (it's rarely sold in New York markets), but she came to Long Island enough summers to appreciate its flavor possibilities. She created a way of cooking bluefish fillets by laying them over thin-sliced Yukon Gold potatoes, first made crispy on a sheet pan in the oven, with a little garlic and a handful of thyme—a dish those of us who knew about it would make all summer long.

WITH MARCELLA, I AM A forever student, sometimes deliberately attempting recipes that seem out of my range. One day, I promise myself, I will finally make that green lasagna I learned in Bologna—no excuses! The Simili sisters' handwritten recipe is still right here, on my desk, just as Marcella is in my kitchen still. Not like in that famous cartoon by David Sipress, as a religious shrine hung over the stove; a young woman turns to her friend and explains, "It's not a saint, exactly. It's Marcella Hazan." (The same Sipress who, in a fond memorial in the *New Yorker*, referred to Marcella as "a tough biscotti.") I think of Marcella every time I dip my fingertips into the jar of salt I keep by the stove as she did, remembering not to add it to my pasta water until it comes to a full boil. I think of her as I am stirring, stirring, slowly stirring her risotto in my deep pot. And as Marcella did, I try to cook dinner almost every night, attempting, by that act, to make home the living heart of a world that seems every day more crazed and less comprehensible.

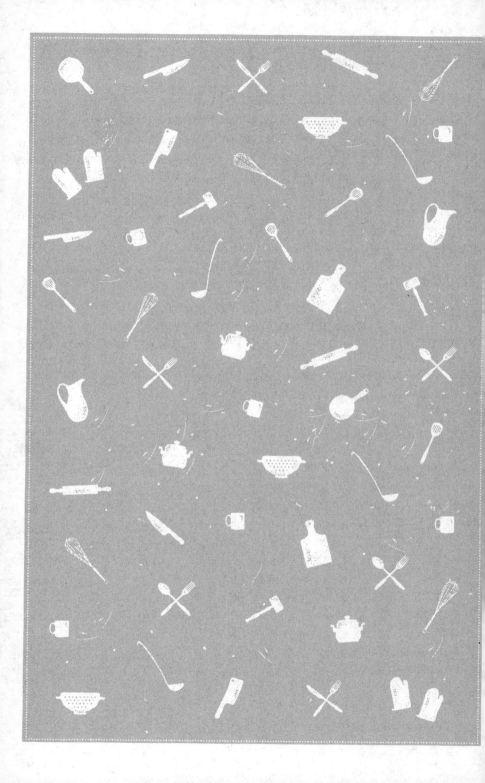

CHAPTER 4

———— ❧ ————

SALT COD & THE MAN

Gundel discreetly inquired about my health, digestion, and eating preferences, and then suggested that I start with *Balatoni fogas à la Rothermere*.

"Just the filet of the fish, boiled in a *court bouillon* made with white wine, then covered with *sauce hollandaise* and topped off with a crayfish *pörkölt*, a ragout in a thick paprika sauce," he said. He made a circle with thumb and forefinger, closed his eyes, and shook his head slowly, and for a moment there was an expression of ethereal delight on his face.

—JOSEPH WECHSBERG, *BLUE TROUT AND BLACK TRUFFLES: THE PEREGRINATIONS OF AN EPICURE*, 1953

IN THE MIDDLE OF A winter over a decade ago, Colman Andrews summoned several dozen of his friends and family members to the restaurant Gundel, in Budapest, to celebrate an important birthday. The choice was no accident: as an editor and food writer, he'd fallen early and hard for the epicurean writing of Joseph Wechsberg, whose rich commentary on the European restaurant scene in *The New Yorker* and in his books spoke to Colman as a young writer. Too, the ebullient restaurateur George Lang, the Hungarian proprietor of Café des Artistes in Manhattan, had told high-drama stories of his renovation of the legendary and nearly one-hundred-year-old Gundel. Since this was an irresistible invitation, Christopher Hirsheimer and I and a gratifying number of Colman's food world friends made the trip.

In the early days of our friendship, Colman and I often cooked together—or rather, he would be cooking, and I would be curled over a cutting board dicing toast for croutons for his soup into impossibly (and to my eyes, unnecessarily) teeny and regular squares. Colman is nothing if not demanding; he cared awfully how his food was presented. I was surprised to read his altogether different version of our cooking escapades in *My Usual Table: A Life in Restaurants*: "By the time we started talking about *Saveur*, Dorothy, Christopher, and I had known one another for at least ten years. We had worked together, gone out to countless meals together, traveled together, and cooked together . . . We had different styles in the kitchen: Dorothy was meticulous and well organized and often seemed to be pursuing some platonic culinary ideal; I was on the rough-and-tumble intuitive side, trying things that worked well about half the time; Christopher would let us scuffle, and then just quietly set about making little masterpieces with a 'This old thing?' modesty." Calling me "meticulous" in the kitchen was either a fanciful misreading or a sign that he was too caught up in realizing his own vision to notice my faults. He was spot on about Christopher, however. Colman was the writer, and I was the editor, and Christopher became the photographer—but she was always the cook.

And okay, I suppose you could call me guilty of fantasizing about unattainable culinary glory. But Colman's "rough-and-tumble intuitive" style? This man is a fanatic for accuracy (I recall an anguished animal howl rising from his office when, late one night, he discovered that a writer had placed a town in the wrong county). In cooking, he is laser-focused on every element and its position on the plate, leading to my characterization of Colman as a "plateist" as opposed to mine as a "platterist." Colman, deliberate as a chef, frets about the way each element appears on the dish that's set in front of a diner. I, on the other hand, tilt heavily toward abundance. I like my food piled on platters that run down the center of the table. One might be tempted to throw around ideas of control versus generosity, but one might be incorrect.

The apotheosis of the "plateist" ideal was that birthday celebration at Gundel. As Colman recalled it later: "When the main course is served, the whole dining room stops to take notice: in front of every place is a large plate covered by a silver dome; twenty-seven waiters surround the table with military precision, and at a nod from the captain, each raises a dome (you can almost hear a chorus of 'Aaahhhs')—to reveal thick, forest-brown slices of roasted Böszénfa roe-deer saddle, which turns out to be possibly the best venison I've ever had, juicy and rich and somehow wild-tasting without being gamy, glistening with intense, dark black truffle sauce and surrounded by an underbrush of grilled carrots, baby leeks, and cauliflower." So. As I said, he's the food writer. Word-perfect but for that unfortunate "underbrush" of grilled carrots.

"I've probably learned a lot from cooks, pro and otherwise," he told me recently, "but as you know, my orientation since childhood has always been looking at food from the point of view of the dining room more than from the kitchen. You look at food from the kitchen out." That sounds right to me. Since his childhood in Los Angeles, son of a screenwriter father and a onetime-ingénue actress who loved the glam of dining out, restaurants have always been, for Colman, all about atmosphere and romance and theater. What showed up on the plate was just the final gesture in the long dramatic arc of the evening's performance.

When Colman cooks (and I would be happy for him to cook for me any day), he wants to control the way his guests experience his food. He wants the plate to tell the story. And I guess I see a bigger picture—the whole issue, if you will, and not just the one piece. Instead of Colman's honed-in plateist focus, for a big dinner, I'd serve a platterist's bounty: my version of pot au feu, for example. I'd make a landscape of slices of boiled beef, a pile of braised short ribs, a chubby boiled chicken, a couple of lamb's tongues (sliced), and lots of smoked sausages, surrounded by little red potatoes (skin-on), carrots (peeled, leaving a little green stem), and parsnips, and turnips, everything brought to the table in a great presentation on outsize trays. Or I'd serve a long-simmered beef bourguignon in the sauce-stained Le Creuset pot it was cooked in, with a loose salad of chicories and a big bowl of wide, parsley-strewn noodles.

Here's a (plateist) menu that somehow survived in my files from an actual (plated) dinner Colman and I cooked (okay, he cooked; I diced) for our colleagues, Dee Nolan and a group of British editors of *Metropolitan Home UK*:

Fritto Misto Siciliano

Winter Vegetable Salad with a Soupçon of Spring
(and a touch of Westphalian Ham)

White Bean Soupe de Poissons, Red Pepper Coulis
et Sa Garniture de Maine Crab Meat

Rôti de Porc with Tomato Chutney

"Champ" New Europe (Puree of Potatoes
& Brussels Sprouts, to you)

Petite Salade of Frisée and Lolla Rossa (whoever she is)

Red Winter Pears & Mountain Gorgonzola

OUR DISPARATE APPROACHES DID MAKE for a bit of tension, but that tension, I believe, was what made *Saveur* so good. Unlike the drill at so many publications today, where top editors impose an autocratic, sanitized procedure of story selection— ideas must be submitted in writing in advance (thereby removing the juice of a writer's enthusiasm, and the sparkle in their eyes, from the editorial pitch)—each of us presented story ideas in person, to our whole staff, in loud and ever-so-slightly contentious meetings. Everybody had a say. Or a shout. Passion ruled. We made sure to include the test kitchen cooks and our assistants (a precious few). Especially them. We were our own best critics. We knew what bad was. Nothing was easily won; every idea was examined, and often loudly rejected for taking the easy—or obvious—way out.

When we launched *Saveur*, we were collectively in the grip of a kind of *nostalgie de grand-mère*—a shared conviction that the only true, the only real cooking came from old and knowing hands, hands that had made their meals from the same ingredients in the same place in the same way since, well, forever. Today, there are entire and legitimate dialogues about the appropriation of food origins, about the very words *authenticity* and *ethnicity*, and even about who gets to decide.

I can only report that in those early days, we saw the food world as being in a perilous downward slide—either publications were so chef-centric that the restaurant recipes they touted were notoriously unachievable for the home cook, or they dumbed down food to "quick-and-easy dinners." We worried that readers were becoming drastically distanced from authentic traditions, from real cooking; we foresaw a future of shortcut culture. In our new magazine, there would be no "Six Ways with Pork Chops." Our collective anti-*Saveur* example was "low-fat cassoulet."

As Colman later explained it, "You can make a dish of beans and turkey sausage cooked with olive oil instead of duck fat . . . and if you're a good cook, you can probably make it taste okay. *But don't call it cassoulet.* If everybody publishes recipes for low-fat cassoulet—or for Tex-Mex cassoulet, fusion cassoulet . . . then at some point real cassoulet is going to get forgotten. And that would be a shame not just because real cassoulet is a wonderful dish but also because it's a tradition, a cultural icon, a complex construction whose every element has historical and social implications. Let's give people the recipe for *authentic* cassoulet, we decided, full of sausage and duck confit and fat, as close to that you'd have in Toulouse or Carcassonne or Castelnaudary as possible. Let's give people the real thing."

We were adamant about what this magazine would not do: assign food stories that sent a chef on a sentimental journey back to their native country to glorify their formation as a cook. However, should said chef have a *grandmother* in India, or Senegal, or Mexico, who taught them everything they knew? Bingo. Neither Colman nor I came all that equipped with grandmothers ourselves, which was most likely part of their allure. Dora, my father's mother, died when my dad was a boy, leaving me no connection but part of her first name wrapped in mine. My mother's mother, Jeanette, who'd come here from Eastern Europe in the early twentieth century, reportedly made strawberry wine on her fire escape in Brooklyn (this was Brooklyn way before hipsters made wine on *their* fire escapes), and hardball-dense challah that she nonetheless managed to produce in her small, hot kitchen every Friday. She eventually decamped for Israel (leaving her five daughters and eleven grandchildren), intending to die there helping the poor. Which she did.

Colman's paternal grandmother died young, too, and though his mother's mom reached the venerable age of 102, she lived mostly in New England, and the only memory he holds of her in his Los Angeles kitchen involved darning socks. Christopher was the only one of us with a memorable grandmother/cook, her beloved Nini, who was still vividly alive in her head. When Christopher shared her memory of learning to rub a whole leg of lamb with garlic and rosemary as an eight-year-old in Nini's Sacramento kitchen, Nini became grandmother to us all.

Before we launched the magazine, we put together a mock-up cover to test potential reader reactions in focus groups, me in New York with the rubber cement and Colman on the phone from Los Angeles, writing the cover lines. Our test cover photo, was, of course, of a charmingly perky grandmother type, straw-hatted and smiling, face radiant with the wisdom of her years, her aproned lap filled with the string beans she was topping. Our lead blurb, "How French Grandmothers Make Crêpes" (we could have chosen a more engaging dish), was followed by "What Winemakers Drink" (pure Colman) and "Eating Our Way Through Morocco" (pure me). The focus groups (which we were to watch behind mirrored glass) were enthusiastic, surprisingly unfazed by a new magazine whose name they couldn't pronounce. (Our publishing director Joe Armstrong's mama, Dorthadele, back in Abilene, Texas, the buckle on the Bible Belt, got heaps of congratulations from her friends for her son's job at that new Christian publication, *Savior.*)

We launched with the cover story "Secrets of Oaxacan Cooking." Neither a grandmother nor a rock star chef, the young Mexican cook we featured on the cover, Rosario Mendoza, from a restaurant in Teotitlán del Valle, smiled at us over three bowls of squash blossom soup.

COLMAN HAD FAMOUSLY (FAMOUSLY TO me, at least) written these lines in *Met Home* a dozen years before: "One afternoon not long ago in Burgundy, I bit into a carrot. It was tiny and neatly beveled, lightly steamed and glazed in butter. I thought for a moment that it was perhaps the most perfect thing I had ever tasted. Its sweetness and intensity of flavor simply dazzling; its texture was astonishingly right. I believe that if a hunk of fresh truffle had been offered to me just then, I would have

turned it down in favor of this common, bright orange vegetable." When, much later, I had the fine luck to drive down
the same deeply forested back road that led from Beaune to
the restaurant-of-the-carrot, Jean-Pierre and Isabelle Silva's
l'Hostellerie du Vieux Moulin in Bouilland, I experienced the
eerie sense of coming home. If I hadn't been born there, I was
convinced I had been born to *be* there. Burgundy became the
subject for our first special issue of *Saveur.*

Searching out a Burgundian grandmother was our first
move. The one we found belonged to a neighbor of Colman's
in Los Angeles, who reportedly made a killer coq au vin. On
the rare occasions when I gave myself permission to leave my
desk and travel on location with Christopher and Colman, I
would be in such a state of nerve-tingling, heightened awareness, my hair would catch fire. This was especially true when
we set out to report that Burgundy issue. Everything seemed
urgent to me; crucial to the story. "Oh my God!" I practically
shrieked as we drove into the charming village of Époisses,
home of my favorite cow's-milk cheese, its rind washed with
Marc de Bourgogne brandy. As we approached the famed Fro-
magerie Berthaut and spied a man in boots crossing the yard,
I cried out, "I bet that's Monsieur Berthaut himself!" with all
the self-control of a groupie. My companions remained singu-
larly unmoved.

Marcelle Gueneau, that grandmother of Colman's LA
neighbor, lived in leafy Avallon. She invited us for Sunday
lunch to sample her vaunted coq au vin (the classic Burgundian dish once involved an old rooster, the bird's own blood,
and even sometimes cocoa powder; our eventual *Saveur* recipe settled on a six-pound capon; lost the blood but kept the
cocoa). Christopher remembers Madame Gueneau's young

nephew climbing through the dining room window to join us. But it was her bright-green salad that set me vibrating.

"What makes your vinaigrette so wonderful?" I excitedly ask her. She scurries to the kitchen and returns holding her secret: a small box of fécule de pomme de terre, potato starch. "This is not a chef's trick; it's a grandmother's trick," she confides, setting a small glass bowl next to me right on the dining table and pouring a tablespoon of boiling water from her kettle. She spoons in a teaspoon of fécule, and, whisking it smooth, adds two teaspoons of Dijon mustard (Amora, I think) and two tablespoons of red wine vinegar. Then, still whisking, she slowly drizzles in six tablespoons of vegetable oil until her dressing is smooth and thick and slips over the tender leaves of her salad like paint. Madame Gueneau gave me that box, and I kept it in my pantry for many years. Just looking at it made me smile. As Colman wrote at the sweet end of our Burgundy issue: "We realize . . . that the food of Burgundy isn't just what Burgundians eat; it's who they are."

DISCOVERING COLMAN ALL THOSE DECADES ago, I discovered, too, a way to codify how I felt about food. Journalism mattered to both of us; food journalism meant going narrow and deep, going against the gushing (or insipid) nature of most food writing then. From the beginning, we believed there was a larger story to tell and a personal way of telling it. Colman found his voice in pieces he wrote for us over the years at *Met Home*, stories such as "Why I Hate Three-Star Restaurants." He was among the first to report on emerging German wines. He called the moment for Franco-Japanese cooking, and shared his excitement about preserving the old ways, too—he was mad for wild boar (sanglier) and wood-cock (bécasse), and the aged plum brandy (vieille prune) at his favorite old-fashioned Parisian bistros. Colman was early and prescient in writing about the singular young American winemakers and cooks who also happened to be his friends (think Alice Waters, Jonathan Waxman, Larry Forgione, Wolfgang Puck). *Met Home* was among the first to brand the emerging food movement the New American Cuisine. Even then, Colman's writing combined sophistication and enthu-siasm, always letting readers in on the excitement of his dis-coveries, generous with his erudition, never self-indulgent, patient with the gap between his knowledge and ours. For a design and architecture magazine, *Met Home* had a knockout food program. Colman was very good. And he was ours.

Here's an image I keep from those years: I'm in my of-fice in freezing New York working far too late (cue the vi-olins), and my phone rings. It's Colman, way past midnight in some enchanted town in the South of France, or along the Ligurian Riviera, where, after driving back to his inev-itably charming little hotel, through gentle hillsides where villages reveal themselves by the cluster of house lights that twinkle in the night sky, following yet another remarkable dinner and any number of bottles of the best wine of the region, he wants to wax on about how wonderful this restau-rant, town, cuisine, special dish, accomplished chef—choose one—that I've paid to send him to cover is, and what a fine story we'll get out of this trip. And I'm thinking, "You're *driving* after that dinner?" There's something about these phone calls that always made me feel like the tallest girl in the sixth grade.

IT'S NOT THAT I'M ALWAYS so easily influenced by my friends, but it took just one minute in a restaurant to kill truffle oil for me. Colman, Christopher, and I were in London, shortly after the launch of *Saveur*, seated at a round table with a few of our colleagues at one of Terence Conran's estimable big restaurants of the time; I think it was Le Pont de la Tour near the London Bridge. And as the waiter brought a platter of pasta—or was it a pizza?—drenched in truffle oil to the table, both Colman and Christopher turned up their noses in disdain at its pretention and slightly synthetic aroma: "Oof! Truffle oil!" Five minutes earlier, I'd had no opinion about truffle oil, but their reaction instantly ruined that food substance. Truffle oil is dead to me now.

In the early years, Colman's Cooked and Raw Vegetable Salad was the whizziest thing I could make. For one thing, that salad gave you permission to use those forgotten ingredients hanging out in the back of the refrigerator—you know, the ones that look up so hopefully every time you open the door ("Choose me!") but eventually become resigned to ignominy; I'm looking at you, jars of pink pickled ginger, lone floating cornichons, the few capers stuck to the bottom of a bottle too narrow to get a fork into. Colman's salad was guilt-free in that regard; it was an all-inclusive game. Forgiving in a way he'd never be with a flabby sentence structure or a lazy word choice. In his salad, almost anything could play: cold boiled potatoes, nubbins of steak, roasted peppers, cooked cauliflower, pine nuts, or peanuts. What saved it from being a Salvation Army of a salad, though, what gave it style and structure, was the ample and unifying inclusion of fresh greens—mâche and/or bibb lettuce, green beans and peas, celery leaves, handfuls of basil, and parsley, and scallions—and its simple salad-bowl dressing: just lemon juice and olive oil.

That was my kind of recipe; it allowed the cook a free hand. It was as casually permissive as Colman was insistent about the execution of other near-sacred dishes. He once gave me (as a culinary challenge?) his recipe for Lamb Carnitas Empanadas with Roasted Corn–Poblano Chile Sauce. That one ran to five typewritten pages and involved marinating the meat cut from an entire leg of lamb for 4 to 6 hours, searing it, then roasting it for 2 to 3 hours. Then you made the cornmeal empanada dough, flattening that dough into three-inch circles and stuffing them with said lamb and herbs and olives and a goat cheese mixture, then frying up the empanadas. Then you got to serve the empanadas with the sauce (all right, you were probably smart enough to make the sauce first, which I wasn't) from the kernels of three ears of sweet corn you'd first roasted in their husks, then sliced off the cob and mixed with roasted and skinned poblano peppers and lightened with crema and cilantro. And, because he was from LA and knew Mexican food, and I was not and did not, and out of a sense of pride—and combat—I actually put myself to the challenge of those lamb empanadas, which I recall serving close to midnight.

BUT NOTHING EQUALED COLMAN'S ENTHUSIASM for Catalonia, which he first wrote about in *Met Home*. When he pitched the story, I remember being impressed with his research in three languages (Spanish, French, and Catalan) and that he thought so hard about what it takes for a cuisine to be its own thing—so distinctive and so long-lasting. The book that research produced, *Catalan Cuisine: Europe's Last Great Culinary Secret*, was definitive then and major still. Not only did Colman call a moment and a movement—the book is both scholarly and cookable—but what he found and codified in that Spanish culture would become, for decades, the most significant culinary influence in Europe. For it was just up the Catalan coast in Roses that the famed modern chef Ferran Adrià began a movement at his restaurant El Bulli that would rock the culinary world (and that Colman himself would eventually chronicle in his biography *Ferran: The Inside Story of El Bulli and the Man Who Reinvented Food*).

What Colman's *Catalan Cuisine* did for me was formative. He made it clear in a personal way—in a cooking way—how every cuisine has its flavor bases, its signature herbs, its authentic ingredients, its unique methods of preparation, all of which spring from the land and its surrounding waters and inevitably add up to its distinctive flavors and the iconic dishes that deliver them. These are ideas we take for granted now. We have become so sophisticated about international food, about terroir, able to parse subsectors of subsectors of regional differences; we know all about flavor profiles, and instinctively match specific ingredients with distinct culinary styles.

But Colman taught me (inadvertently, that is; his intent was never—or, rarely—didactic) nothing less than how to learn a cuisine from the ingredients up. Something of a walking culinary encyclopedia (with a merry ego to match), he showed me how to keenly observe the seminal ingredients of a cuisine, to pay attention to what works with what. Once you've figured that out, I realized then, you will always be able to trace the roots of almost any kind of cooking (Turkish or Thai, Persian or Peruvian). You will be able to sense relationships of flavors and cook in a spirit true to its history. All this seems self-evident now. But I was a young cook then; I had never really thought about food that way.

Neither had Colman, as it turned out. In *Catalan Cuisine*, he explained: "I came to Catalan cuisine as a novice, an outsider—and immediately fell in love with it. I was taken by its freshness and vitality, haunted by its resonances of the past, thrilled by its forthright, vivid flavors. But I think what fascinated me most of all about it, and what seemed to define it best, was precisely its unexpectedness, its surprising way of doing unfamiliar things with familiar raw materials . . . It's an accessible cuisine to us, I think, but at the same time an exotic and mysterious one." Who wouldn't want to learn a cuisine that could deliver like that?

CROSSING THE PYRENEES FROM FRANCE into Spain—or tunneling through—you are at once in a very different place. The land gentles. The trees spread out; playful umbrella pines spring up; silvery olive trees climb hillsides where even the undergrowth looks greener and softer. Farms cluster in un-French ways, which is to say they're less deliberately organized, outbuildings painted warmer colors—and even though you're only miles away, and just as close to the Mediterranean, you feel the difference of another country.

Four decades ago, Colman made that same drive from France, a place he knew intimately, to a Spain still foreign to him. His first stop, just miles from the French border, was the Motel Ampurdán (today known in its upgraded Catalan form as the Hotel Empordà) in Figueres, a town named for its fig trees, not far from the beaches of the Costa Brava. Besides being the place where Colman Andrews discovered Catalan cuisine, it's known for being the hometown of a certain Salvador Dalí, where the Dalí Museum shows a collection of the ebullient artist's works. The restaurant that drew Colman, which has since been christened El Motel, in honor of the establishment's origins, was where—according to the European food buzz he'd heard—a chef named Josep Mercader was doing a modern version of Catalan cooking, itself then a mystery to Colman, as well as to most of the rest of the world.

When Colman walked into the place decades ago, he found his future. "Immediately, I realized that the smells were different." In the kitchen, they were cooking piles of onions in oil, adding tomato, then patiently simmering that mixture down until it had the consistency of marmalade—this was sofregit. Other cooks were pulverizing piles of blanched almonds and hazelnuts with garlic and fried bread in mortars, adding toasted saffron, parsley, and oil, and even bits of chocolate, to make a thick paste called picada. "Looking at those two flavor bases," he remembers, "I felt in my bones that something important was going on here." Those first impressions eventually led him to write *Catalan Cuisine,* which would be published in the next few years, but not before we'd assigned him a couple of articles defining the cuisine first for *Met Home*'s readers.

TODAY, TO CELEBRATE YET ANOTHER of Colman's important birthdays, many of us who've only read about El Motel (and edited and published what we've read) are there at last in person. The group is some thirty souls, drawn from all pockets of Colman's life, from half a dozen countries and dozens of cities. We gather and greet at 2:00 p.m. around a bar in the hotel's marble-floored lobby. This is a simple place, unpretentious but undeniably polished, its values in the right place. Surfaces are unadorned, elegant but well thought out, like the waiters, in their white jackets, correct but not stuffy. Glasses of sparkling cava are poured from a trough of iced bottles on a long table. And on the bar . . . what *is* that curling provocatively out of footed bar glasses? Can it be? Yes! The deep-fried spines of anchovies. This idea is so stunning, it bears repeating; you pick up a delicate fried anchovy spine and experience the saltiest, crunchiest bite, a bite so unexpectedly satisfying, French fries would weep in comparison. It occurs to me that there is nothing random about these salty entremeses. Colman has put the might of his culinary erudition into every course of the remarkable lunch that follows.

Slim platters of fried "potato chips" appear next. But look again. Two of the thinnest potato slices you've ever seen are held together by a smear of what's called call "garum," not the ancient Roman fermented fish sauce but a Mediterranean paste of black olives and anchovies. For a salty, crunchy girl like me, those two aperitius would have been sufficient. But they are followed by croquetes de marisc, seafood croquettes: a delicate bread crumb crust rolled around an interior of chopped shrimp and their crustacean friends, and fried. Then come thin toasts topped with an even thinner slice of black truffle. These are not just hors d'oeuvres; they're little celebrations, made even more fragrant by the lemon that Peter Ward, the irrepressible Irish food advocate, kept waving in front of my nose to smell—he'd just snatched it from one of the trees on the restaurant's lawn that were heavy with them. Ward lives in Nenagh in Tipperary, and you can call him a "grocer," with a wink, because his worldview is wide, embracing the best food values: local, sustainable, traditional, realistic—beliefs he'll musically share at the slightest provocation. Ward became an instant friend of Colman's years ago when he spoke frankly at a food symposium about the integrity of Irish food, and the two of them together (oh, what a torrent of words!), with Colman's award-winning book *The Country Cooking of Ireland*, have helped alert the world to the most authentic food traditions that country has to offer.

No sooner are we seated in the generous, sun-filled room, all thirty of us around a vast rectangular table that allows for small talk and group banter both, than lunch proceeds. Looking down at the printed menu on my plate, I think Colman has put as much thought into creating this meal as into an entire issue of a magazine. History and imagination are at work. I picture him arguing with himself (and not me!) about which dish best balances the nuances of salt against sweet, of texture, and provenance. Sequence? What should follow what? As the meal proceeds, plate by plate, I see the result of deliberate intention; each plate is a frame for one powerful idea, voluptuous in its austerity, containing this thing and only this thing.

First come tiny, barely cooked squid, their soft bodies shirred like satin on slim wooden skewers, sauced with a tarragon vinaigrette, and simply, perfectly, paired with a crunchy nest of lightly fried fideus noodles. A shallow bowl follows, with sea cucumber cut in pieces swimming in a garlic emulsion made pale green with herbs; it's really the fleshy interior membrane of that slug-like creature, and has the toothsome texture of a big squid. "It's the only part of the animal that's edible," Colman leans over to explain.

Next comes a white plate with two big red local shrimp, barely cooked through in a crust of coarse salt. Then and at last, the salt cod—bacallà—as the Motel's first owner, Josep Mercader, originally made it in this restaurant: one small square of cod, thick and elegantly white, brushed with a bubblingly hot garlic mousseline—a whipped cream–mayonnaise sauce. Lovely. Then comes the becada—I know this bird as the French bécasse—roasted woodcock, its rare breast draped over a bed of seasoned rice, its tiny head with its overlong beak perfectly bifurcating the plate. Next, smiling waiters appear, dipping their silver trays of whole Muscovy ducks (from the Empordà), roasted Peking-style, in front of us. Waiting carvers then reduce the ducks to discrete portions, plating them with pear chutney, a classic Empordà dish.

BEFORE COLMAN, I WOULD HAVE been just another person walking by a fish counter or through an Italian market, never recognizing the desiccated powdery white slabs of salt cod for the vital foodstuff they can be. I would not have known that it takes just a couple of days in the refrigerator and the simple addition of cool, clear water to coax that slab into sweet white resurrection—to something worlds away from its dead flat, salty, dehydrated state. Salt cod reminds me of those Magic Rocks we had as kids, bits of metal salts that you would drop into a bowl of liquid (sodium silicate, it turns out) and watch as they grew, fantastically, before your eyes, into tall multicolored towers. There is a purity in this act of rehydration that quite appeals. Salt cod is like that; it goes from nothing to something—something really special—in just in two days. I am forever moved by that humble transformation.

For me, the very words *salt cod* are elemental and ancient. Salting fresh cod for preservation has been done since the Middle Ages and is inseparable from the difficult times when finding good things to eat was difficult, too. The writer Paul Greenberg makes the distinction between "holiday fish," like salmon or striped bass, and working-class fish, which is cod all over. Cod—this groundfish that lives and feeds on the ocean floor—may not be glamorous, but it's never to be taken for granted. Cooking with cod is itself redolent of history and danger, of generations of born fishermen fitting out their boats, and braving the laws of the sea, and fighting the weather, in places as far flung as Scandinavia and the West Indies, as Basque Spain and Cape . . . Cod!

Always with you, too, are stories of catching and curing, of overfishing and underregulating, of lost fishing grounds and even lost species. These stories of squandering our natural resources are told in two remarkable books, *Cod: A Biography of the Fish That Changed the World*, by Mark Kurlansky, and Paul Greenberg's *Four Fish*. Reading them, you'll be humbled by cod's tumultuous history and how that fish even lands on your plate.

"Cod isn't particularly favored in the United States," Colman wrote in *Catalan Cuisine*. "It suggests frozen fish sticks somehow and, of course, cod liver oil. Add the dreaded word 'salt' to it, and I reckon you might as well be talking cat food as far as most Americans are concerned. But I've decided to be bull-headed about the matter . . . Because salt cod is a vital staple of Catalan cuisine. And because the stuff is wonderful."

I ASKED COLMAN TO COME and cook salt cod with me in my kitchen. I'd begun the meal prep a few days before, with a slab of dried cod I'd found in my funky Long Island fish store and soaked for two days and two nights, changing the water three or four times a day, carefully balancing the watery pan as I carried it from refrigerator to sink, pouring off the salty, fishy, liquid, then adding more cool water. It is never lost on me how this flat shoe sole of a food substance gradually and miraculously takes the water into its body, transforming itself, until at last the flesh itself is plump and white and sweet-smelling and it becomes something good to eat. This requisite foreplay only adds another layer of ceremony to the preparation of salt cod, heightening the anticipation of the dish it will become.

When Colman—a large man—cooks in a small kitchen, his movements are small, too. All his intelligence is focused on the task at hand: chopping garlic, the knife held just so, the cloves rolling on the cutting board held steady by his fingertips with their well-bitten nails. He occupies only the space required to accomplish each task. Stuffing a kitchen towel into the waistband of his pants, he begins with a sofregit, the flavor base that makes food taste Catalan in the same way that the soffritto of Italian cooking and the sofrito of Spanish cooking give deep flavor to those cuisines.

He starts with onions, about three of them, chopping them roughly and, adding the chopped garlic, cooking them slowly in a deep pan with lots of olive oil until they've turned golden brown. This is a pleasant process and always takes much longer than you think. Then, about six ripe tomatoes—seeded, peeled, and grated on a box grater if fresh (a great Catalan tomato secret Colman taught me years ago) or canned if out of season—are added to the pot and stirred until they melt into the onions. While the sofregit bubbles, Colman drains the big white beans I'd soaked overnight and cooks them in a pot of water until they're soft.

Soaking the cod, I was tempted to lay a bay leaf or two over the fillets, for looks as much as anything. When I casually mention this to Colman, he responds curtly, "Bay leaves are not Catalan." He cuts the now-pristine soaked white cod into small cubes, and after drying them with paper towels, rolls the pieces in flour. Pouring ample olive oil into a large skillet, he gently sautés the cod pieces until they turn golden on all sides. As he cooks, his kitchen chat is easy, his mood light; he talks about his daughters, Madeleine and Isabelle, grown into tall young women now, in a casually revealing way he never would across a restaurant table. When I turn all poetic and platonic-ideally about his cooking rituals, he dismisses the praise. "I'm just making lunch!"

AS SOON AS THE SOFREGIT has cooked down to its mythical marmalade state, Colman stirs in the lightly browned cod, spoons in the cooked white beans, and lets the flavors meld. Looking deep into the pot of tomatoey, oniony white beans, I lose myself in memory. *There are so many people in this pot*, I think.

There's José Andrés, and the lessons I've learned from his book *Tapas: A Taste of Spain in America*. José wrote that book with Richard Wolffe, a fine journalist who was then *Newsweek*'s senior White House correspondent. Propelled by his love of food, Richard had become a close friend of José's. During my tenure as *Newsweek*'s executive editor (and because I'd come from *Saveur*), I wrote a yearly review of cookbooks, just because I thought it important. But this book by José, a major Spanish chef, written with my *Newsweek* colleague, posed a bit of an issue. What if I didn't like it? I took the book home and cooked from it (a practice one expects of all cookbook reviewers). My concern was unwarranted, it turned out. I loved the book and still make the Asturian bean stew with clams, ordering the elegantly long white fabada beans grown near José's birthplace in the north of Spain from tienda.com.

Still focused on the stewpot, I wonder what I'll do with the rest of the soaked salt cod we didn't use. *Aha, brandade!* I think, recalling that Provençal cod and potato puree, brandade de morue, so similar to baccalà mantecato, the Italian whipped-cod-and-potato appetizer you see on the counters of every Venetian bar at sundown. Brandade is easy and so delicious. I cook it in my mind: Gently simmer several peeled, cubed Yukon Gold potatoes in a small saucepan of milk and add a bay leaf (!) and some snippings of fresh herbs. After about 10 minutes, add the soaked salt cod and cook until it softens, about 15 minutes. Over low heat, mash the potatoes and milk and cod together in the pot and slowly whisk in olive oil until the mixture becomes creamy. Spoon the fluffy stuff into a shallow baking dish and slide it under the broiler with a bit of butter until the peaks on the top begin to brown. Serve it with lots of toasted bread.

Suddenly, and who can explain these things, that pot flashes me back to Los Angeles before Colman moved east to edit *Saveur*, when he was a restaurant reviewer for the *Los Angeles Times*, known all over town. He'd take me on restaurant crawls, to the beach in Venice, home of what was then the epitome of California cuisine, Bruce Marder's fresh and local West Beach Café. I'd trail in behind Colman, his arrival causing loud squeals of delight from all the young ladies who ran the bar, and the servers, and the maître d'. And when we'd had a glass of wine at the bar and were ready to cross the street to the café's sister restaurant, Rebecca's—a wildly exuberant Frank Gehry–designed California Mexican place—those ladies would be so heartbroken to see Colman leave that I wouldn't have been surprised if they had followed him across the street, attached to him like limpets, those snail-like shellfish that stick to rocks. I called them the Limpettes. But they never knew the salt cod side of him.

AS COLMAN AND I SIP wine with our stew, he tells me how his cooking has changed, confesses that he's become—he hates to admit it—something of platterist at home these days. His current specialty is Whatever You Have Stew. He explains the method: Start by browning (or broiling) whatever protein you have—lamb, pork, beef, chicken, or ground meat. Meanwhile, in a deep stewpot, cook down a bunch of sliced onions with olive oil and bacon fat until they're soft and dark. Cut up garlic, carrots, parsnips, or whatever veg you have and sauté them, too, in the stewpot. Add the browned meat to the pot along with any pan juices, then pour in a bottle of red wine, cover, and cook slowly for about 3 hours. "These days," he tells me, "I cook by feel, sticking close to the ingredients and what they need. Maybe we're less food snobs than we used to be," he admits, smiling. "Maybe because we know more."

—— ❦ ——

CHAPTER 5

THE PHOTOGRAPHER IN
THE KITCHEN

PEOPLE TELL US WE LOOK like each other. We look nothing like each other. She's blond; I'm not. We're both tall, and we laugh at the same things. The only time we ever looked alike was when we looked so unlike those around us, photographing at 6:00 a.m. on a crowded street corner in the Tsukiji fish market in Tokyo, two gargantuan gaijins; we were actually recognized by a Japanese restaurateur from New York who'd come there to work with his suppliers.

Our story began a lifetime ago and fittingly, in a restaurant—the now-defunct Washington Square Bar & Grill in San Francisco's North Beach. Only it happened in the bathroom. I had just met Christopher Humphreys, the beautiful sweetheart of my great friend and colleague Jim Hirsheimer, an hour before. And yet there we were, two girls crammed into a teeny loo, Christopher holding a big bottle of San Pellegrino, offering sips and dampened washcloths to help calm my alarmingly unsettled stomach. One would be tempted to characterize our whole relationship as figuring out how to get out of tight spots. But calm caring is just one of her attributes, and not the most exciting one.

Emily Dickinson's poem "Tell All the Truth but Tell It Slant" perfectly captures Christopher's take on the world. It is a question not of probity but of delivery. She never fabricates, but like all artists, she processes the world (you could say she "cooks" it) and makes it her own. She tells me I can recount a trip to Europe and make it sound like a visit to the supermarket: "I went; I came back." Christopher's storytelling can make a trip to the supermarket sound like *War and Peace.* When she tells me, as she often does, "I know how to do this," I always believe her. When she asks me (or I ask her) "Am I crazy?" the answer is always "No!" Christopher cooks with such style and such internal conviction—with so little fuss and drama—she is her own Kitchen Whisperer. But I am fortunate that she's mine, too.

Once, I was invited to dinner at the home of a self-proclaimed "serious cook." He parked me on a stool at a bar facing the kitchen (his stage) and I was a captive—his command audience—as I watched him perform with any number of robot-thises and coupe-thats. His energetic flinging of ingredients and brandishing of knives lasted for hours. I mean hours! He was all theater. Dinner, when it came together at last, was forgettable. Christopher in the kitchen is the opposite of such culinary flash. "I've learned to touch everything just enough to keep the plates spinning," she'll say.

Watch Christopher cook, and despite what's running 'round her brain (I know that mind is working overtime), she seems forever calm and focused. But never in the performative way that self-styled "gourmet" cooks have of drawing attention to their every move. ("Do you have a *really* sharp knife?") Christopher just gets on with it, all the while telling whoever's in the kitchen with her, apropos of nothing at all, how, for example, when M. F. K. Fisher was in Strasbourg one winter before the war, she'd separate the segments of a tangerine, set them on newspaper on her hotel's radiator to plump up, then move them to the packed snow on her windowsill to chill briefly before devouring them—their skins crisp with cold, their insides still juicy. (Roger says that Christopher displaces so little space in the kitchen, and you're so riveted by whatever she's talking about, that you never notice that she's cooked dinner for eight and quietly cleaned up after herself. Suddenly the story is over and dinner is ready.) "You know I cook with my left hand," she'll say, ducking the praise. Christopher came into this world somehow knowing how things should be done.

Born in San Francisco, she grew up in Hawaii; then Sydney, Australia; then back to San Francisco. "Living in Hawaii, our fun was dipping slices of green mangoes into soy sauce. When we went to Chinese restaurants as a young girl, my big blond father would take me back into the kitchen and speak to the cooks in fluent Cantonese." But starting young, every summer, she'd leave her family (notably her four brothers) and get to be an only child at her grandparents' house in Sacramento. "I loved staying there," she tells me. "My grandfather was a wonderful shopper. He'd take me with him to his favorite places—where they made the best sausages, sold the best cheese. He would buy white peaches, which I loved. And strawberries. My grandmother, Nini, was a simple salt-and-pepper cook, but she did everything so beautifully."

Nini was a Rogerson, and as Christopher tells it, the Rogerson girls were born with their hats on. In her hectic *Saveur* traveling days, Christopher was all Rogerson: she'd sail out the door saying, "I was born with my hat on," to photograph a story in Morocco, or Thailand, or, twice to Alaska. "Nini would make angel food cakes and let me beat the eggs," she recalls. "She always made her food the same way, and it always came out the same way—perfectly! I learned excellence in her un-air-conditioned Sacramento kitchen, where the temperature would soar to over a hundred degrees. That's where my most vivid food memories come from. I was aware of every move Nini made. At an early age, I somehow knew that she was never fussy. She had what I recognize now as a real respect for her ingredients. Everything she made was delicious. I learned so much from her; I was always tuned into her kitchen." Grandmother Nini must have recognized early on the young Christopher's precocious competence, and not just in the kitchen; "Next time, Crissy," she warned her, "come back as a clinging vine."

CHRISTOPHER'S CONVICTIONS AS A COOK slip out as conversational by-products. "Water is a great liquid to add, not always stock, or wine," she'll toss off as she loosens a tomato sauce in a skillet by pouring in a bit. "I'm always trying to get flavor into my cooking. I'm looking for a high note," she'll say as she squeezes in half a lemon's juice, or adds a generous shower of salt, or mashes in an anchovy. And, "You need fat to carry the flavor, too—like olive oil or butter." And, "I'm crazy about hot pepper these days," before sending me a packet of spicy Cambodian long peppers that look like chocolate caterpillars. She is deliberate, for example, in the proper ratio of oil to vinegar (or lemon juice or soy sauce) in a salad dressing. It is 4:1. "You're just using the vinegar to wake up the flavors." (Four to one, I murmur to myself over my salad bowl.) Now that we no longer work together, we have what-did-you-make-for-dinner phone chats, she in her Bucks County kitchen, me in New York. "I made chicken soup," she'll tell me. "You know, the kind where you pull apart the poached white meat with your fingers and put it back in the broth?" I listen, tucking away her cooking wisdom for future use. Among the important things Christopher inadvertently taught me is to s-l-o-w d-o-w-n in the kitchen. To think before I cook.

On Christmas, despairing of getting our families together, we share menus instead. I email her my version of La Vigilia, the Christmas Eve Feast of the Seven Fishes:

American Black Hackleback Caviar, Toasts, Champagne

Ceviche of Peconic Bay Scallops

Spanish Tuna Belly with Piquillo Peppers

Gramercy Tavern Cured Arctic Char

Baby Portuguese Sardines, Roasted

Squid with Squid Ink Pasta

Oyster Pan Roast

She replies: "Dee-vine . . . so elegant. I am doing the Feast of the Six Fishies . . . I'd better think up one more!

Home-Cured Gravlax with Mustard Sauce

Crudo of Ahi with Really Good Olive Oil, Kumquat Zest
and Maldon Salt

Cracked Dungeness Crab with Louie Dressing

Calamari Stuffed with Smoky Hot Italian Sausage and Braised
with Fennel and White Wine

Mussels with Scallions and Cream Served with Frites

Escarole Salad with a Lemony Anchovy Vinaigrette

Oh, and I'm doing prime rib and horseradish for Christmas dinner."

ONE NIGHT A FEW YEARS AGO, Christopher surprised me with a birthday dinner *at my house*, all the components of which she'd secretly cooked herself in her Pennsylvania kitchen and lugged to New York.

"How did you even do this?" I wrote the next day, attempting to thank her:

1. You had to think up the idea in the first place.
2. You acted on it and didn't just brush it away, as we've often had to do with so many of our best intentions these days.
3. Which meant you had to get Roger on the case.

4. Then you had to make sure the day went as you figured it had to, time for that great lunch with Colman, time to hang in my office, time to run out and "buy your lettuces," even time for a mani/pedi.

5. But before that, you had to secure those beautiful chickens and the eggs, and the green beans, the cipolline and the prunes, and the kabocha squash and the lemons and the bacon and the smoked salmon, the parsley and the and the . . .

6. Then you had to boil the eggs (always with ½ cup salt added to the water) until they were perfectly done.

7. And tediously peel every single one of them.

8. Then figure out something secure to carry them in from Pennsy.

9. Then make the buttery mayo and find the right-size something to fit that sauce in.

10. Then get on the horn with Charla and somehow cajole her into coming.

11. And even manage to get Jim on the case (and to New York, yet!) and figure out the driving arrangements so he could bring the cooler, later.

12. Back to the cooking/prep, you had to sauté those beautiful leetle chicken pieces and gently layer them in plastic bags so they would ride well.

13. And then you had to roast the kabocha squash and puree it with lots of lemon and pimentón: yum, yum, yummy. And find containers large enough to hold all that soup.

14. And fry the bacon croutons and carefully dice them and put them in another bag.

15. Then you had to confit those lovely cipolline onions with prunes and pack them separately so they would stay whole and beautiful.

16. Then somehow figure out how to transport the wine-braising sauce in its own container.

17. And the million other steps/calculations it takes to single-handedly pull off a surprise dinner for sixteen people on a weeknight!

18. Then you had to fit all of the above into a giant cooler before you jumped in your car and drove to New York, so that Jim wouldn't have to do anything but get the cooler in his car to drive in later.

19. Then you had to get me to be so completely oblivious that even when I opened my door and saw Jim with two cases of wine, I thought, "Oh, how wonderful! A family dinner with just us and the kids." And I meant it. I really did.

I can't remember if that was the year she made a chocolate birthday cake whose top layer she intended to suspend, Greek temple–style, on little gold-flecked plastic columns. As she was installing that layer, however, the whole thing collapsed. A lesser cook would have collapsed, too. And run for the nearest bakery. Christopher, however, was unfazed, turning that cake into temple ruins, standing some cake shards on end, leaning a column here, another there, until she had a perfect Athenian landscape of a birthday cake. Roger loves to tell that story as an example of Christopher's grace under pressure.

I DISCOVERED CHRISTOPHER'S KITCHEN SKILLS with a defining *plop*. In my kitchen, we were serving up a pot of little green lentils we'd just cooked to accompany a braised pork stew. I grabbed a long gray Granite Ware serving spoon I loved, and *slop!* went the beans onto a plate. Christopher quietly opened a drawer and chose a much smaller spoon, a soupspoon, and ever so gently delivered those beans onto the plate. And in that moment—and this was decades ago—I saw my own gesture for what it was: gross and unrefined. Lacking the finesse those delicate beans deserved. *OMG*, I thought, *I am an oaf!*

I watch Christopher prepare her signature deviled eggs—pressing hard-boiled yolks through a sieve, mixing them with mayo and mustard, and, tenderly, with two teaspoons, delivering those fluffy (never mashed) yolks into the waiting egg whites. Flavor, for Christopher, begins with the way food looks. And not just on the plate. It matters what it looks like on the cutting board. It matters what it looks like in the market before she even buys it.

Christopher's all-around virtuosity stealthily revealed itself over the decades. We were friends. We cooked together. She showed me how to cut the backbone out of a whole chicken with kitchen shears and open the chicken like a book, and how to make "stuffing" the way her grandmother Nini did, by tearing the tender insides of a loaf of good bread into soft pieces, mixing them with salt and pepper and lots of finely chopped parsley, and sliding them under the spatchcocked bird and into the oven. When I replicate those moves, that stuffing, it's the closest I come to a Nini.

Our families would try to have Easter dinner together; we loved to roast a whole lamb that we'd order from John and Sukey Jamison in Western Pennsylvania. But it was not until Christopher dropped off a box of fine shortbread cookies at my door that it finally dawned on me: This girl should be a food editor. And after a while, she became one at *Met Home.*

WHENEVER I AM FEELING BEREFT of both ingredients and imagination as dinnertime approaches, I almost never order in. Though I know it's good for restaurants, the food that shows up rarely survives the voyage. At those moments, I stop and try to imagine what Christopher would do. Lack of groceries would make her laugh; she'd be energized by the challenge. At *Met Home*, when we decided we could not stand silent as a magazine while the designers we covered—our readers and our friends—succumbed to AIDS, we managed to pull off the industry's first magazine-sponsored fundraising effort: a showhouse with top-tier designers and architects that occupied an entire midtown town house, and a gala dinner to raise money for DIFFA (Design Industries Fighting AIDS). The gala was a big deal. Robin Williams and Bette Midler performed. Which meant that Christopher, as food editor, was in charge of providing megabucks-worthy dinners, in two vast and empty New York armories. *With no kitchens.* Which meant she had to beg for donations of high-end ingredients, the participation of big-name chefs, kitchen space, prep cooks, waitstaff, you name it. She called it "cooking for twelve hundred from a taxi." Surely, I think, I can find some pasta in the cupboard for supper.

THE IDEA FOR A NEW kind of food magazine (which would eventually develop into *Saveur*) came about, well, slant. Christopher, as food editor of *Met Home*, had taken a (rare) press trip to Norway to investigate how that nation values their salmon, why that fish is so crucial to their culinary identity. On that trip, she learned *everything* about making the cured salmon called gravlax. She returned with tales of salting salmon fillets, wrapping them in newspaper, and burying them in the backyard for the winter. Quickly, the idea of curing salmon at home spread among the staff. We were all mad to do it.

Gravlax made it into *Met Home* a few issues later, as part of a food story on weekday entertaining we called "Lamb on the Run." Clever title, but who, I now wonder, could even imagine pulling off a leg of lamb on a weeknight? Anyway, charmed by Christopher's stories, I decided to make the recipe for gravlax she'd developed. I took myself to the fish market, where I dutifully purchased (at no small cost) two luxurious salmon fillets, both sides of an entire fish. (It was not Norwegian.) When I got the salmon home, I went over each fillet with tweezers, pulling out all the little pin bones. Then I made a mixture of salt, sugar, and white peppercorns and ground them in a mortar, mixed in lots of chopped dill, and rubbed that gritty paste onto the salmon flesh. I flicked some Cognac over each side of salmon, placed one fillet skin side down on a baking sheet, and on top of that, tail to head, the other fillet, skin side up, and covered the fish with plastic wrap. Then I put another baking sheet upside down on top of the two fillets and weighted it with two heavy cans of tomatoes. Then I had to make room for that entire contraption in my refrigerator. And there it stayed. For the next *four* days!

Every day, I dutifully tended my salmon, draining the inevitable liquid from the pans, turning and resetting the two fillets, the two baking sheets, and the two tomato cans. I paid so much attention to those salmon, they might as well have been pets. When the time was up, I removed the fillets from the fridge, carefully washed and dried them, and sliced them with a long fish knife—or maybe I begged Christopher (who can make slices of salmon on a platter look like waves on a pink ocean you can't wait to dive into) to do it. At last, I was ready to serve the gravlax with slim toasts and the honey mustard sauce we doted on then.

That the salmon was ten kinds of delicious was, to me, almost beside the point. In the magazine, the gravlax story was as buried as those Norwegian fish. In a double-page photograph of the entire meal—including the lamb!—it occupied two square inches. To find the recipe, you had to work really hard. Just ten lines of copy for what had taken me days to make. It appeared some fifty pages later, at the back of the magazine, with all those black-and-white three-inch ads for custom table pads and thin-slatted window blinds. Talk about burying the punch line. If I hadn't known where to look for it, I'd never have found it. What was wrong with this picture? Gravlax—learning the saga of its provenance, tasting its delicate salmony saltiness—had been a revelation. Making it had taken days of my life! How, I wondered, could we open up our storytelling to convey that kind of food experience? How could we share that history and romance and process with our readers?

Could a fish help invent a magazine? *Met Home*, devoted as it was to leading-edge design and architecture, was no place to tell a story like that. A story like that needed its own magazine, one that prized the origins and traditions and process of making the food we wanted to learn about and to cook. Christopher and Colman and I got together to dream about a food magazine that could deliver such deep, original stories. We even went so far as to make a mock-up of our ideas, which we called *Home Cooking*, the rough pages of which are lost in the mists of time. Turns out we were a bit ahead of ourselves. It would take another few years for *Saveur* to become a reality.

IN A SIMILARLY OBLIQUE WAY, Christopher became a photographer. It was midnight in Waukesha, Wisconsin, and I was on press at Quad Graphics with our first issue of *Garden Design*, the sister magazine of the not-yet-launched *Saveur*. It took all night. Our pages were fraught with errors (our *GD* staff was small and frenzied) remedied by our creative director, Michael Grossman, who, though digitally savvy, had not lost his skill with an X-Acto knife and rubber cement, which proved crucial when we discovered that several photos were in the wrong places. Chance is strange, for in that very same Midwestern town was the world headquarters of Penzeys, which the first issue of *Saveur* was about to call "the Best Little Spice House in America." Despite the all-nighter on press, I knew I had to spend the next morning with Pamela and Bill Penzey, the brother-and-sister owners.

Deep in the dizzying aroma of their warehouses, I asked for samples of their raw materials to bring back to show our editors: foot-long curls of cassia cinnamon bark from Sumatra, whole star anise from southern China, sinewy black Madagascar Bourbon vanilla beans, Kashmir Indian saffron threads, whole cardamom pods—black from India, green from Costa Rica, and white from Guatemala—dried Jamaican gingerroot, and whole nutmeg from Grenada, with something you rarely see, its lacy covering of mace intact.

Wowed by those spice treasures, Christopher asked, in her offhand way, if she could take them home and try to photograph them. We said, "Yes, of course," never imagining where this would lead. Not only did Christopher make memorable photographs (she had to borrow her husband's Canon) in what would become her signature style—sunny available light, minimal props, direct and emotional contact with the food—using those spices, she developed a recipe for Spice House Pears, then prepared and photographed the finished dish and wrote about it for the Penzeys story. Looking at those pictures today, it is astounding to see how she nailed her vision on that very first food shoot.

By then, Christopher had been producing food stories for years. She'd run her own small restaurant in the Midwest. She saw those spices with the same knowing eyes—a cook's eyes, a poet's eyes—demonstrating a luminous style that eventually would lead her around the world to photograph many of *Saveur*'s most memorable stories. She was born with her hat on. After *Saveur*, Christopher would go on to shoot books for the greats—Julia Child, Jacques Pépin, Lidia Bastianich—and to produce award-winning Canal House books with her business partner (and former *Saveur* food editor), Melissa Hamilton. Christopher's recipe for those spiced pears is still a favorite in our house. I make it with peaches, too, peeling and poaching the whole fruit in white wine and sugar with curls of lemon peel, using all the celebrities of our spice story: star anise, vanilla bean, cinnamon sticks, and saffron threads.

I THINK OF THE KIND of cooking Christopher and Melissa produce at Canal House as forensic. They dive into the history and culture of a dish and come back with only the attributes that count. The essence of the thing. This apparent simplicity is the result of knowing so much and choosing only what really matters. Their deliberate approach is worlds away from the just-add-a-shot-of-sriracha-and-we're-good moves of hipster cooks. But it's equally equidistant from fussy restaurant preparations so contrived you can't remember by morning what you had for dinner the night before. Canal House is measured nonchalance; anti-cheffy, but just as precise. Those ladies are as deliberate in what they do as in what they do not do.

In a recent review of Canal House Station, Christopher and Melissa's restaurant in a renovated 1870s train depot, and their recent book *Cook Something: Recipes to Rely On*, both nominated for James Beard Awards, Craig LaBan, the *Philadelphia Inquirer* restaurant critic, gave the restaurant his high accolade of three (Liberty) bells (!), describing, "Rustic slabs of pâté marbled with chunks of pork, herbs and Cognac-scented chicken liver. A milky bowl of chowder steeped Irish-style with smoked whitefish. A duck confit so perfect, its tawny skin glowed luminous atop caraway-roasted apples as the afternoon light beamed in gently from across the river."

Sunday dinner at Canal House Station is everything you want to eat. Deliberate. Just one single, perfect menu is offered. As an example, here's an Autumn Apple Dinner from a Sunday in October, printed with the date and a sweet note: "It's Dorothy's birthday!"

TO WHET YOUR APPETITE
Pâté with Apple Jelly & Melba Toast (handmade)

Maitake from Across the River & Scallion, Tempura-Style

TO BEGIN
Fall "Leaves" Dressed with Vinaigrette

Mt. Tam Cheese with Seeded Toast

MAIN COURSE
Roasted Duck Legs

with

Baby White Turnips, La Ratte Potatoes

& Roasted Honeycrisp Apples

DESSERT
Apple Tart with Soft Whipped Cream

Deliberate is a funny word to use with Christopher, because once, after we launched *Saveur*, on a transatlantic flight, possibly immediately after watching the tearjerker film *Like Water for Chocolate*, she turned to me and confessed, "I don't know if I can do this job. I'm so drifty." I hope I had the grace to suggest to her that the most imaginative ideas come from the drifty side of the brain.

IN *SAVEUR'S* EARLIEST DAYS (in reality latest nights), to compress the writing/editing process (and to meet our looming deadlines), Christopher and I would write together, chairs side by side at my computer. For a section at the back of the magazine simply called Kitchen that carried her byline, we would dive into the cooking part of our feature stories. In this, we replicated our experiences cooking together when we'd laughingly ask each other, "How does she do this again?" reminding ourselves that "we" were the "she" and that the story of the dish is more important than the recipe.

"What Am I Making for Dinner?" is an example of an early piece we wrote as she was finding her voice. It sounds a little bit like me and a little bit like her. "Even though I guess I fall into the category of 'food professional,' I feel like just another working girl [her] when I stand in front of my refrigerator and think, I wonder what she's got in there? [me] But for me there's nothing like the challenge of a refrigerator dinner—making something from nothing [me]—to get my juices flowing. I'm on my toes. I'm bobbing. I'm weaving [her]. I'm on a cooking high. If I've got Italian rice, a can of chicken stock, and a carrot, I'll add a little saffron and I've got a golden risotto [her]. Just three eggs, an onion, and the end of any cheese make a frittata [both]. A can of cannellini beans doctored with olive oil, garlic, and a squeeze of lemon juice is great on toast [her]. I roast canned plum tomatoes with garlic and herbs and spoon them over polenta [me]. Simple things like that. Heaven!"

FOOD PHOTOGRAPHY, WHEN I WAS a young editor, was a full-scale Hollywood production. Photographers used an eight-by-ten-inch beast called a view camera. This hulk, this Terminator—and determinator—of a camera was fixed on heavy wooden legs, and in order to even see the image on the camera's ground glass, you had to duck under a voluminous black cloth. And unlike with a single-lens reflex camera, *that image was upside down*! So, say you were shooting a Thanksgiving turkey (which all home magazines were condemned to do). The setups were so cumbersome that the turkey had to be almost nailed to a table. You could move props around it, but once you decided on the shot and the super-hot lights were fixed on their metal stands, the camera itself did not move.

With a fixed camera, you had to figure out where the watercress should go and put it in the shot and then scurry back under the black cloth and turn your head upside down to see if you'd got it in the right place. Try making an enticing photograph under those circumstances. (Eventually, a Polaroid film holder was developed that could be attached to the 8x10's ground glass so we could take test pictures and see the image the right way.) I learned from Carol Helms, design editor of *Met Home*, how to navigate such a photo shoot. It was miraculous to watch her get the watercress right, every time. (Well, give her any five unrelated objects and she'd work her magic and make them look as if they were born that way.)

Those old photo setups required a blinding blast of light on the set that further distanced the image from the real thing.

None of this fit our editorial vision of making our pages look cookable. It took many unnecessary years for separators to accept film from smaller format cameras. (Believe me, I know how nutty this sounds today, when we're used to holding up a small rectangle to our eye and digitally recording our every bite.) You'd leave a photo shoot with frustration; when you eventually saw the printed page, the last emotion you'd feel was the burning desire to cook the food.

Met Home was owned by the big Midwestern publisher Meredith. Before the success of our magazine earned its move to New York, we had to produce photo shoots in the basement of the corporate headquarters in Des Moines, Iowa, rummaging among the blue-flowered CorningWare and piles of polyester napkins in the vast prop rooms of *Better Homes & Gardens*, testing our recipes with olive oil I'd have to carry from New York (small wonder they called Iowa then the "land of two Velveetas"—with pimentos and without), borrowing our bowls and plates and platters from antiques shops in West Des Moines, relying on the goodwill and unfailing eye of Jim Hirsheimer, editor and antiques dealer (and eventual husband of you-know-who).

By the time we launched *Saveur*, we would not even think about photographing our food in a studio. We moved into a sunny loft in SoHo with great old factory windows and abundant available light. (Light so awesome that if we were lucky, we'd look up and see the sunset caught in Rachel Whiteread's glass water tower on a rooftop a few blocks away.) We would cook in our newly installed IKEA kitchen and carry the dish to a big worktable in our common space to shoot it. No fake barn-board backgrounds, no fantasy sets, no extraneous props. No watercress. No food stylists! Or prop stylists! Our food would look the way we editors wanted it to look. Just-cooked. Doable. Authentic. Delicious.

All of this played directly into the way Christopher wanted to shoot food. She was the right girl in the right place. She learned photography the way she learned cooking, by looking and doing, perfecting her skills ("Keep pushing the buttons!"), and trusting her artist's instinct for what was right. It was the value of visual storytelling—truth-telling. The food we showed on our pages would come a whole lot closer to the food readers could cook in their own kitchens; it had the advantage of being real. Christopher's photographs—bathed in natural light, emotionally immediate, beautifully composed—moved readers; she helped to reduce the frustration and fear of failure inherent in all kitchen endeavors and established a style that continues to be seductive to this day.

I have a memory of Christopher sitting on the floor in some hotel room somewhere in the world, surrounded, like the statue in the center of a fountain, by a daunting array of equipment: cameras and backs of cameras and pieces of cameras and all manner of lenses and filters and techy matte-black tripods and piles of film rolls (yes, there was film!) and cans of shot film. And she was just chatting away as she calmly organized those disparate parts, serenely making sense of it all. How remarkable, I thought. She has taught herself to know exactly what to do with every one of those little black pieces. ("Like with like," I can still hear her singing in the process of organizing whatever chaos she confronted.)

With Christopher shooting many of our stories and Colman writing them, instead of working as editors with a photographer to produce the pieces and a writer to report them, we increased our editorial fleetness. Unlike the magazines we competed with—with their enormous prop and travel budgets and a cast of dozens—we had neither the money nor the inclination for such overblown productions. We could travel lighter, argue more, discover the real story as we went along.

Undaunted and unflappable, Christopher rode on the back of a scooter in Hanoi to photograph the celebration of Tet. She made a couple of sentimental journeys to Australia, once with Colman, which involved covering so many wineries I feared they'd never return. And one night, she called me from Valencia to report that all the snails they'd bought for the paella shoot had escaped from their baskets and were crawling up the walls of her hotel room.

I DID GET TO TRAVEL and report a few stories with Christopher, but a highlight for both of us is the crazy-fast trip we made when, just as we were putting together our third book in the *Saveur Cooks Authentic . . .* series, we realized to our chagrin that we had holes as big as Italy itself in our coverage of that country. So Christopher and I set off on a frenzied itinerary to Rome, Milan, Bologna, and Palermo to capture the Italy we were missing. Colman sent us to his favorite trattoria, Casale, which was, as he promised, on the Via Flaminia, one of those roads that all lead to Rome. In front of an open kitchen, where a whole lamb, fragrant with fat and rosemary, rotated on a spit, two tiers of tables were covered with a landscape of long white rectangular dishes, one more voluptuous than the next. To us, it was the antipasto at the end of the rainbow.

Maybe it was the smoky aromas, or the dizzying high of escaping the office, or maybe it was just being in Italy, but that vast food landscape took our breath away (when we weren't distracted by the Italian soap opera playing on the trattoria's TV). Casale was lodged permanently in our collective imaginations, influencing not just what we cooked but the way we wanted our food to look. The photographs we made that day became powerful shared memories; when we got to cook together at home, it was those Casale platters Christopher and I had in our heads.

Each dish held only one thing, but that thing in abundance: slices of roasted eggplant in herbs and olive oil, say; or peppers of all sizes, roasted, too, split, and stuffed with rice; or just a simple layering of marinated green zucchini and plenty of fresh herbs. From this repetition came a pattern. We photographed bright rows of tomatoes fattened with risotto and basil; yellow zucchini blossoms, cheese-filled and fried; wide bowls of ventresca—the meaty belly of tuna (happily, it comes jarred)—with rings of red onion; big borlotti beans in oil with garlic cloves and whole sage branches; twice-peeled green favas with slim slices of mild young pecorino, and still more white platters holding every kind of cured meat, and the cheeses: bufala mozzarella and fresh ricotta and provolone.

Christopher and I eventually figured out (well, mostly she figured out) how to make some of those platterist fantasies. I watch as she fries zucchini blossoms from my garden, not in the extra-wide skillet I'd have chosen but in a small, deep saucepan, dipping each fragile blossom in a rather austere little batter of equal parts white wine and flour with a pinch of salt, then frying only a few at a time, draining them on paper towels, and salting them. She crisps sage leaves with the same treatment, a surprising hors d'oeuvre. When batter-frying anything—recently it was shiitake mushrooms—I close my eyes and rehearse Christopher's moves: *Small saucepan. Not too much oil. Batter: half and half, wine and flour. Drain well. Lotsa salt.*

We'd make cipolline in agrodolce, those lovely little flat onions in a sweet-and-sour braise of white wine vinegar—the onions a pain to peel but the dish a pleasure to prepare—and spaghetti alla puttanesca, pasta in a lusty sauce of both black and green olives, a hailstorm of red pepper flakes, and chunks of peeled tomatoes. (Like Marcella with red peppers, Christopher likes to peel raw tomatoes.) And carciofi alla romana, whole artichokes pared down to their edible essence and gently warmed—spa-bathed, really—in good olive oil and white wine, with (preferably Roman) mint, their peeled stems in the air.

Looking at Christopher's photographs, you can almost smell the food as you revel in the light. I think of her style as Being There, worlds away from the dour and chilly New Nordic look that's so trendy these days. You know, those photographs where the food—drained of color, seemingly wrung out and worried—is invariably shot against a background of unironed knobby linen (hand-)dyed in somber seaweed colors, redolent of fermentation, tree bark, and moss. To us, that style (or any style, really, that distances readers from the food) impedes connection and gives it an intellectual overlay that's more satisfying to the producers than the readers.

On that same Italy trip, we discovered strattù, the pungent Sicilian paste made from tomatoes dried on platters in the sun, whole mounds of the stuff, displayed on shaky tables at la Vucciria, "the madhouse," Palermo's gritty, operatic street market. Strattù gives me new respect for the costly jarred stuff: its deep flavor can make a meal. We were drawn to the cucina povera that's the frugal essence of Sicilian cooking—

foraged herbs and toasted bread crumbs instead of the more costly cheese. We learned dishes like bucatini con le sarde, in which the pasta, hollow like a straw, is tossed with dried currants, and the fennel fronds that grow with wild abundance on the dusty roadsides, and sardines scooped up from the surrounding seas, with plenty of those homemade bread crumbs. Each time we cook these dishes at home is an attempt to re-create that experience and, almost, their flavor.

We drove into the Madonie Mountains to a grand old agricultural estate where some buildings date to the thirteenth century (our room was in a converted horse stable) to learn the deep secrets of arancini, "little oranges"—croquettes made from day-old risotto with a hidden surprise of soft mozzarella and ham inside, rolled in bread crumbs and crisply fried. (Just last week, Christopher and Melissa made suppli al telefono—a version of arancini without the ham, where the mozz stretches out like telephone lines—for Sunday dinner at Canal House Station.)

I have a photograph Christopher gave me from that shoot. It's a dining room. A shaded hanging lamp spills light, pink with promise, over a long wooden table and onto the tile-patterned linoleum floor. Six simple pine chairs with rush seats surround a scalloped plastic lace cloth that hangs down a foot on all sides. Plain white plates, everyday wineglasses. An opened green glass bottle of wine, another of water. *This*, she was telling me. *This is all you need.*

WHEN I ASKED MARCELLA HAZAN where we should go to report on the cooking of Bologna—the famed ragù Bolognese; the lasagna, with wide noodles made green with spinach; the tiny pork-and-prosciutto-filled tortellini en brodo—she introduced us to Valeria and Margherita Simili, who'd been Marcella's cooking assistants when her cooking school was based in Bologna. Those estimable ladies, twins, one a foot taller than the other, welcomed us into their own cooking school and gave us days of priceless education as we captured their process. Christopher says she'd like, one day, to look just like the Simili sisters: slim and neat, their white-collared linen blouses open at the neck to reveal a simple strand of pearls. Ragù Bolognese became one of Christopher's favorite things to cook (there's a knockout recipe in *Cook Something*).

WE WRESTLED WITH THE DECISION to travel to Barcelona in February 2020 to celebrate yet another momentous Colman birthday. It's winter in our imaginations, too, we said. We need to remind ourselves who we are, we told each other. We need to change the movies that are playing in our heads. It was a big deal: Christopher and Melissa had to close their restaurant for a week. I had to not feel guilty about leaving my desk, where this book was being written. Christopher and I had gone from years of seeing each other every day to years when we could count our in-person meetings on the fingers of one hand; from traveling a whole lot to being strangely rooted in just one place. We convinced ourselves that we had to make that trip.

Once we made the decision to go to Spain, we decided to go somewhere else for a few days first. Christopher, now cooking in her own restaurant, felt the need to connect with some real French food. And I, now working alone in my office, was starved for primary inspiration.

After some research, Christopher suggested Lyon, mostly because of its famed bouchons, those traditional typically Lyonnais restaurants that serve the kind of old-fashioned food you can hardly find anymore. The kind of food that after all these years still matters to us. In the middle of the peninsula that shapes that fine city at the confluence of two mighty rivers, the Saône and the Rhône, we rented an Airbnb in a graceful nineteenth-century building with south-facing windows overlooking the Place Carnot. And even though it had a perfectly fine kitchen, we agreed not to cook. We were there to experience the food, not make it.

Through our friend David Tanis, we connected with Bill Buford, the writer who'd lived in Lyon for five years cooking and researching his book *Dirt*, which was just months away from publication. Bill generously told us about his two favorite bouchons, the Bouchon des Filles, on the very street where he and his family had lived, and the Comptoir d'Abel, telling me, "It's the only bouchon (that I know of) that serves a quenelle as it was made by La Mère Brazier (it's really a piece of history, like something from the thirties)."

He had me at quenelles. Those poached dumplings of seafood mousse, ethereally light and often formed with two soupspoons, and thus usually egg-shaped, are traditionally served with a sauce, often of lobster or crayfish. Quenelles, a Lyonnais specialty, are old-fashioned and pretty much out of style everywhere else; they were the first thing I ordered when, during my junior year in Paris, somebody's parents would come to town and take us to a real restaurant.

Bill was kind; he steered us right. We could have stayed in Lyon for years! Our first dinner was around the corner from our apartment, at the Comptoir d'Abel, which did indeed make an estimable quenelle de brochet (pike), their version so puffy it looked like a Portuguese man-of-war on a dinner plate, browned on top by its run under the broiler. That quenelle lived up to its history, as it was made by Eugénie Brazier, aka La Mère Brazier, the most famous of the Mères Lyonnaise (they called them "mothers," the women who were once the most important cooks in that city). La Mère Brazier founded the restaurant where Bill worked the punishing *stage* about which he writes so painfully and superbly.

At Comptoir d'Abel, we couldn't take our eyes off a traditional salade lyonnaise, served in a huge white bowl: abundant greens with big rough-cut olive oil–toasted croutons and hefty bacon lardons, and on top, a peeled soft-boiled egg, its golden yolk oozing out over the torn greens. A salad to replicate as soon as we got home. We celebrated Valentine's Day in one of the great eating rooms of France, the nineteenth-century Brasserie Georges, where every five minutes it was somebody's birthday and the lights went out and the waiters stopped to sing "Bon Anniversaire"; but they would just as happily come to your table and perform the traditional ritual of steak tartare. We ate lusty pied de cochon (pig's foot), and devoured with our eyes the table-size platters of choucroute garnie, with its traditional hunk of skinned ham hock, a plate-size slab of bacon, three kinds of sausages, and peeled boiled potatoes, all hugging a mountain of sauerkraut.

In the small, cozy room that was Bouchon des Filles, run by two women and crammed with families celebrating, well, just Sunday, and each other, we were wedged in at a teeny corner table. By then we knew to immediately order a pot de vin, the Lyonnais clear carafe of house wine. We shared another quenelle, this one of red mullet in a pastry crust, with sauce

Nantua—crayfish sauce—and a surprisingly delicate pot-au-feu, long-cooked beef with demure pieces of salsify, carrot, and turnip in a strong, clear, beefy broth. Lyon, we now appreciate, is a city in no hurry to run away from its past.

On our last morning in Lyon, Christopher called me to the window of our apartment, saying: "DK, come look what I've arranged for you." And there, like a dream, our food fantasies had come to life. Opening the French windows by the cool arabesques of their handles, I beheld a Sunday market that had set itself up on the Place Carnot as we slept. Running down the marble steps to the street, we discovered a poultry rotisserie truck, with skewers of birds in descending sizes from fat turkeys to plump poulets de Bresse, their blue feet demurely crossed and tied with string, turning on hefty skewers in front of heating elements, succulent juices dripping onto trays of roughly chopped potatoes below, just waiting to catch them.

There were tables of breads in all the iconic shapes—miches and ficelles and épis—and even though it was February, there were plenty of vegetables: bunches of pink turnips with bright-green tops, and round red kuri squashes. And even though this tiny market ran just a block at the north end of the square, there was a mushroom seller, too; and a cheesemonger, with five versions of the soft, round Saint-Marcellin of the region that we'd already come to love; and a stand hung with rough country sausages. There was an elegant pâté maker, who offered tall loaves of layered meaty bits wrapped in flaky golden pastry, their tops fancifully scattered with pastry leaves whose veins were etched on ever so carefully with the tip of a knife.

IN THAT EARLY-MORNING FRENCH SUNLIGHT, who could have imagined we would return to an America forever changed. I to New York City, then the heart of the pandemic, where, just three weeks later, the scream of ambulance sirens down now-empty streets would become the soundtrack of our lives. Where ordered groceries could take ten days to arrive. Where we sprouted scallions on windowsills, hoarded the roots and peels of every vegetable we could get our hands on for stock. Where cooking every meal, and planning for it, would become an obsession. Where Black Lives Matter was painted in bold yellow letters twelve feet high on Fifth Avenue in front of Trump Tower, three blocks away. Where on the sidewalks, playroom restaurants would pop up, all plywood planters and plastic walls, strung with lights, as fanciful and fleeting as the forts my sister and I used to make in our pitch-black basement, throwing white bedsheets over shaky card tables, navigating by flashlight. Who could predict that worrying would became our prime occupation?

When Christopher returned to Canal House Station, she and Melissa invented take-out pop-ups for fried-chicken sandwiches and "the best BLT on the planet Earth." And every Sunday, they offered, for pre-order and pickup, an inspired five-course dinner, different every week. And every Sunday, they sold out.

CHAPTER 6

—— ❧ ——

THE STOMACH CLUB

MANY YEARS AGO, MICHAEL ANDERSON, an editor at *The New York Times Book Review*, confessed to our San Francisco–based writer friend Tom McNamee that he was an obsessive wine collector—but that he never drank the wine he collected. Indeed, he had bottles stashed under the bed and in the coat closets of his Upper West Side apartment. And there they stayed. Immediately, Tom saw it as his responsibility to relieve Michael of such an embarrassment. He suggested that a small group of us—passionate cooks all—could make a splendid dinner to accompany such wines as Michael saw fit to contribute. This simple premise would become a tradition: decades of dinners known as the Stomach Club—our very own version of Dickens's Society of the Pickwick Club—where we could cook together, experiment with recipes, and drink very good wine. And learn one another's cooking moves firsthand.

For years, Michael overdelivered; one dinner featured a roast pork shoulder with a flight of 1982 Pomerols; another centered around rare Saint-Émilions—Château Cheval Blanc, to be precise. We served cucumber soup with Puligny-Montrachet Les Combettes, 1992. Tournedos, sautés au madère (no one promised unpretentiousness), were paired, for the purposes of comparison, with four different 1985 Bordeaux—including those show-offs, Lynch Bages and Lafite Rothschild. And because we were all writers, or actors, or filmmakers, or editors, the Stomach Club planning process itself—emails frantically pinging from coast to coast—took on a dizzying life of its own.

Here's an example of the deliberately pretentious exchange between Tom, the Stomach Club's gifted chronicler, and Miles Chapin, our actor/real estate friend:

Tom: So, Miles. I was planning on a chocolate dessert— somewhere I have a recipe for the three-flavor mousse from New York's old Café Chauveron, the greatest chocolate mousse in history—but Michael wants to bring Sauternes and he says chocolate with Sauternes is an abomination. On the other hand, he's also bringing a flight of 1986 Pauillacs. What do you say?

Miles: Part of me wants to say, "Michael, you'll have your d'Yquem with chocolate and you will like it." But of course, since he's being so generous sharing his cellar with us, we can't do that. So. Maybe we could have a Sauternes with an earlier course, like foie gras, or a blue-type cheese? It matches well with both and is kind of unexpected for most people. Or, I guess, I suppose, we could change the dessert. How about some junket?

Besides loving the chance to experience those wines, and the always-chaotic camaraderie of working in the kitchen with friends, I managed to learn a whole lot of cooking from the recipes and culinary styles of our friends. Tom was fanciful and fussy about his recipes, worrying over every ingredient and its preparation; Miles, well, Miles just walked in the door and started cooking. For one such dinner, he arrived after work at about 6:30 p.m. and served a pitch-perfect tenderloin of beef an hour later. The finicky tenderness of tenderloin always terrified me. How do you keep what is essentially a roll of filets mignons—an investment cut, costing into the three figures—from overcooking? Miles delivered succulent pinkness using tricks he'd learned from his sainted mother, Betty Chapin, who did a whole lot of social entertaining. She made it look effortless. So does her son.

Finding the right cut, he advises, is key. Good butchers will prepare a tenderloin properly, by skinning the gristly membrane off a four- to six-pound roast without disturbing the tenderloin's meager fat. But good butchers are not easy to find. Miles admits to sometimes buying the tenderloin Cryovaced at Costco and dry-aging the beef at home—a simple process, he promises, which involves resting it on top of a whole lotta paper towels for a few days at the bottom of his refrigerator.

When you're ready to cook the tenderloin, Miles advises, take it out of the refrigerator at least an hour before roasting and bring it to room temperature. Pat the surface of the roast very dry, then liberally sprinkle it with kosher salt, freshly ground black pepper, and dried rosemary. Plop on a goodly amount of Dijon mustard, and rub the seasonings all over the meat. Place the tenderloin directly on a baking pan (don't use a rack, because you want every bit of goodness that sticks to the pan to end up in the accompanying sauce). Lay on a few branches of fresh rosemary and pop it into a very hot oven—450°F at least—and cook until done, only about 10 minutes per pound. Medium rare is about 135°F. Remember that the meat should rest for 10 minutes after it's out of the oven.

Miles likes to serve the tenderloin with a fruit-based sauce. "You don't happen to have any currant jelly?" he challenges us dubiously. Imagine Roger's delight at the one-upmanship of producing a jar of our very own, made from the currants on our own bushes!

BUT AS GOOD AS OUR dinners were in those early years, one could argue that they truly took off when the real cooks—Christopher Hirsheimer and Melissa Hamilton of Canal House—joined the Stomach Club. Because of their absolute competence and good-natured willingness to do whatever it takes (such a winning combination), I suddenly found myself smack-dab in the middle of planning foreplay in the protective role of guardian of their well-being.

Christopher: Canal House will make and bring the pigs in blankets. And a bottle of some lovely bubbles and perhaps a good pinot. We will provide the truffles for Dorothy's chicken (poulet en demi-deuil), and we can all make that when we arrive. How's that sound?

DK: Now, Crissy, I don't want you springing for no stinkin' truffles. We can make a succulent fresh thyme or tarragon butter to slip under those chickies' skins.

From the moment Canal House arrived at their first dinner, the Stomach Club abruptly shifted from being all about the wine to being mostly about the food. And, as it turned out, Michael Anderson eventually decided on the wise course of selling his (remaining) collection instead of squandering it on the likes of us. Reflecting on the shift, I rationalized: *All those storied vintages are just a bunch of empty bottles in the morning.* The menu-deciding emails took on a boomeranging life of their own. Tom would suggest, Christopher would counter, and I'd have to step in to make sure she and Melissa didn't wind up doing all the cooking in advance. Christopher suggested guinea hens for their first dinner. I could see where this was going.

DK: How this *does not work* is that you two cook the meal and bring it!!! We have been known to split expenses at the end if anyone is still awake. Assuming the birdies need a bit of time to braise, I will get them here and wait for all of us to arrive and let them cook as we prepare the rest of the meal and consume obscene amounts of good wine. We'll all weigh in before the menu is locked.

But we haven't even gotten to the part where Tom hates everything and we have to go back to the drawing board.

Melissa: Dear Stomach Clubbers, I haven't had the nerve to pipe in to say my New Year's resolutions are to be allergic to dairy, shellfish, and nuts, and I forget what else, oh yes, I'm trying to follow a gluten-free, fat-free diet. By the looks of this delicious menu, I see I'm doomed (or incredibly blessed!).

Can Christopher and I add an escarole salad to the courses to come before (or with) the cheese? I'm very much looking forward to eating and drinking with all of you.

Tom: I'm allergic to escarole, Melissa. Can't be in the same room with it.

Tom: Just kidding.

IT'S THEIR DARK MEAT THAT makes guinea hens so flavorful, like the wild partridge you find only in autumn, even if they are farm-raised. I'd never cooked guinea hens but always loved eating them. And as I watch Christopher pan-roast the hens on the stovetop for that Stomach Club dinner, cooking them turns out to be much easier than I expected. (Watching her do anything always makes it looks much easier than you thought it would be.) She seasons the pieces of the quartered birds with salt, pepper, and cinnamon (great touch). In our largest skillet, she takes a few minutes to brown diced pancetta, then cipolline onions and peeled chestnuts, in olive oil, then scoops them out onto a serving platter. She browns the guinea hen pieces in the same pan and removes those, too. Then she pours in red wine and chicken broth, cooks it down a bit, scraping the flavor bits into the sauce, then returns just the legs to the skillet, adds back the pancetta-onion-chestnut mix, covers the pan, and cooks the legs for a half hour.

We munch on the pâté Tom's made from the guinea hen livers he sautéed on the spot and watch as the breasts are returned to the pan. After about 15 minutes more, Christopher spoons the guinea hen pieces onto the platter, scatters the pancetta, cipolline, and chestnuts on top, and cooks down the sauce a bit more before pouring that, too, over the waiting birds. Meanwhile . . .

Melissa is over by the sink preparing an escarole salad as if she's practicing some intense martial art. Each move is energetic and deliberate. *Pow!* She cuts out the core of an entire voluptuous head of escarole and separates the leaves. (I remember another of Melissa's kick-ass moves: She once opened three dozen oysters. With a screwdriver.) *Swish!* She vigorously washes the leaves. *Crack!* I'm surprised to see her breaking off the white bottoms of the hefty leaves, favoring them, along with the tender inner ones, and "saving the dark green tops for another use," as we used to say in recipe writing. *Oh!* I suddenly get it. She doesn't use the green tops! So that's why her salad is always so crispy and crunchy! I watch as she takes the time to thoroughly dry each leaf separately in a dish towel. *Yes!*

Then she grabs our largest salad bowl—a handsome dark wooden trench once my mother's—and, with a fork, mashes a half a garlic clove with salt against its sloping side. She loves to add preserved lemon rind to her escarole salad, plus the juice of half a lemon. "Sometimes," she explains, watching me watch her dice the rind of about a quarter of the preserved lemon she's brought, "I'll add in some mashed anchovies instead of the preserved lemon." Then, rather ferociously, she whisks in about six tablespoons of olive oil, tasting with her fingertip as she goes. She loosely measures out about six cups of the groomed escarole leaves and tosses them vigorously with the dressing. Now, that's a salad to remember!

Stomach Club dinners are usually held at our New York

apartment, a conveniently central gathering place for travel-
ers, with an open kitchen we can all work in together. Reviewing the photographs and videos we've taken over the years,
I'm touched by how beautiful everything looks, and by how
hard we work to make our celebrations special. How every
dish is served with such style and warmth, because we know
how lucky we are to be in this place, with these people, at this
moment, eating this food.

WITH THE NEXT MEETING OF the Stomach Club on the horizon
comes my now-inevitable admonition to Tom:

DK: We simply cannot invite our Canal House ladeez and
expect them to come cook for us like they did the last time.
Why don't you write them a McNamee-ish note and invite
them with that stipulation?

Tom: Darling ladies: There is an unfortunate aspect to your
having joined the Stomach Club, and it has fallen to me to
tell you. You are so much better at everything we have been
trying to do—e.g., chopping, stirring, simmering, frying,
roasting, thinking, bringing—and so generous with your
skills and your genius and your provender, that when you
appear bearing treasures galore, having already imagined
the glories they might, in your hands, become, and you
then (as we look on, goggling and drinking) produce those
glories with evident ease, well . . . how can I say this? We are
covered in shame.

So, with face red and eyes downcast, I am deputized to request that you bring less food, please, next time, and don't cook it quite so good. Okay?

Then there would be the inevitable kvetching over prospective menus:

Tom: The problem is: Everything sounds good, but in aggregate it sounds sickening. It's too much. It's too rich. We're not Henry VIII. Please let's edit.

Roger: As you know, I don't get terribly involved in Stomach Club menus. Not, that is, until it becomes absolutely necessary. I agree with Tom that the menu is much too rich. For that reason, I would add a leavening course, a new recipe I found for foie gras with pineapple cream sauce. You'll love it.

Tom: Do you like butter soup? It's really really simple, and light; really just a beurre monté. Or you can do it as a beurre blanc, with a base of shallots, lemon juice, and white wine.

Christopher: Why bother with all that folderol? Just one block of Kerrygold Irish butter on each of eight plates (remove the wrapper first) with a sprig of parsley. Serve with a stack of toast. Sometimes this is served with a Lipitor chaser.

Tom: Yum. You're so right. The parsley is a brilliant touch.

SEVERAL TIMES, THE STOMACH CLUB traveled to Canal House. One spring, we gathered at their studio in Lambertville, New Jersey, but not without the tsunami of planning emails. The Canals love the idea of paschal lamb, farm-raised from "the illustrious Jamison Farm in Latrobe, Pennsylvania. It could be chops, shanks, legs, or even a springy navarin." Miles is mad for shad roe, can't stop talking about it, and makes an educated pitch for how to cook and serve it. Tom, however, is having none of that: "I'm doubtful about the shad. For one thing, there are only about three people left on the planet who know how to bone the damned thing, and poorly boned shad is a throat-stabbing nightmare.

"What if I were to just be rude and say, hey, what about we off the shad? Maybe it's some sort of northeastern-anadromy [fish migration] myth to start with? Some nostalgic survival from poverty days up the Hudson and the Delaware? I think back on the hundred and more times I've had shad roe, with the bacon, with the beurre blanc, poached, grilled, breaded and fried, whatever the hell, split, splitting, spilling out like some poor relation's old beat-up sofa, and all I can remember is, well, you know, it didn't really taste all that good."

Miles caves on the shad, and Tom counters with quail but eventually comes around: "Spring lamb sounds great, and to hell with the quail parade."

TWO SPRINGS AGO, WHEN CHRISTOPHER and Melissa opened their restaurant, Canal House Station, after a renovation that, like all renovations, took far too much time, far too much money, and far too much anxiety to complete, they suggested we have a Stomach Club dinner there to inaugurate the space. This was an invitation devoutly to be wished. Planning reached a fever pitch. Travel was involved! And designated drivers! And invited guests; there would now be sixteen of us!

To mark this auspicious occasion, I decide to make my favorite Burgundian terrine, jambon persillé, an acrobatic effort involving several whole days and two calf's feet (a dish that Lincoln, who came with us to the dinner, was to call meat Jell-O and refuse to touch). That terrine of pink ham in its parsley-studded jelly made its indelible impression on me years ago in a small restaurant in Paris where a bunch of French editors I was working with took me to for lunch. I can still see the round table in the corner by the front windows where we sat.

That restaurant served an all-pâté menu—the idea irresistible to me. Servers came to the table cradling white bowls of smooth chicken liver mousse, and earthy vegetable terrines, and chunky pâtés de maison. You chose spoonfuls or slices of whichever appealed. (Did I dream this? I could never find that place again!) It was there that I experienced my first jambon persillé; I later helped perfect a recipe (now in *Saveur Cooks Authentic French*) for *Saveur*'s Burgundy issue. In the years since, it has remained a singular pleasure to get my hands on a seven-pound bone-in cured ham, cut it into fat chunks, and, in my biggest pot, cook it slowly for about 5 hours with two now-difficult-to-procure calf's feet, a bottle of good-enough white Burgundy, and fragrant aromatics. I love the drama of it all: Slow-cooking the ham, then removing it from the pot. Clarifying its pungent broth with a whipped-egg-white raft that magically attracts all the impurities and, when removed, leaves the stock crystal clear. I love the feeling of shredding the cooked ham into a bowl with my fingers, mixing in an abundance of chopped parsley, then adding the stock by the ladleful and chilling it all overnight.

Tom got it into his head to make crispy duck patties, the pan deglazed with white wine, orange liqueur, and a sauce of slivered orange rinds. Even he cannot remember the inspiration. Miles made spaetzle and brought plenty of Riesling. The Canals served up a salad of little spring lettuces, lots of herbs, and tiny flowers—spring on a plate—and, for dessert, made a beautiful apple galette, exactly the tart I have promised myself to ask Christopher to teach me. Someday.

Here's the breathless fangirl note I wrote to Christopher and Melissa after seeing their new restaurant for the first time:

Dear Ones,

I knew the Station would surprise and delight, but I was unprepared for the level of thought, refinement, inspiration, and just plain magic that greeted us yesterday. I know it has been a project of love (and pain), and I feel for you all. But beginning with the grand opera entrance: the kitchen in all its soaring whiteness, its hanging light fixtures big as ocean liner smokestacks suspended over that generous deck of glorious white marble, and the pièce de résistance—that chorus line of wildflowers in old canning jars creating an eight-foot curtain of blossoms. That is a gasp-er, as we used to say in *Met Home* days.

And then the myriad discoveries: the garden so full of promise and fig trees; that inspired wallpaper in the entrance; the way you made the dining rooms (former station waiting rooms!) seem to stretch out beneath their gorgeous gables; the rigor of the bare windows, and the splendor of the (Jim-made) lamps. I could go on.

And all of that infused with your generosity and welcome. I still cannot believe how great thou art! And how lucky we are.

VERSIONS OF STOMACH CLUB DINNERS, I'm happy to report, have continued to happen, whenever and however we can manage to get Tom on the East Coast. As worldly as we all like to seem, we continue to learn from one another, cooking together, making new traditions. One spring, it happened that four of our members were nominated for James Beard Awards: Roger for his documentary film *The Restaurateur*, about Danny Meyer; Tom for his definitive biography *The Man Who Changed the Way We Eat: Craig Claiborne and the American Food Renaissance*; and Christopher and Melissa for their big book, *Canal House Cooks Every Day*. Now, that was an occasion to celebrate.

Over the years (and reviewing all the smart-ass emails I saved, always kinda hoping it'd be Tom who'd put the Stomach Club in a book), I discovered that there was no dish mentioned more frequently than pommes Anna, or its variant, gratin dauphinois. And I figured out after the first few years that it was not just the gratin we craved—all those thinly sliced potatoes, carefully layered one by one in a shallow pan in a rosette pattern, made crispy on the bottom by all that clarified butter, sometimes cheese. Rather, it was the *idea* of the gratin. It was the experience we longed to recapture. The gratin meant to each one of us—no matter where we grew up or when in our lives it happened—that little French bistro we just happened into one chilly night, where the lights were low and the tables were close, where checkered napkins stood peaked and ready on thick white plates, a carafe of red was poured, and we would order . . . gratin dauphinois. And after our appetizer of hors-d'œuvre variés—grated carrots, dilled cucumbers, a slice of pâté, shiny sardines in oil—the practiced server would bring out with our entrecôte an oval pan of sliced potatoes baked in butter. It was not so much the potatoes we longed for; we were hungry for the experience of being charmed. We craved those vivid feelings of delight and well-being, neither of which, of course, could ever be recaptured. But with the Stomach Club, at least we could try.

CHAPTER 7

COOKING WITH
YOUR HANDS

I MET DAVID TANIS'S ADMIRABLY crunchy bean salad long before I met the man. Lunch, upstairs at Chez Panisse Café in Berkeley, was a simple plate of tiny green French lentils, breathtakingly executed—each bean distinct but flavorful, punctuated by even tinier cubes of bright carrot and celery, heightened by a sharp sherry vinaigrette. That something so humble could be so good in observable ways had never even occurred to me, but I did suspect that cooking this simple had to come from a complicated place. I didn't think to inquire about the salad's creator, but I tried to replicate it for years, making the obvious mistake of adding the carrots and celery to the raw lentils, where they quickly surrendered both color and texture to the long boil. It wasn't until I had David's most recent book, *David Tanis Market Cooking*, in my hands that I saw my error: You briefly sauté the diced carrots and celery with diced onions *first*, then add them to the *cooked* lentils, then dress the salad.

Duh. When I told him this story recently, he smiled and said, "Oh. You cooked the carrots *with* the lentils?"

I HOLD AN ADVANCED DEGREE from David Tanis U. in Swiss chard—the vegetable that's all voluptuous leaves on important stalks, developed by a botanist in Switzerland from the beetroot plant. The swagger of those majestic leaves is awesome. Once, in the course of reporting a special issue of *Saveur* on California (home state of my two cofounders), Colman rented us a funky little 1950s house in the coastal town of Trinidad, in the damp and foggy extreme north of the state. That first night, we decided, each of us would choose a local ingredient to bring back to that odd little kitchen, cook it for our dinner, and photograph it for the story. Colman eschewed his usual meaty boy food for the local hot-smoked salmon we found at a nearby smokehouse, gently breaking up a center-cut fillet and folding silky salmon pieces into pasta with shiitake mushrooms. Christopher made a dessert crisp from the organic blueberries that were sold from tables along every roadside. And I was seduced by brilliant branches of rainbow chard at a local farm stand. It was only when we returned to the house with our shopping that I realized—more than embarrassed—that I had *no clue* what to do with the armload of chard I'd bought. I can't even remember how I managed to prepare it, but both their recipes (plus photos) made the issue, while "braised red and yellow chard" was precisely the amount of ink I got.

I had to wait years to really learn chard, to when I slipped, briefly, out of my *Newsweek* office for a quick trip to Paris with

Christopher to report a story for *Saveur* on David Tanis's cooking style. Christopher, who would photograph David's first two books, *A Platter of Figs* and *Heart of the Artichoke*, believes he's the most natural cook she knows. We wanted to discover where all that finesse lives, which, as it turned out, was in an apartment on the Rue Saint-Jacques, in a seventeenth-century building in the 5th Arrondissement, for six months a year. For the other six he would return to Chez Panisse, where he was head chef. (I was so happy to find every note I made from that trip.)

This was our idea for the story: We'd take David shopping at all his favorite local markets, and Christopher and I would get to buy anything we wanted him to show us how to cook. "*Anything?*" he asks, dubious. "Anything!" we decree. Game on! We were about to play WWDD: what would David do.

Heading to his favorite outdoor market—on the Place Maubert, in the 5th—we spy two plump whole lobes of foie gras at the poultry seller. That man, David tells us, is part bird himself: "Watch! With little provocation, he'll crow like a rooster." Show us how this duck liver becomes a pâté, we challenge him. "It's really no big deal," he says, unperturbed. We scoop up a forest floor's worth of wild mushrooms—trompettes de mort, chanterelles, girolles, pieds de mouton, what we call hedgehogs—and ask him how to clean and cook them without killing their signature shapes and fragile texture. "Only wash them if they're really dirty. Then, just a swish. And *no* mushroom brushes—they break up the delicate mushrooms. So what if you get a little dirt?" As for cooking: hardly! Just a fast sauté in garlic-scented olive oil—the sturdiest mushrooms first, then the most delicate. A handful of chopped parsley at the end. Done!

Pork loins have a discouraging way of turning dry and flavorless if you look at them the wrong way. When I asked David once about how he prepares his succulent pork roast, he confided his secrets in a note: "Massaging the roast with lots of good olive oil. Never be afraid of touching the meat! Seasoning ahead with lots of fennel seeds, sage, and rosemary, coarse salt, and pepper. Refrigerating overnight. Roasting hot. Taking it out of the oven soon enough. Letting the cooking finish slowly during the resting period. Result: moist, flavorful, and still a tad pink." To prove these points, we cross the bridge to the Île Saint-Louis and his favorite butcher shop, Charcellay, where the handsome butcher, M. Charcellay himself, prepares two beautiful two-pound loins of pork—one on the bone, the other boneless. We ask David to cook both of them, to compare their flavor and succulence. (An exercise, incidentally, that, in David's hands, turns out to be a difference without a distinction; he roasts them both precisely the way he told me in his note. Both were excellent. Back home, I find the bone-in version juicier.)

"A restaurant is only as good as its simplest green salad," David wrote in *Chez Panisse Café Cookbook*. Making a salad, he believes, is the true test of a cook. "I'll never understand why the salad station—garde manger—is where restaurants put their least-trained cooks," he says as we walk. "A lot of restaurant cooks feel insulted if they can't be on the hot line, shaking pots and pans around. But it takes such knowledge and finesse to make a good salad. Only a good cook knows how to make a salad right." From a sea of greens, David chooses a whole leafy palette of colors and textures for our story. "Going through a market and seeing vibrant, perfect, just-picked lettuces—that's my cheap thrill!" he confesses. "Oh, and do *not* buy those precut bagged salad mixes. They always put in the wrong things. I don't want to deal with someone's three-day-old chopped radicchio!" As we leave the market, I spy a glorious display of Swiss chard, and I know that very soon I will have, at last, the answer to my secret shame!

We follow David home, up steep stone stairways hollowed by centuries of footfalls, and into his little kitchen. Spread your arms wide and you can touch both walls. "People can't believe that I cook all this food in here, in a five-by-eight-foot space. But what do you need in order to cook, really? Fire. And water. A table. And a knife!"

Turning to the chard we've bought, he's patient with his explanation. "Chard is really two vegetables. There are the leaves, and there are the stalks, and you must treat them differently." The impish skepticism that often colors David's worldview never spills over into his cooking. About cooking, his attitude is forever a sunny and inclusive "Isn't it all obvious?" Cooking comes so easily for him that he believes it should be no mystery for the rest of us.

David's hands, I quickly learn by observing him work, are his principal utensils, his secret weapons. His fingers are so articulate that they make up in deftness what they lack in length. Tom McNamee, who hung out a lot in the Chez Panisse kitchen, reporting his biography of Alice Waters, once said to me about David's hands: "Looking at them, one would think the delicacy they are capable of would be impossible." David never hesitates to get in there with his fingers, performing the tasks that lesser cooks think they need fancy gadgets for. Observing him make a Swiss chard gratin is a pleasure and a revelation.

After thoroughly washing the leaves, he lays them one

by one on a cutting board on his sliver of a kitchen counter. With a sharp knife, he cuts out each leaf's hefty stalk, then he makes a pile of the leaves, and trims and slices the stalks into slim batons. These he blanches briefly in a pot of salted boiling water with a bay leaf. (I remember those stalks from Marcella's table and remark how different is David's prep from her diced stalks, their 30-minute boil, then a sauté in olive oil!) Next—and this is a technique I continue to use with every leafy green I cook—he stacks the leaves on top of each other in a pile and rolls them up tightly into a fat cigar, making it ever so much easier, then, to slice the leaves crosswise into thin ribbons. He sautés the sliced leaves in a bit of olive oil and minced garlic, then lets slip another comment I remember every time I cook them—"The flavor of all greens benefits from a little red pepper"—and sprinkles on a pinch of hot pepper flakes (red pepper plus greens, check). I've seen him reach for a tin of pimentón, too, and give it a generous shake.

David grabs a heavy copper saucepan to whisk up a simple béchamel—stirring flour into melted butter and then adding cold milk, just a spoonful at a time. He grates in lots of nutmeg (nutmeg plus greens, check!) and continues whisking the white sauce until, he says, it has the texture of a good milkshake. Buttering a large baking dish (always oval, French, and old), he piles the still-green sautéed chard leaves on the bottom, the blanched stems on top. Then, giving another couple of hits of nutmeg to the béchamel, he ladles the creamy sauce over the chard and grates a generous layer of Gruyère over the top. When I made it for Thanksgiving that year, David's Swiss chard gratin was a universal hit. And then it became mine.

TURNING TO THE PÂTÉ (which is technically a terrine, because cooked, the liver remains itself; it's not made into a paste), David generously seasons the twin lobes of foie gras with salt, pepper, bay leaves, and thyme, explaining, "Foie gras and truffles have become so 'haute' that people forget they're not at all delicate: both started out as peasant food. There are really only two good things to do with foie gras: sear slices in a very hot pan with no oil or poach the lobes and watch them slump into a terrine, then chill and spread on warm baguettes." To demonstrate, he settles the well-seasoned lobes into a deep oval earthenware dish, then lowers the terrine itself into a large roasting pan and pours boiling water about halfway up the terrine to gently render the fat. He waits until, eventually, the lobes obediently "slump," and register 100°F on a meat thermometer. Then David covers the terrine and refrigerates it overnight. He'll serve the foie gras the next day on still-warm baguettes from his favorite baker, Maison Kayser, whose shop is just around the around the corner on the Rue Monge.

Christopher and I are smitten with those authentic Maison Kayser baguettes. ("Imagine!" we marvel. "Éric Kayser is your neighborhood baker!") She can't stop photographing the long breads with their distinctively pointy ends, ever so-slightly burned, poking from the bag hanging nonchalantly on the handle of the kitchen door. (In the be-careful-what-you-wish-for department, however, years later, Maison Kayser invaded New York with more than a dozen shops offering excellent buckwheat-flaxseed baguettes, pretty patisserie, expensive and uneven food. Until suddenly, like so much of pandemic midtown Manhattan retail, sadly, all the shops closed, and are rumored to be reopening as . . . Le Pain Quotidien.)

David washes his salad greens with the care of a jeweler cleaning an antique clock, and dries them carefully, too, with a tender roll in a clean dish towel. "French housewives would use a pillowcase," he says with a smile. "But never a salad spinner!" he warns. "They bruise the tender leaves." (I'm hoping the David-cam is not on in my kitchen to witness my total and shameless dependence on my own such device!) Often—unless I'm too rushed to stop and think and then I just wing it—I consciously make a vinaigrette David's way: dicing a shallot into a big salad bowl, adding about a tablespoon of vinegar and a big pinch of salt. Then comes the most precious ingredient: patience. *Let it sit for 10 minutes!* he advises. The vinegar and shallots need time to influence each other, and, in fact, to let the shallot pickle slightly in the vinegar. Only then comes the olive oil. And not that much of it; only about three tablespoons. David's dressing makes just enough so the leaves glisten. ("People use far too much dressing!") Only just before he's ready to bring the salad to the table does David toss the greens. With his hands.

HAPPILY, OUR VISIT COINCIDED WITH a singular event David and his partner, Randal Breski, created during those many half-years they lived in Paris. They launched, in their small apartment, an informal dining club called Aux Chiens Lunatiques (named for their beloved dog, Arturo, with a wink at old Parisian bistros like Au Chat Qui Fume). Randal presided with the confident flourishes of the hospitality pro he is (among other things, he ran the dining room at Chez Panisse). "I got to shop for everything at the flea market—the *marché aux puces*," he recalls. "It was heaven. I could buy fine white linen sheets for ten dollars. By the time we left, I couldn't even find them for a hundred dollars. And all the flatware!" Those oversize, heavy eating utensils the French love, mismatched, and as full of character as the people who once owned them. Deep soup spoons, and long-handled salad forks, and knives with wide blades and handles that feel like the weight of history in your hand. "The idea of starting Les Chiens came from necessity," Randal recalls, "because as soon as we moved to Paris, everyone we knew kept sending us their friends and the friends of their friends, and we simply couldn't afford to cook for them all!"

For a Chiens meal, Randal would make one long dining table by pushing together every surface in their small living room, joining them with drapings of many of those white linen sheets. Not surprisingly, every seat at a Chiens dinner would be filled. Parisian friends came; Americans bumped into other Americans and brought them along. Several times a month, more than a dozen good souls would gather around that generous table. David, alone in his minuscule kitchen, would turn out his soulful food, sometimes slow-cooked Moroccan lamb, and once, even paella from their fireplace. Here's the menu from a luncheon that happened while Christopher and I were in Paris. It featured pintade, that estimable French guinea hen with ever so much more character than chicken, and . . . our Swiss chard gratin. The meal began, as always, with an aperitif, usually a petite cocktail made from good, little-known French Champagne, a splash of Pastis, and a sprinkling of crushed fennel seeds, served in Randal's perfectly unmatched flea-market glasses.

Steamed Fennel with Caper-Anchovy Vinaigrette

Braised Guinea Hen

Wild Mushrooms

Roasted Pumpkin

Chard Gratin

Cheeses

Fig Crostata

The cheeses, presented on a generous white porcelain platter (oval, French, and old), included various flat, chalky chèvres and the Corsican sheep's-milk Brin d'Amour, its white rind bristling with fragrant dried herbs. At the end of the meal, a jar was passed for grateful diners to fold their euros into.

MUCH LIKE THE SUBTLE WAY he cooks, David is sly, a virtuoso of the understatement. Once, when we were working on his first book on Long Island, I heard myself whining about not having grape leaves to wrap around a whole bluefish I was preparing for the grill. David studied me for a minute, then walked me outside: "Aren't those figs you have growing up against the house?" he asked, eyes twinkling, adding after a beat: "Those leaves would do nicely to wrap the fish." Though that stand of Chicago fig trees I'd planted (against all climactic odds) had never yielded enough fruit for even one jar of jam, there were, indeed, leaves enough to wrap the entire catch from the fleet out of Montauk. And after all, wasn't David's book called *A Platter of Figs*? (Even though, at the time, its working title was *My Grandmother's Cadillac and Other Recipes*. Go figure.)

That *Figs* found its way to its eventual publisher is thanks to Christopher's intervention. She stepped in after the first acquiring editor became daunted by, among other things, a series of David's menus that featured . . . rabbit! Christopher connected David with Ann Bramson, Artisan's publisher, who had no such rabbit qualms, and who eventually asked me to help edit the book. Chapter 2 proudly led with a menu called "How to Cook a Rabbit," where David commented, "Rabbits are hideously misunderstood in this country, except by a few of us quiet loyalists who persist in our devotion." I kinda know what he means. Last week, when I made lapin à la moutarde (I had to order the rabbits days in advance), I answered Lincoln's "What's for dinner?" query with a deliberate mumble that made it sound a lot like chicken. In Europe, rabbits are food—you see as many prepared rabbits in a French butcher shop as you do chickens. Here, they are pets.

I remember the lapin à la moutarde from one of those French grandmothers of Sandrine's whose cooking ideas still hover around my kitchen. Today, I cook David's mustard rabbit in the oven, and I always make two; leftover rabbit is good! This recipe reminds me of David's warning that American mustards, even those so-called French-style brands, are never quite as sharp or flavorful as the French mustard, marked "forte," you see everywhere, even in a French supermarket. I grab a few jars of Amora whenever I can.

DURING THAT SAME *FIGS* WORKING session, pages spread out on the dining table, David and I became aware of Lincoln, then about thirteen, banging around alone in the sweltering kitchen. Investigating, I found he'd gotten it in his head to make croquembouche, of all things, from the cookbook *Saveur Cooks Authentic French*. Please do not ask why he chose that impossible dessert on that impossibly hot day. He was attempting nothing less than a pyramid of cream-filled puff pastries, stacked one atop another, forming a sort of dessert skyscraper. Indeed, the legendary French chef Antonin Carême, who famously claimed pastry as a branch of architecture, was said to have invented croquembouche.

The scraping sound David and I heard was Lincoln struggling to incorporate eggs into his pâte à choux. "Wait a minute," I said to him. "You have one of the best cooks in America in the next room, and you're attempting to make this without asking him for help?" Proud Lincoln preferred to struggle, but he conceded when David slipped in to show him a pastry trick he'll never forget—he was being uncharacteristically timid with his dough. "Elbow grease was the trick, LOL," Lincoln texts me. "He taught me not to be afraid of it!" Forever after that, and for reasons known only to him, Lincoln referred to David as "the man with the face." Later, Lincoln took his fascination with stuffed puffy things to a world-class gougères game, and tangentially, to macarons. Last Mother's Day, he made a PB&J version: perfect ivory-colored meringue discs filled with . . . peanut butter and strawberry preserves.

Lincoln turned fourteen the year *Ratatouille* came out, and he became obsessed with making the title dish precisely the way Remy the rat chef prepared it in the movie. Lincoln learned this from *Binging with Babish*, his favorite YouTube cooking show, where, in his mellifluent voiceover, this Mr. Babish (in reality, the filmmaker Andrew Rea, whose thing is to re-create recipes from popular culture, and who named himself after Oliver Babish, *The West Wing*'s White House lawyer) coaxes his viewers into thinly slicing plum tomatoes and using a mandoline to reduce yellow squash, zucchini, and eggplant to impossibly sheer discs. These slices, layered like a poem over a blended tomato sauce, are then baked and served in a timbale-shaped stack. This was the precise version that sent the movie's restaurant critic, Anton Ego, into an ecstatically emotional reliving of his own mother's dish. As for the humble, chunky (and très correct!) Provençal version perfected by David and made by Lincoln's very own mother (each ingredient fastidiously cooked separately, their flavors only later allowed to mingle in an earthenware bowl), Lincoln does not want to know.

ONE MORNING, READY TO WORK with David on his second book, *Heart of the Artichoke*, I walked into the house in the Berkeley hills where he and Randal lived when he ran the kitchen at Chez Panisse. When I saw a pot of stewed apricots on his stove, I felt a bit embarrassed for him, like he hadn't quite gotten to putting away the food from last night's dinner. But I quickly realized that this was (of course) an intentional pot, left to sit out all night because David had discovered the resulting jam to be richer and thicker for its overnight sleep. Apricot jam, he explained, is a fleeting thing, and perfect only when apricots are truly in season, which is only briefly, and then perfect only for the few days after the preserves are made.

Making apricot jam, he continued, need not be a big production. A modest yield is totally fine, even desirable. Its rarity underscores its value. He tells me how he would sometimes surprise a Parisian neighbor by leaving a small jar outside her apartment door. As he spoke, my mind slipped down the hill to Chez Panisse, where, once, at a lunch with Colman and Alice Waters, she was served a small plate of two blushing apricots. All of a sudden, we saw her childlike features darken, grow severe. She summoned a server, held out the plate, and delivered a lecture: "Never, ever, serve an unripe piece of fruit!" Alice sent back those apricots. In her own restaurant! Nobody at that table would ever look at an apricot the same way again.

In the twenty-two minutes each year that apricots are in season on the East Coast, I have Alice in my head as I surreptitiously smell the fruit at the Greenmarket before I commit to buying it. Back in my kitchen, I hear David's voice, at first cautionary—"Don't be tempted to skimp on the sugar; even very ripe apricots will never be sweet enough for jam"—and then encouraging: "Make a few pints now! I am not making it for posterity. I am making it for breakfast."

THANKS TO DAVID, I WENT from a world where nothing was persimmons to one where everything was. One day I didn't know the flat, tomato-like fuyu from the misleadingly heart-shaped hachiya, and the next, the world was divided into the sweet and the acidic. Suddenly, I was making David's persimmon pudding (from *A Platter of Figs*) for holiday dinners, serving the sweetened, flan-like cake with his barely whipped cream. The device-averse chef, for whom a mortar and pestle is the best food processor, would pour a pint of heavy cream into a cool metal bowl and pass it, along with a large balloon whisk—companionably and communally—around the dinner table. By the time each guest had had their way with it, and before it could become a chore, voilà! barely whipped cream. For years, I served that persimmon pudding with bright slashes of the raw, peeled, soft fruit for friends to marvel over. No one ever guessed what it was they were eating.

The persimmon images in David's head were all wintry Italian, which—like most of his potent food ideas—came directly from observed life; he remembered seeing the fruit growing in the Veneto. His dessert was the surprise ending of an Italian menu: saucy lamb (instead of veal shank) osso buco, with a gremolata of orange, lemon, and capers. Persimmons, for me, were, until David, purely decorative. The bright-orange fruits always look like sculptures of themselves: orbs of cinnabar, that prized sunset-red Asian lacquer, their quatrefoil calyx of four equal rounded leaves always seeming more carved than real. I, too, had seen those bright-red fruits hanging from black, leafless branches, mine against an autumn Tokyo sky, graceful as brushstrokes. Kaki, the Japanese call their native fruit. But eating the fruit called persimmon never even occurred to me.

Though they're grown in California, even in their autumn-to-winter season, you can hardly find persimmons in the store. David says that no matter whether fuyu or hachiya, the fruit must be ripe before you eat it or cook with it, a subtlety lost on supermarkets where they're sold—tough as rubber balls—indiscriminately, interchangeably, and inedibly. Buying them, I could never remember which was the good one and which the sour. I figured this much out: *h* for hachiya are heart-shaped; *f* for fuyu are flat.

I would see persimmons, bruised and shivering, catching their death of cold, on the stands of my neighborhood street-corner fruit sellers. And I'd walk on by. David says both types of persimmon are okay to use as long as they're soft, ripe, and peeled, though the fuyus I found at Eataly in New York (immaculate, and expensive at $1.50 each) were branded with those obnoxious fruit stickers and their misleading marketing hype: "Doc's Delight. Eat Hard Like an Apple." Yet as quickly as they had rolled into my life, persimmons rolled right out.

Then, suddenly, three persimmon encounters (was the universe talking to me?) gave me reason to believe this: Persimmons are winter's tomatoes. Fuyus showed up at the photo shoot for Mike Solomonov and Steve Cook's book *Zahav*. To make *Zahav*'s Israeli salad when tomatoes are out of season, they use pickled persimmons (or mangoes, or passion fruit, or even grapes) instead. I marveled at that idea. *Of course* you could not use out-of-season tomatoes in that fresh salad. For *Zahav*, we photographed glorious whole fuyus on a heavy coal-black pedestal stand I found at a Philadelphia flea market. On the facing page is a Pyrex dish of quartered persimmons—close-up and intimate—bathing with dates, black dried limes, garlic, cardamom, and other fragrant pickling spices, just waiting to become salad.

Another persimmon winter salad surfaced just a few days ago on *Zahav*'s Instagram. Now the kitchen sliced golden Sharon persimmons—a product of Israel's advanced agronomy that breeds the astringency out of the fruit—and sprinkled them with rose water, olive oil, coriander crumble, bits of tangy Bulgarian feta, and little leaves of pink radicchio. Two days later came another salad, this one served at Canal House Station, where mellow quarter moons of flame-bright fuyus, sweet and ripe, were sliced and set on top of maroon-speckled pale-green leaves of Italian winter chicory. There they sat, topped with oven-roasted pumpkin seeds and dressed with a lively lime vinaigrette. Same notes, different strokes.

DAVID CARRIED HIS DEEP CULINARY knowledge, and his non-chalance, with him when he eventually moved to New York and became a food columnist for the *New York Times*, only a touch discouraged by finding on this coast a food landscape of "canned beans, coconut milk, and sheet-pan suppers." His are the recipes I most download, his spicy, lacquered chicken wings the way I make my peace with the Super Bowl.

I stop before I start to make polenta, remembering David's complaint that most people do not cook the grains long enough to develop their full corn-y flavor. His polenta (never instant) is the result of at least forty-five minutes of patient and in-termittent whisking. I recall, too, David's take on roasted peppers. He believes the put-the-blackened-peppers-in-a-bag-to-steam thing turns them mushy. Kills their sweet fruitiness. A cooling rest on a plate is fine by him. By me too.

On a night shortly after he and Randal moved into their brownstone apartment but before a working kitchen was in-stalled, David pulled off dinner for a whole bunch of us using just two toaster ovens and a hot plate. In most chef's kitchens, and especially in most high-end non-chef's kitchens, you'll find a row of shiny appliances that signify mastery to the Williams Sonoma crowd but in reality only telegraph a quick Amazon trigger finger. (Just because they're there doesn't mean they're used, or used well.) In contrast, the shelves in David's kitchen hold a formidable row of fleshy marble and stone mortars, their pestles akimbo—as imposing as a lineup of sumo wrestlers just waiting for their chance to *crush*! Everything goes into David's mortar: spices to scatter over the lamb stew he's just made; herbs as the base of a salad dressing; Rocambole garlic, pounded into submission, the pestle light in his hands.

David cares about garlic. Much of his cooking begins with it, "but most people get garlic wrong," he tells me. "You have to approach it with small, mindful moves. It doesn't make sense to peel a garlic clove by smooshing it with the side of a knife on a cutting board—you get garlic oil all over the knife. And the cutting board. It's not a bad thing to do if you're using it right away, but if you aren't, I don't want that smelly garlic clove hanging around my kitchen. Rather than attack garlic with a big knife, I cut it with a paring knife; it's more controllable. But I'd prefer that you peel garlic any way you like instead of buying pre-peeled garlic. You just do not know where that garlic has been! Nature has perfectly designed garlic heads to stay fresh—each clove is individually wrapped! What you want to do is pop the clove out of its skin with your fingers." Well, his fingers.

"If you need a fine puree of garlic, smaller than knife-minced," he continues, really into it now, "put some rough-chopped garlic in a mortar and use the pestle to pound it with salt. Or, if you need just a bit of smashed garlic, use the French housewife's trick of pressing a fork flat on a cutting board and rubbing one peeled clove over the tines: instant puree! Lately, I've been grating a clove of garlic on a Microplane, or a ginger grater. And yet another lovely way to get a smooth, even mash of garlic is by cutting it into bits, then chopping it small with a big pinch of coarse salt."

DAVID HAS AN ANTHROPOLOGIST'S REVERENCE for the indigenous bite. He remembers exactly where, and in what circumstance, he has tasted each delicious thing that lodges in his memory and motivates him to cook. Like Wordsworth's definition of poetry, "emotion recollected in tranquility," cooking, for David, is a process of retrieving memories. That's where the talent lies, I've thought often. He appreciates the authenticity of an experience before he even begins to try to recapture it. David sees flavor-pictures in his head, images so vivid you can taste them. Just the way he talks about food makes me crave what he craves.

For example, when I think about making Mexican tacos, my thoughts do not immediately travel to fish from the Caribbean, cooking on a smoky barbecue under the palm trees on the beach at Akumal; or to the sublime sopa de tortilla Mónica Hernández served at her beautiful restaurant at Hacienda Katanchel, a onetime henequen plantation near Mérida; or even to the superb tacos al pastor, delivered in diminutive double corn tortillas, made by the admirable chef Alex Stupak at Empellón, just a few blocks away from where I type. Even though I've enjoyed all those dishes, when I cook Mexican food, I want what I never had; I want the beachy tacos David once told me about—the broiled-fish tacos with shredded cabbage and fresh lime that he used to eat "in a tiny makeshift seaside joint near Veracruz, Mexico"—after he'd gone home and figured out how to re-create them.

As his unlikely story goes, one day in Paris, during a heat wave so intense the French have a term for it, *la canicule*, our David craved those Veracruz tacos. Gathering his ingredients from far-flung sources (he couldn't just rush around to the corner bodega), he somehow located authentic Mexican corn tortillas—small and earthy. He tracked down a great slab of white-fleshed fish, with plenty of ice to get it home fresh. This he broiled briefly with a rub of chile, garlic, oregano, and olive oil. And though I've never been to Veracruz, or, as a matter of fact, had Mexican tacos in Paris, I often make David's lunch from that hot French day. The soft char of the white fish, the welcome crunch of cabbage instead of wimpy lettuce, the shredded leaves lightly salted, then given a brief sit in a bit of lime juice to soften—this has always made perfect food sense to me.

With the fish tacos, David makes a salsa of just-ripe tomatoes and green cilantro and tomatillos (in Paris?) that's brighter than any jarred mix (forget about flavors like pineapple and fire-roasted mango). And an avocado salad using "just ripe and a little firm" avocados that stops just short of guacamole, with chopped scallions, crispy radishes, and lime juice. To scoop up the salsas, he cuts day-old corn tortillas into quarters and fries them in lots of peanut oil for homemade tortilla chips (not far from the chilaquiles he once showed me—leftover tortillas lightly fried, sauced with tomato, and topped with fried eggs for breakfast). And with that, ice-cold Corona beers in those longneck bottles you stick a wedge of lime into before you drink.

DAVID'S PARISIAN TACO FEAST BEGAT our own taco ritual, one I'm not so sure I want David to know about. Call it Food of the Week in Review. We begin, at least, with good tortillas (I do have my standards), sometimes ordering Caramelo Sonoran-style flour tortillas from Lawrence, Kansas, or the exemplary Mexican corn tortillas from Tortilleria Nixtamal, in Queens. These we heat over a gas burner, trying not to incinerate them in the process. But this meal of many dishes is as inauthentic as it is delicious. Any hard cheese we happen to have is grated onto one little plate; avocado with lime juice and oregano is smooshed into guacamole on another. Onto more little plates go shredded bits of last night's roast chicken, or grilled fish, or beef; chopped tomatoes, if we have them, or leftover cooked veggies—fresh corn if we're lucky; beans, not refried but re-heated; sliced radishes and chunked cucumbers; shredded any-kind-of leafy greens. The red pepper relish we make and preserve every August is our salsa. Pretty soon, the table is covered with a mosaic of little plates, along with random bottles of hot sauce and a bowl of sour cream. Not Mexican, but close in spirit. Pretty beautiful if photographed from above.

I'VE BEEN FORTUNATE TO LEARN so much from David, but I knew I was asking a lot when I begged him to teach me about chiles. Now, you might think that the former editor of a food magazine and producer of dozens of cookbooks, who's even grown chiles in her garden, would *get* chiles. But the truth is, I've always been a little scared of them. I love to char sweet red bell peppers, peel them, and slick them with olive oil and garlic and herbs; I learned to stuff charming little Spanish piquillos with lemon-scented ricotta and bake them. I'll sprinkle pimentón or a pinch of red pepper flakes or ground chile powder on anything from eggs to greens without a second thought. But every time I come near a jalapeño, it manages to jump stingingly into my eyes. And all those leathery, dried chiles confound me, because there's nothing that comes naturally about using them. They don't even look like something good to eat.

What, you might wonder, could a boy from Dayton, Ohio, teach me about chiles? I remember from working on his books and tasting his food how masterfully David uses chiles in his recipes and at his restaurants. I know how thoughtful—and more than a touch scholarly—he is about studying the sources of the ingredients he loves. David spent years living in Santa Fe, where he had a restaurant, Café Escalera. I loved his story about having his dried chiles ground; it involved a trip to the Badlands, where an old man powered his mechanical grinder set in the middle of an old barn by hooking it up to the engine of a tractor he'd leave running at the barn's window.

Which dried chiles should I buy? I wanted to ask David. They come packaged; so how can I tell if they're good if I can't even touch them? And what's the best way to reconstitute and roast them? What I needed to understand—just like my experience with salt cod—was how these dried leathery things became food. While thinking hard about chiles, I happened to be reading Jeff Gordinier's *Hungry*, his fine book about cooking with René Redzepi in Mexico, where I discovered a similar awe. Writing about mole, the complex chile-based sauce, he says: "Taking apart mole was like taking apart a river. Mole was fluid and endless. Its very nature was elusive. You couldn't 'get to the bottom' of it."

The first thing David does is to press into my hands his copy of *The Art of Mexican Cooking*, his friend and mentor Diana Kennedy's classic book that's so rich I want to eat it. And that venerable and ever-so-feisty British lady quickly throws the credit back to Mexico. "Without doubt," she writes, "the apogee of chile cultivation and use has been reached in Mexico." Kennedy confirms my concerns, writing that dried chiles are confusingly named, and we must make sure the chiles we do find are not too old, are still flexible, have some life in them. Which I take to mean be careful where you buy them.

David and I agree to make slow-cooked carne adovada, from his *Heart of the Artichoke*. *Adovada* means "marinated," which is another way of saying pork cooked in red chile sauce. "Larger leathery ruddy red chiles—such as New Mexico, ancho, and guajillo—are the ones to use for sauces, marinades, stews, and soups," he says. "Toasted lightly and seeds removed, they are then simmered before being blended into a paste." It's one thing to edit his words, quite another to act on them. I head to Kalustyan's, where I find dried red New Mexican chiles still looking plump and fresh in their clear package; then I find smooth, long guajillos and blackened ancho chiles, which I knew to be the dried form of the poblanos I once grew.

When David opens the clear bags, he smells the chiles appreciatively, and likes what he calls their "beautiful, leathery consistency." He declares them excellent. Phew! Before we begin, he pulls from his bag three small containers of ground chiles—pungent red New Mexican, a chunky mild Korean red he uses in kimchi, and some pretty strong Aleppo pepper from Syria—he's brought for us to taste with our fingertips, an excellent way to compare their subtleties of flavor.

To begin cooking the sauce for the pork, David weighs a mix of the three dried chiles, using more of the New Mexican reds and about the same amount of guajillos and anchos. We need eight ounces, which pile up to more chiles than you'd think: about two dozen. Then he heats a large, dry cast-iron skillet and tosses in the chiles, saying, "We just want to lightly toast them, to warm them up. For this recipe, we don't want them to blacken." The smell is so fragrant, like chocolate, like fruit—which, technically, as the blossom end of the plant, peppers actually are. He slices open the toasted chiles, tossing their stems, and I get in there with my fingers ("There's a lot of heat in the veins") to help deseed them.

We boil the warmed and seeded chiles in water just to cover for about 10 minutes. I am riveted watching the cooking water as it rapidly turns red brown; dipping in a finger, I find it tastes as good as it looks. Then David transfers the chiles to the blender, with just enough of the boiling liquid to cover them, and whizzes them up.

In a deep, heavy Dutch oven, he warms a diced onion in oil, cautioning, "No color; no browning." He adds about six cloves of chopped garlic, a teaspoon each of ground coriander and ground cumin, and a bay leaf. Then he sets a strainer over the stewpot and dumps in the chiles from the blender. Slowly, slowly he pushes the puree through the strainer. "You do not want chile skins in there," he says. "They're too chewy and do not help our sauce." Once strained into the pot, the chiles darken to a seriously deep red-brown color. We cook the sauce down for a few minutes, then let it cool before we settle a lovely three-pound piece of pork shoulder deep into the sauce and decide to let it marinate in the refrigerator overnight.

The next day, I put the pot in a 350°F oven for 90 minutes and prepare a pot of polenta, and a platter with little lettuces, avocados, sliced oranges, cukes, and radishes. David returns for dinner with Tortilleria Nixtamal corn tortillas. Peering into the pot, I am deeply moved by this stew, by its aroma of smoke and fruit and mystery, and by its very old, very deep color, the burnt sienna of Rembrandt's shirt in a self-portrait, with lowlights of vermilion and highlights of gold. The sauce seems alive with the ancient knowledge that produced it. When I taste it, I think, "These chiles have come a very long way from the ristras, those endless strings of drying peppers that hang from doorways in sleepy Mexican towns." David's note the next day: "I did think the red chile sauce was deeply delicious and velvety, but ordinarily it would be a bit more picante—it wouldn't hurt to punch it up with a little cayenne or Aleppo or Tabasco." Chefs!

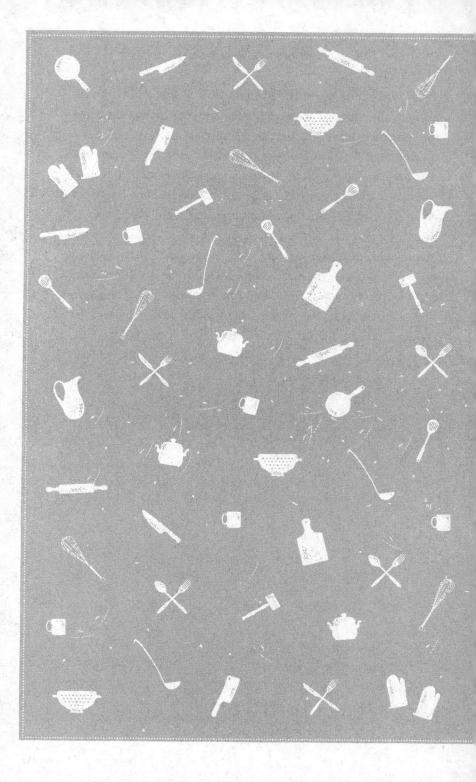

CHAPTER 8

THE ALCHEMY OF FLAVOR

I KIND OF HATE IT when Michael Anthony goes out of town. I mean, with his whole family. Especially in winter. Because our neighbors' vacation means one thing above all: mu radishes. When Mike and Mindy generously leave a box containing their CSA (community-supported agriculture) allotment from Norwich Meadows Farm—always welcome; I don't want to seem ungrateful—at my door like a basketful of stray kittens, I feel responsible for the contents. But these are not tiny cats. These are dead-of-winter root vegetables: ugly-beautiful rutabagas; kohlrabi, that weirdly protuberant cousin of cabbage with a soft stem and a pure white heart; long, tapering parsnips; lavender daikons and thin, icy-white ones; and China rose radishes big as softballs. There are the oddly knobby Jerusalem artichokes, lavender-top turnips, watermelon radishes, pale yellow carrots and deep purple ones, a handful of potatoes, a few heads of garlic, and a big, sweet celery root. Plus one golden beet. In short, the gnarly bits.

This year, I promise myself, I will not throw the contents indiscriminately into a huge pot for a March of the Root Vegetables Soup. I will treat each vegetable individually, calmly, giving it the mature respect it deserves. This year, I will not be defeated by mu radishes. I breathe. I do some research and immediately learn that *mu* is the Korean word for radish. So all these years I've been referring to those greeny white roots as "radish radishes." Pickled mus, I discover, are often served with fried Korean chicken wings. Okay! There's my flavor profile. So I use a classic formula to tame those roots into crunchy white pickles: peel and cube a pound of radishes and submerge them in a solution of ⅓ cup white vinegar, ⅓ cup sugar, 1 tablespoon salt, and ¾ cup water. After a few days in the refrigerator, the little cubes of pickled radishes are so perky, they seem to animate everything I serve them with.

Pickling is a virtuous circle; it enhances the flavor of the thing itself, which in turn enhances the flavor of everything those pickles touch. As I worked with Michael on the cookbook for New York's Gramercy Tavern, where he is executive chef and partner, he encouraged me to pickle practically *anything*. I roamed the restaurant's basement, awestruck by whole shelves of pickled ramps in ten-gallon plastic containers that captured that wild leek's fleeting season. Tubs of scored whole Meyer lemons were curing in spices, sugar, and salt. But, I learned, most of Gramercy's pickles—the secret spark to so many of the restaurant's dishes—are made quickly. And very simply. In small batches. And used right away. The way you'd do it at home. The way I tamed the mus.

Michael's pickling recipe is simple, and he uses a similar process for shallots and rhubarb, and ginger, and petite cauliflower florets, okra, baby carrots, Japanese mushrooms, and the little killer red hot peppers called ají dulce, and for salsify and sunchokes (a happy ending for Jerusalem artichokes).

Boil together ¾ cup rice vinegar, ¼ cup water, ¼ cup sugar, and 1 tablespoon salt. Pour over a bowl of 2 cups of the pickle candidate. Cool to room temp. Refrigerate.

Of course, because he's the chef and he knows such things, Michael can't keep himself from inventing clever variations: to pickle whole Bing cherries, he adds a clove, a vanilla bean, and half a cinnamon stick, and uses champagne vinegar instead of rice. He turns circles of sliced cipolline onions bright red by adding beets, then places those crimson rings along the top of a GT favorite—fillet of smoked trout. (Sometimes I pickle the onions and buy the trout!) He pickles the stems of beets (the part you usually throw away), creating tangy shards guaranteed to wake up any soup bowl or salad plate they're scattered on.

Making pickles, however, uses up only some of the contents of that CSA box. Looking deeper into it, I realize that the way I handle each vegetable mirrors what I've learned from Michael over the years; he's teaching me without even being here! Holding whole heads of garlic in my hand, I remember the garlic seed Mike's great-grandfather brought here from southern Italy, and how Mike was able to find a farmer in upstate New York to grow that family heirloom, and that this descendant of Anthony garlic is used today in the kitchen of Gramercy Tavern.

Grabbing a hairy celery root, I recall with a smile a moment Michael recounted in our book *V is for Vegetables*, about when he was a young cook in Daniel Boulud's kitchen—how that exigent chef would stand behind him, breathing down his neck as he peeled away the pockmarked skin, always chiding him for removing too much of the root: cutting away the profits! Now whenever Michael goes to peel a celery root, Daniel's looking over his shoulder; but he admits it's pretty impossible not to lose some of the root in the process. He showed me how to take celery root beyond the requisite (and delicious!) mustardy rémoulade on every hors-d'œuvre variés platter in every Parisian bistro. He likes to puree the cooked roots and serve them just like mashed potatoes. Going further, he turns that celery root puree into an unctuous soup, adding lots of cream and roasted chestnuts and topping it with teeny cubes of skin-on diced raw apples.

To thinly slice watermelon radishes, revealing their rosy hearts, I reach for the small and inexpensive handheld bright-red plastic Japanese mandoline I bought the minute I observed cooks using that tool to prep veggies in Gramercy's kitchen. Kohlrabi is an unexplored novelty; I could peel and quarter it and roast the pieces like a potato, finishing it with a shower of pimentón, patatas bravas–style. Or, I could entertain a roomful of young folks by peeling and slicing the mystery root and offering those thin white slices raw, instead of potato or pita chips, as a sturdy deliverer of dips. As for the rutabaga? A flavor lesson in itself.

Food historians contend—though I find it a bit hard to believe—that carrots growing wild, say a thousand years ago, were pale yellow, like the four short specimens in my box. Historians posit that the *carrot* carrot color was bred into them in the seventeenth century by the Dutch, to honor the House of Orange, their royal house. Well, we know the Dutch are fine growers. As for that story? Who knows? (I do know that I once bet Colman Andrews $500,000,000 that the carrot is not related to Queen Anne's lace. Of course it is. Expensive lesson.) Less widely known: wild carrots were once purple, too. And when Michael, then safely ensconced at Gramercy, returned to Japan and, while prowling Kyoto's legendary Nishiki Market, chanced upon purple carrots with hearts that glow golden, he managed to track down enough seeds to encourage Zaid Kurdieh at the same Norwich Meadows Farm to grow them. "The summer crop was a failure," Mike recalls, "but the fall was magic. Suddenly Kyoto carrots were a thing at the Union Square Greenmarket. A thing with a story. Everyone knew about them. I love that people can learn from vegetables."

ONCE YOU GET TO KNOW Michael Anthony, you become aware of how quickly his mind spins behind his amused eyes. He's the polar opposite of the overheated, pot-slamming, invective-hurling histrionic chefs who use their restaurant kitchens as their own personal performance space. Michaél is no less passionate. He's just not that kind of guy. He's been there, seen that. Won all the awards and garnered all the accolades. Instead, he chooses to make his kitchen the next step in his cooks' formation, his impulse a generous one: "I want to graduate great chefs." Danny Meyer told me, "Mike's level of taste and ability to cook good food are rare enough; add to that his refined sensibility and his willingness to teach other cooks, his kindness and his humility, and you have a combination that's almost unheard of in the world of professional chefs. Mike's food at its best creates an experience that causes you to drop your conversation—and your fork—in amazement and delight."

Michael, I have come to realize, is that favorite professor you're always wanting to please.

MICHAEL HAD DISCOVERED FRENCH EATING—ALTHOUGH not yet French cooking—during a revelatory junior year abroad in Strasbourg and Lyon. "When they saw my joyous discovery of the food they cooked and served, my French family discouraged me from cooking. It was not for me, they believed (and this was not that long ago!). 'You have to be born into a family of cooks,' they told me. 'Cooks here begin their apprenticeship as teenagers.' For me, pursuing my love of food was a great way to learn the language and the culture."

Counterintuitively, the day after Michael graduated from college in Indiana, he left for . . . Tokyo. He had no formal plan. "I was swept up with a romantic notion—I fell for Japan for all the wrong reasons: the aesthetics, and the Western notion of Japan as this wonderful, mysterious country. I'd studied Japanese in college, and I found a job teaching there in a language school. My parents expected me to go to law school. They were pissed. I moved to Japan, and it was a year of being lonely and introspective. I kept asking myself: What do you want to do? I knew by that time that my passion was food, but I didn't know what to do with it.

"Women in Japan have clubs, and a student at the language school I taught at introduced me to the Hiking, Poetry, and Cooking Club—mainly a bunch of women, aged fifty to seventy. Through them, I learned another side of the Japanese kitchen: home cooking. We made stews—like chicken mizutaki—in the nabe, the Japanese hot pot; we fermented roots into pickles, and made chahan, Japanese fried rice, and tonkatsu, breaded fried pork. The intense flavors of these homey dishes have stayed with me and influence my cooking today."

During most of that year in Japan, when he wasn't teaching or hiking or writing poetry or pickling, Michael was working in his first real restaurant job (if you don't count part-time high school and college gigs, which he doesn't), in the tiny kitchen of a twenty-seat restaurant alongside its French-trained Japanese chef/owner, Shizuyo Shima. Shima, he says, is a woman "iconoclastic in every way and brutal in her training. There isn't a day I don't think about what she taught me: A chef always thinks ahead! Use the right tool for the job! Be prepared! Work clean and tidy! Be organized! Sometimes during that year I wondered, *Is this going to kill me?*" Michael's tough training ended well. He'd planned to continue his studies at the most famous cooking school in Japan, the Ecole Hôtelière Tsuji, in Osaka. But Shima convinced him that since he would eventually cook in the West, he should study in Paris, where she'd trained, at the rigorous vocational culinary school Ferrandi. "She not only steered me there, but a few weeks into my first term, Shima actually came to Paris and introduced me to the famous (and infamous) old-generation Michelin-starred chef she'd worked for, Jean Delaveyne, who eventually hired me at Bougival."

At Bistro Shima, Michael came to know dashi, the lifeblood of the Japanese kitchen, a broth made fresh every morning from dried kelp—the broad seaweed called kombu—and dried bonito flakes, katsuoboshi. The flavor of dashi is delicious: a little smoky, a little salty, dashi is umami incarnate; it seems as old as cooking itself. As the stuff of Japanese folklore, dashi is the aroma a sixteenth-century traveler would long to catch a whiff of as he approached his home. Making dashi is the most elemental kitchen task in a Japanese household, and if you are lucky enough to spend the night in one, or in a rustic ryokan, it is dashi's distinctively mellow perfume that awakens you in the morning.

To make dashi, sides of bonito fish, a fierce cousin of the tuna, were once dried into mahogany-colored slabs and prized as an artisanal product. The slab was grated over a sharp blade inset in the top of an ingeniously crafted box fitted with a pull-out drawer below to catch the bonito flakes, aka katsuobushi. The best kombu comes from Hokkaido, Japan's northernmost island, where kelp is harvested from the Sea of Japan and the Northern Pacific. Today you can buy a plastic bag of shaved bonito flakes on the internet for less than $10. Ditto for dried kombu. So much for poetry. And to be honest, these days, many Japanese home cooks make dashi from a powdery mix that comes in a packet. But not Michael Anthony! And not me. Mike shops for the best katsuobushi and true kombu at Japanese markets; he makes dashi to enhance the flavor of his food in many subtle ways. (Sometimes he'll add in a few drops of a favorite elixir, shirodashi—a bottled flavor enhancer made from dashi and a hit of white soy sauce. When I can find it at Japanese groceries, I've come to depend on shirodashi to rev up everything from a raw salad to Asian noodle soups.)

As a young cook in Japan, Michael mastered kinpira, a delicate simmer of slivered root vegetables cooked in dashi and served as a salad. He often makes kinpira with daikon and carrots, sometimes with celery root and salsify, too, frequently adding lacy slices of lotus root and shavings of the peeled roots of burdock. The burdock I know is a nuisance weed—its leathery green leaves and deep brown roots invade my garden beds, and, in fall, its prickly burrs grab on to my pants and won't let go. But because the Japanese have long prized burdock root for its mild flavor and powerhouse medicinal benefits, I've learned to respect it.

In rural Japan, you see just-harvested white daikon radishes hung to dry by their leaves, roots down, strung across the facades of little houses like icicle Christmas lights. Michael may have passed such daikon-festooned neighborhoods on his hour-and-a-half rail commute from the small town where he lived to Shima's restaurant in downtown Tokyo. However it happened, daikon, previously unknown to him, permanently lodged in that Midwesterner's head. And in his kitchen. He showed me a favorite little Japanese daikon grater: just a simple shallow plastic box whose removable lid is pierced with sharp holes to rub the root over. Staring at the tiny pile of snowy flakes that result, I recognized an old friend. Daikon *oroshi* (grated) is freely used in Japanese restaurants—as a condiment on teriyaki-grilled anything. It's what they stir into the dipping sauces for soba noodles, and tempura, too. Michael likes to serve grated daikon as a topping for the pan-roasted fish I learned in the kitchen at Gramercy.

I set about making kinpira the way Michael showed me, the way much Japanese cooking begins, with the simple act of making dashi. I put a small pot of water on the stove. Then, when the water's just short of boiling (which would turn the broth bitter), I add a few pieces of dried kombu and gently simmer it for 20 minutes. When I remove the pot from the burner and stir in a cup of loosely packed pink bonito flakes, I can already smell history. Then I attack the roots that remain from the Anthonys' CSA box.

Remembering how I've watched Michael prep kinpira, I think for the millionth time, "Cooking is cutting." I've seen him square each root by slicing off the rounded bits ("Save them for stock"). Then, he makes deliberate and easy slices, about ⅜ inch thick. In his hands, those slices practically fall into matchsticks. This is a skill I fail to master. My matchsticks are modern art: odd little free-form cudgels that do not affect the flavor, only the look—which is everything in the Japanese kitchen. I sigh and move on, happily reducing purple and white daikon, those China rose radishes, Jerusalem artichokes, and lots of carrots into a slightly messy but colorful pile. Finally, when the matchsticks meet the dashi with a shot of mirin and soy sauce, a squeeze of lemon juice, and a scattering of toasted sesame seeds, I realize that even though I have traveled throughout Japan on three food-related editorial reporting trips, in showing me how to make kinpira, Michael has opened a simple path into cooking the true flavor of that country.

Refrigerated, my kinpira will last days. And the dashi that remains? I do as Mike suggests, stirring in a tablespoon of light miso, a handful of sliced shiitakes, and a sprinkle of scallions, and almost instantly I have a lovely mushroom soup for lunch. Several days later, I gently heat the last of the kinpira in the cup or so of dashi that's left and pour it over a bowl of soba noodles.

FROM WORKING WITH HIM ON *The Gramercy Tavern Cookbook* (in fact, from the first of his meals I had at the restaurant), it was clear to me that Michael is a chef with a great deal to say about everything—an elegant philosopher/cook, and a generous one at that. None of the roughness of his early kitchen formation remains; except, perhaps, the deeply felt conviction of *what not to do*. He has so much to teach the rest of us, I realized as I wrestled with how to make the GT book richer than just an anatomy of a great restaurant—I was determined to make it useful for home cooks and for the restaurant's fans as well.

Michael and I purposely chose recipes that, while representative of GT's cooking, did not depend on the stratospheric skill level of the restaurant's kitchen; recipes that were immediately seductive, ingredient-driven, and replicable at home. Like those many instant pickles. Like duck confit made by burying duck legs and breasts overnight in salt, sugar, fresh herbs, and lemon peel. "Duck is the new pork," the headnote proclaimed, demystifying the process, and demonstrating in step-by-obvious-step photos how confit can easily deliver seductive texture and flavor at home. At 3:00 a.m. on the day after Thanksgiving, we photographed the inspired floral designer Roberta Bendavid transforming the Tavern into an instant Christmas wonderland, making it a magical place to be at holiday time. We recorded the pastry chef's every move as she invented the best chocolate chip cookie ever made. In this way, I was a typical reader, unwilling to replicate cheffy fussiness or plates tarted up with tweezered herb leaves at home. We photographed the food in an accessible way, too, deliberately avoiding the pretentious holy-cathedral-of-high-art images you often find in high-end restaurant cookbooks in favor of a warmer, more intimate style.

We shot lots of raw ingredients, lots of hands on the food, and lots of how-to photos. Happily, I absorbed many of those lessons. For example, to pan-roast fish, season a skinless, boneless fillet on both sides with salt and pepper; heat a bit of olive oil in a small skillet and lay the fillet flat in the hot pan; flip after 3 minutes; cook a couple of minutes more; add a smashed clove of garlic, a sprig of thyme, and a knob of butter; squeeze some lemon juice into the pan to emulsify the butter; and, with a soupspoon, baste the fillet with the butter and lemon juice. *Et voilà!* Pan-roasting is a skill I managed to master (but I still like to check those pictures to make sure).

I took the train to Locust Valley, New York, to interview the restaurant's architects, Peter and Susan Bentel of Bentel & Bentel, to understand how their design choices resulted in one of the most feel-good restaurants on earth. It was the first restaurant project for this family firm that's gone on to design dozens of winners—among them Le Bernardin and the Modern. Peter told me, "Our first thought was to reject the GT assignment, telling ourselves, 'We went to a very nice graduate school of architecture! We don't do restaurants!' But of course we were just being high-culture idiots." He recalled how Danny sent him and Susan, who were newly married, to Italy to visit his favorite trattorias, to figure out what they had in common, what made them feel so good, so welcoming, so hospitable. Peter made a great discovery: the width of the dining rooms in those small trattorias was determined by the height of the trees used to make their ceiling beams. In the GT book, we included a floor plan of the final restaurant space to show how that perfect square was deliberately divided, made to feel like an Italian suite of rooms in an American inn.

AFTER THE GT BOOK WAS published, I was convinced that Michael had more—much more—to say. I knew that above all things, he is passionate about vegetables, about terroir, about what he likes to call "the taste of here!" I looked for a way to share his always-wise philosophy: "Our reflex should be to use what we're connected to naturally. To ask, 'What do we have around us? What's right there in front of us?'" Pete Wells, the *New York Times* restaurant critic, wrote a three-star review of Gramercy Tavern in which he perfectly captured the vegetable essence of Michael's cooking: "It's as if he has fallen in love with everything he puts on the plate. He's like somebody who goes to the farmers' market hungry, ends up buying everything he sees, then figures out a way to make it all come together. . . . Mr. Anthony gives you a sense of what's going on that week in the vegetable patch that few chefs can match."

Book ideas come from unlikely places, and in a small shop in Vézelay, France, my hand fell on an irreverent paperback called *Abécédaire légumophile* (loosely translated, *ABCs for Vegetable Lovers*). Whimsical black-and-white line drawings of vegetables, the odd recipe, and amusing commentary ran through the alphabet: "A comme Aubergine [eggplant], B comme Bette [beet], C comme Chou [cabbage]."

I couldn't wait to get home and show Michael the book. Perhaps not so coincidentally (there are no accidents!), years before, I'd bought a (reproduction!) edition of forty-six gorgeously illustrated individual nineteenth-century color prints of vegetables, drawings that had once illuminated the lavish catalogs of the great French seed producer Vilmorin. What if we could do our own alphabet, I wondered, building on Michael's unique love of—and remarkable recipes for—vegetables and using those Vilmorin illustrations (if somehow, we could secure the rights)?

Happily (and thanks to our beloved agent), we landed a contract for *V is for Vegetables*. *V* was never meant to be a vegetarian book, but Michael's ideas are no less subversive—his intent is to turn the entire Western diet on its head. To flip the equation. In a *V* world, meat and fish become condiments, and vegetables are at the center of the plate. Michael went so far as to question whether we needed plates at all. What about a bowl, he wondered—a prescient idea that became reality a few years later, when you had to kick grain bowls and takeout organic salads out of the way to get down the street.

We thought hard about how to make the book in an effective, personal way. We decided to produce it in my kitchen, which is open to the living room. Four times that year (once for every fresh produce season), we turned the whole place into a photo studio. It was an easy choice to reassemble the principals who'd worked on the GT book. Photographer Maura McEvoy, whose beautiful, careful images had so effectively made Gramercy feel intimate, began as a young design editor at *Met Home* before she stunned me one day by closing the door to my office and telling me she'd decided to become a photographer. With her fine editorial eye and polished photography skills, she'd succeeded. We've happily worked together producing books both here and abroad. Kathy Brennan, a former senior editor at *Saveur*, a skilled cook, and herself a cookbook author, had been the recipe editor on the GT book; she played that role and more on *V*. We added my creative director collaborator, Don Morris, with whom I've produced magazines and many books—a fine editor as well as designer. And we asked Sue Li, an accomplished cook, to be our sous-chef.

Because there could never be too many layers to what we envisioned as an encyclopedic book, we asked the accomplished artist Mindy Dubin (who happens to be the chef's wife), to make line drawings of each vegetable, drawings that would eventually illuminate every letter of the alphabet that Don strategically placed at the top of each page in the elegant, serifed Wessex typeface, each printed in a different vegetable color. Oh, and did I mention that as another layer of information, we'd decided to photograph every vegetable in its recognizable raw state, before it was transformed by cooking?

Michael's singular passions drove his choice of vegetables; only occasionally did we have to satisfy an alphabetic requirement. "I is for iceberg lettuce" is a bit of a fifties foodie joke, but legitimate when wedges of the stuff are uncharacteristically seared on a hot griddle. To buy us the letter Q, Mike deemed quince an honorary vegetable, inventing a killer recipe for mostarda, stewing quince with pears and apples in white wine, mustard seeds, and toasted walnuts as a condiment to serve with his favorite Jasper Hill Farm cheeses. And X? X was easy. "X is for extra-virgin olive oil," of course! In truth, Michael Anthony has never met a vegetable he didn't like, but in the end, in addition to a Vilmorin illustration on the opening spread of each letter of the alphabet, we edited our vegetable stars to sixty-one. Sixty-one Mindy drawings. Sixty-one veggie portraits. And more than 150 recipes cooked right in front of our eyes. It was Michael Anthony from A to Z—Chef Mike's cooking school. And we loved it.

Growers were so starstruck by the possibility that their entire cranberry bean plants, their feathery fava bean fronds, their heirloom tomatoes, had a chance to make it into Mike's book that they drove their vegetables in from farms in New Jersey and Long Island. So much seasonal produce arrived by the basketful and the boxful that we asked my super, Martin Dowd, to stash the overflow on his terrace, which occasioned his almost daily visits (somehow always at lunchtime!). We were delighted when Rod Lamborn, son of the very same Dr. Calvin Lamborn who had invented the sugar snap pea in 1968, hand-delivered a box of just-cut sugar snap pea plants for us to photograph.

So it was that a tiny team of us gathered around my kitchen island, watching as Mike, in his Wilco T-shirt, cheerfully cooked his way through the alphabet, developing recipes that ranged from homey—Grandma Anthony's Pickled Eggplant—to haute: his version of the flaky leek quiche he'd learned at cooking school in Paris (which still terrifies me). Working this way meant no distance all between the way recipes were created and the way they were written. It meant we learned those dishes instantly and never forgot how they were made. It meant we observed Michael's gentle, intelligent, organized approach and immediately calmed down ourselves.

Kathy, never shy, was the voice of reality and would call out as he cooked, "Mike! No home cook would ever go to that much trouble." Or "You can't ask me to make a sauce and then to make another sauce for the same dish." Maura remembers—and now practices—the way Michael spread a dampened dish towel under his cutting board to steady it before he sliced. I repeat that act almost nightly, loving the intentional, quasi-religious ritual of preparing the prep space. Hearing Michael gently telling me, *Stop. Take a moment. Focus.* Slowing down was a lesson to be learned.

We watched each recipe as it was transformed from its featured ingredient to finished dish in real time, tasting everything. And we washed lots of dishes. Sometimes we'd deliver goodies to Roger's film production office next door, savoring the whoops of appreciation for hot and crunchy potato and cheese croquettes, or a particularly piquant chimichurri sauce ("*H* is for herbs") on grilled steak.

Cooking expertise travels in an ever-changing game of recipe telephone, I realize as I watch Michael make an omelet of garlic scapes ("*G* is for garlic"). Drawing upon every omelet he's ever prepared in every kitchen he's ever cooked in, Mike's sigh encourages the rest of us. (Omelets are frustrating for him, too.) "I've practiced for years and years," he says, "and maybe one day, I'll get it right." But as soon as he achieves just the right fold of eggs with snipped garlic scapes inside and out, taking the time to wait patiently for the top to set, he's nailed that omelet. Next up in this telephone game is for me to cook that omelet. And as soon as I understand that it's not so much in the wrist as it is a matter of practice, and make it often enough, that recipe becomes mine. And the moment a reader sees that recipe and decides to make that omelet in their own nonstick pan, on their own stove, in their own kitchen, it becomes theirs.

Maura and I would take each cooked dish and figure out how to photograph it, choosing from tables full of plates and platters and bowls. With a click, she'd forward the images to Don, who, perched right there at the counter behind his laptop, could instantly download them and begin to design pages. Our process compressed the normal production flow; but even better, it let everyone in on the action at the precise moment the most crucial decisions were made.

This might sound dead logical—how else would you communicate with readers? Take it from me: some chefs never touch the food in their cookbooks; some have no say about the styling, or images, or props. Some stay in their restaurant kitchens while a separate team produces their book.

UNDERSTANDING MICHAEL'S LESSONS REQUIRES THINKING hard about what he brings to his cooking. Fundamentally, I've been influenced by his devotion to extracting the most flavor from the ingredients he cooks with. (I've become obsessed, in fact, by how important it is to get the most flavor from anything I set out to cook, but I certainly do not always know how to make flavor happen.)

"I really think recipes are so limiting. Recipe language doesn't help you understand flavor," Mike tells me when we discuss it. "We have a sous-chef at Gramercy Tavern named Aretah Ettarh who's in charge of making soups. She comes up with a different soup every week. *It's all in her head!* She wakes up and falls asleep dreaming of soup. She's always wondering, 'Should I add a bit more of this? Or a bit more of that?' Without fail, Aretah's soups are exceptional delicacies. I recognize what she makes like hearing notes on a piano. Aretah's cooking is amazing; it's consistent, steady, predictable cooking. What she does is so clear to me as a chef. But how can you teach people to cook like that? Cooking is really the process of transplanting the ideas that play in your head into reality."

I'm relieved that Michael's lessons still play in my head. I remember him telling me once that the last spoonful of a dish should be every bit as defining of the dish as the first spoonful. "I like a good deal more sauce than the Italians do," he explained, which means having enough liquid left in the pan—or on the plate—for the ingredients to fully share their flavors.

In the case of Michael's sweet corn fettuccine, for example, the liquid in question is a corn soup, based on corn broth made from the cobs after the kernels are cut off. Nestled into that plate of corn soup is a spoonful of barely cooked corn kernels in a tangled curl of spinach fettuccine—the pasta turned out that very morning in the narrow basement hallway that was then GT's pasta station. (As I passed by the cooks so deftly extruding their perfect dough, I smiled and reminded myself how glad I was to be over the romance of making pasta at home; how eagerly I eventually gave away that fancy Italian chromed-steel pasta machine—so heavy with its own seriousness—bought once in a frenzy of authenticity.)

Making corn broth from stripped corncobs, however, was a breakthrough concept—and one I use every summer. Don't discard those cobs, Mike counsels. Instead, conserve every bit of flavor by boiling them up with chopped onions, carrots, celery, and garlic in a big pot of water for about 30 minutes. Corn broth! What an elegant and elemental way to capture fleeting flavor. When I look down into the pot of milky-yellow liquid, I smile to hear Mike telling me I have made something out of almost nothing!

Michael is a born teacher; it's no wonder so many excellent chefs have graduated from his kitchens. Water, he advises, is the simplest, cooking-est thing to think about, yet water's not the first thing that comes to mind as you look down at a pan whose juices are fast disappearing. You might think stock, or wine. But water's a better answer (Christopher says the same thing). "When you're finishing a dish, adding a drop or two of liquid brings out its best qualities. A skillful cook of green beans would want to have just enough cooking liquid left in the pan, then add a squeeze of lemon juice, a silver of garlic, a sprig of thyme, and a drop of olive oil to produce a light glaze." (Reminds me of the way Mike pan-roasts a fillet of fish!) "Another obvious example is Grandma's tomato sauce. Remember how she would instinctively add a spoonful or two of pasta cooking water to give the sauce the right consistency and shine."

Pasta water! I grew up making pasta like my mother did (only we called it spaghetti): Boil water in the largest pot available, add the spaghetti, test it, then drain it in a colander, pouring all that pasta water *down the drain*. Then *rinse* the pasta with more water. Rereading *Heat*, Bill Buford's fine book about learning to cook Italian food in Italy, I understand why he believes floury pasta water should be bottled! About making pasta with clam sauce, he writes, "At six minutes and thirty seconds, you use your tongs to pull your noodles out and drop them into your pan—all that starchy pasta water slopping in with them [the clams] is still a good thing; give the pan another swirl; flip it; swirl it again to ensure that the pasta is covered by the sauce. If it looks dry, add another splash of pasta water; if too wet, pour some out. You then let the thing cook away for another half minute or so, swirling, swirling, until the sauce streaks across the bottom of the pan, splash it with olive oil and sprinkle it with parsley: dinner."

Today, with those voices in my head, I make whatever sauce I've decided on in a large skillet next to the pot the pasta's cooking in, transfer the slightly underdone pasta to the skillet along with the water that's clinging to it, and freely stir in spoonfuls of that valuable pasta water to slightly thicken the sauce.

RECENTLY, I ASKED MICHAEL ABOUT something that has bugged me ever since we produced *V.* Under *R*, there's a recipe for rutabaga gratin made with dates, a recipe so wonderful it actually makes me long for cold weather. In this gratin, slices of that rough, onetime barnyard-animal fodder are transformed into pale-gold, silky sheets of flavor. But the process? It's all about the cardinal principle that every good chef knows: evaporation concentrates flavor. *"How can that even happen?"* I ask him, unable, somehow, to wrap my head around the counterintuitive concept. "If the liquid evaporates, then *it's gone*, right?"

"Well"—he smiles at me, because we've had this conversation before—"it's through reduction. The act of deglazing a pan is a classic French cooking technique. It's part of our formal training. You know how recipes ask you to 'stir three times before adding the next ingredient'? That's just homey kitchen wisdom for reduction—it's what Mom and Grandma did to mimic that formal training."

To help you understand what still confounds me, here's an excerpt from the recipe for rutabaga gratin:

> Pour in the brandy and cook until the liquid has almost evaporated. Repeat with the wine. Take your time. This is where the special flavor is born . . .

"How can evaporation create flavor?" I bug him again, trying (but failing) not to seem dense.

"Evaporation," he patiently explains, "is just one point, one deliberate step, in the middle of the one, two, three of cooking. Here's an example: The French start a soup or a sauce or a stew in one pot. All the ingredients are meant to cook together. First there's an allium: an onion, or some garlic, a shallot, or a ramp, cooked in a little oil." (Hence the garlic and shallots softened in butter that are the base of the rutabaga gratin.) "Then you add a bit of aromatic: an anchovy, say. Or a spice, like cumin. Or even a chunk of summer squash." (Sliced Medjool dates play this role with the rutabaga gratin.) "You concentrate the flavors by sweating, not by adding liquid. Finally, you add just a splash of liquid. In Western cooking, it's frequently acid, like wine or vinegar or a spirit."

I made the rutabaga gratin again last night, cooking down first the brandy, then the white wine, with the garlic and shallots. Looking (and smelling) hard, I observed that if you do not cook down the brandy enough, instead of conserving the flavor, you risk making it too potent! I was pleased to discover, by nibbling a bit, that the garlic and shallots had actually absorbed the flavor of the wine. I poured the cream, two cups of it, made sweetly mellow by the dates, and then slightly sharper by the alliums, over two layers of mandoline-sliced rutabaga in the baking dish, each with a covering of grated Parmigiano, and then baked the gratin. I can taste in the finished dish how the rutabaga has eventually absorbed the flavors of its creamy sauce. In fact, I realize, the rutabaga has become its sauce!

"Recipes differ, but the process is the same," Michael tells me. "Controlling the heat and the timing allows the liquid to evaporate, rapidly or slowly. I think of it as adding just a few drops of liquid that coax out the flavor. This happens through the simple, long-proven act of simmering. If you rush it, you'll never get the payoff of building flavors. It happens,

I promise you. And when it does, in that magical moment, people fall in love with cooking." So it turns out I've been unknowingly practicing the concept of reduction for decades. The awareness-of-the-chemistry part is just another life lesson I've learned from Michael.

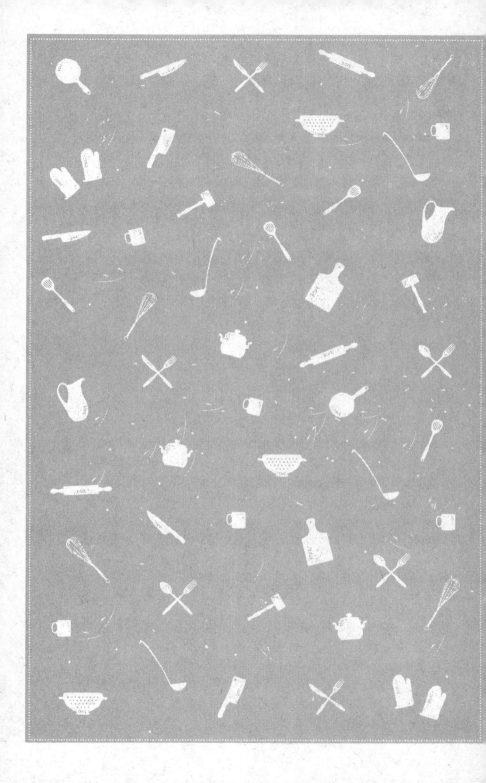

CHAPTER 9

THE COOK & THE GARDEN

I PLANTED MY FIRST GARDEN in Iowa—in the pre–*Met Home* days—on land as vast and undifferentiated as the state itself, whose dense sod required a rented industrial rototiller to break it down into that famously rich loamy soil. Crouched like a toddler expecting a beanstalk, I push lima bean seeds (the dried miniature of the bean itself) into marked rows, tenderly, each by each. Over the hot summer months, those rows were hand cultivated—with a hoe. But that onetime field didn't understand that it was now a garden. This was the Midwest; that garden thought it was still a prairie. Everything that once grew there still wanted to grow there. This was summer in Iowa, with spectacular, biblical storms, operatic thunder and lightning. Suddenly, weeds appeared, Godzilla weeds, from nowhere, threatening the beans. Volunteer sunflowers—really the yellow blossoms of native Jerusalem artichokes—shot up everywhere, their gawky stems higher than my head. Then came even more tenacious invaders: horsetail and foxtail, pigweed, and quack grass, and witch grass, and the tender, weed-like lamb's quarters (whose leaves, I learned from Edna Lewis's *The Taste of Country Cooking*, are good to boil and eat).

This life-and-near-death battle continued until, at last, the lima bean pods formed. And began to fill out. There were *beans* inside! Finally, it was time to harvest them. On my hands and knees down there among them, I felt the pods. The lima beans were ready to pick. These pods, I discovered, are as sturdily constructed as hazmat suits and seem to have an exaggerated sense of their own importance. The *pods* should be the thing you eat. But those suits are just the package the lima beans come in. Shucked, they're good only for compost, but when you manage to pry them open, the pale pearly green beanlets inside make you gasp.

Except, what was this? After all those months of careful cultivation, after all that smiting of weeds, and braving of storms, the entire lima bean harvest amounted to little more than one single package of Birds Eye frozen. Even worse, gently steamed with a little butter, they tasted, well, pretty much like frozen baby limas. Which led me to this life rule: Never grow anything that's indistinguishable from what you can easily buy.

AFTER THAT EARLY ATTEMPT, AS soon as I could manage a garden, I always had one, always on weekends, always on Long Island, even though back then I had little awareness of the profundity of the pond whose surface I was skating on. I was determined to have a garden at the cottage we had on Three

Mile Harbor in East Hampton. As we planned it, Roger said the prophetic words "You know, the garden doesn't have to be a square or a rectangle. We can make it any shape we want." And in that moment, the Octagon was born, its frame made from lengths of beefy eight-by-eight-foot posts, the larger beds marked by double rows of old brick, with an inner circle of smaller herb beds. And in the center, one singular rosebush: a blowsy David Austin English number whose pink blossoms spilled out over a fat terra-cotta pot.

We grew all the usual suspects: lettuces and mints and arugula and Sweet 100 tomatoes, all the basil in the world, the best of thymes—lemon and woolly and silver—and an entire row of creeping thyme that we encouraged to climb over the edges to cover uneven carpentry. My drawing had the detail of medieval apothecary gardens. At *Met Home*, I wrote an editor's page with the too-cute-by-half title "So Many Weeds, So Little Thyme," which did, however, get at the heart of a weekend gardener's dilemma: "Should I weed it, water it, talk to it, prune it, rotation-plant it, mulch it, stake it, rake it, double-dig it, fertilize it (with ecologically correct fish meal, of course), photograph it, paint it, draw it, cook from it—or cultivate it?" I was as good a gardener as I could be, given my part-time status, thrilled to be able to run outside and pick a handful of herbs and a few veggies for dinner.

As a Christmas present one year, Roger and I made a book of photos and recipes for our friends and family and called it *Cooking from the Octagon*. In retrospect, what chutzpah! The first entry was a recipe I'd figured out called Smoky Gazpacho that captures the wood-smoke flavor of grilled summer vegetables. It was illustrated by a photo of red, yellow, orange, and green bell peppers; baby eggplants; and yellow and white onions on a grill, with a whole tray of plum tomatoes on deck. A total cheat! Not one of those vegetables had come from anywhere near the Octagon. Nor, with its high overstory of oak trees, would anything more robust than a whole lotta herbs and the occasional cherry tomato ever grow well there. But you could *see* the garden from the grill. And that *was* a great summer soup: the roasted tomatoes and eggplant pulp pureed with oil and vinegar and lots of basil, all the other smoky vegetables plus a crisp cucumber chopped and stirred in.

The garden is humbling. There is never time enough for the work the garden expects of you. Things will inevitably die. The garden had so many lessons to teach me; I just needed to be smart enough and patient enough to slow down. I had to learn to give it the respect it deserves. When I stopped to listen, I heard a whole lot of voices talking at me: the older Brits, like Gertrude Jekyll and Russell Page, and the younger ones, no less wise, and cooks, too, like Allan Jenkins and Nigel Slater. And the Americans, Katharine S. White and Elizabeth Lawrence. But mostly I found hope and humility in what Thomas Jefferson famously wrote in August 1811; as the season waned, he calmed his spirits: "But though an old man, I am but a young gardener."

LAST SUMMER, THE CHEF/OWNER OF the Michelin-starred restaurant Annisa, Anita Lo, cooked an alfresco lunch—a benefit for Early Girl Farm, run by our mutual friend, Patty Gentry, a gifted organic farmer who grows vegetables on three acres of Isabella Rossellini's Mama Farm in Brookhaven, Long Island. As Anita meticulously hovered over long prep tables (set up in Isabella's garage) where sixty rimmed soup bowls of vichyssoise awaited their final touches before being carried out to a tent on the lawn, she carefully spooned five just-shucked Great Gun oysters (from a local shellfish farm) into each bowl, spacing them deliberately clockwise. Then she supervised a clutch of eager volunteers as we set about garnishing the soup. I, as the first helper, was to deliver one to three minuscule cubes of tiny-diced pickled red onion on top of each oyster. I kept ham-handedly dropping on five to maybe seven cubes, to Anita's mild disapproval. A second helper followed, dabbing a just-so touch of wasabi on each oyster with his fingertip; the next added threads of lemon zest; and the last helper sprinkled on tiny bits of dried shiso leaves. When I had the good fortune to sit down and enjoy that soup, I realized that Anita was not just being chef-fussy with the *look* of it. Each oyster in each creamy spoonful held a play of flavors that leapt from her imagination: the sharp crunch of pickled onion, that flash of wasabi, that hit of lemon, that minty shiso. Anita meant each spoonful to *be the dish*. With her deliberate garnishing technique, she was cooking down to the last second. That's the difference between a cook and a chef, I thought, and not for the first time. Anita sees the world in a perfect bite. I make dinner.

Happily, Roger and I were across-the-street neighbors with Anita for almost two decades on Long Island. We'd eaten at Annisa many memorable times; we would celebrate the Fourth of July together, often with a picnic, and when her busy schedule aligned with ours, we'd have dinner. Anita's moves in the kitchen are subtle. Watching closely, you detect her knowing confidence—and recall with a jolt, this girl is ferocious! She won *Iron Chef*! Anita makes the crispiest fried soft-shell steamers from clams she's dug that day on sandy Bird Island in Moriches Bay. She slides the shucked clams into a bowl of buttermilk, dips them in flour with a touch of corn-meal for texture, then drops them right into 375°F oil. And in the time it takes to pull open a bag of Doritos, we're crunching on fried clams. Anita's a fisherwoman who loves to cook her catch—say, a lovely black bass—by steaming it whole on a rack above boiling water, its flesh gently scored and piled with slivers of scallion greens and fresh ginger, with a quick pour of soy sauce, and peanut oil, and sesame oil over the top.

I try not to be intimidated by my friend when I cook for her, but one memory still rankles. Anita was a bit sick, with a flu of some sort, so I made a chicken soup, which I planned to walk over to her. At the last minute, I remembered the teeny carrots that were just coming up in my garden. How beautiful they'd look, I thought, miniature lacy tops and all, just floating on that chicken soup. Ever so gently, I pulled up the carrots, wiped off the soil, and plopped them into the soup. Well, you can foresee (as I did not) what happened. The second those infant carrots, and their greens, delicate as a Dürer engraving, hit the hot soup, they . . . well, they melted into it. That's the difference between a chef and a cook, I thought once again, as my heart sank into the soup with the carrots. Anita would have predicted the outcome. She would have waited till the last second to drop the carrots onto the soup.

AND THE FARMER, PATTY GENTRY? Well, this farmer went to cu-linary school and worked as a chef for twenty-five years before she ever grew a radish. Cooking drove her passion to farm, to perfect the quality of the vegetables she cooked with and those she supplies to the chefs she serves. As a cook and a farmer, Patty never does one without thinking about the other. And I do not touch so much as a leaf of her vegetables without reflecting on the expertise—and the angst—she's put into raising that plant. I'm smitten with the suave layout of her fields and the way she cradles an elegant head of just-picked frisée lettuce like a newborn. Which, of course, it is.

Patty's reverence for the life cycle of farming is evident in her every move. The varieties she chooses to plant at Early Girl Farm are the things she can't wait to cook: Asian greens like the nutrient-dense gunsho (a yellow-flowered sprouting broccoli), and a branching cauliflower called Song. Patty looks at seeds with a time-traveler's eyes; seeing in them the first stage of a vegetable on its way to becoming a salad. Or a stir-fry, a stew, or a soup. Her hands may be in the dirt, but her eyes are always on the stove. Patty delivers her produce to a few discerning restaurant kitchens, both in Brooklyn and on the East End, whose chefs appreciate her devotion to excellence. I've watched her easily compost anything she would not be excited to cook herself (to me, those discards still look good enough to eat).

Every week during the season, Patty supplies vegetables to more than a hundred families through her Long Island CSA program. With her poetic imagination and her cook's eyes, she's a vegetable proselytizer. Her delight in sharing her passion is evident in the crack-of-dawn Saturday emails she writes to her CSA members, just before they arrive to pick up their weekly share of vegetables.

"Yet another bag of washed lettuces. Listen, people. These lettuces are special. *Please eat them tender stems and all.* For me, the stems are the best part. The lettuces germinated so intensely that they grew up tall yet tender with long stems. Don't be afraid of those long stems. They hold all the sugars and vitality of the plant. Also, we've been using biodegradable biobags. But to keep your lettuces longer, wrap them in a damp paper towel and put them in Tupperware. I know plastic works best, but . . . it's hard to look at photos of a two-hundred-year-old sea turtle swimming with a plastic bag on its head!"

Patty's never too busy to stop and explain, blue eyes sparkling as if she gets her own jokes, how she cooks what she grows. I try to stand close enough to hear her tell a CSA member how to slice those long, sweet Italian Jimmy Nardello peppers and cook them down with onions, or tell another that yes, you can eat the skin of a Delicata squash, so slice it thin and roast it flat. I smile as a woman asks her if she peels her carrots. She does not. "Why would she?" I think. "She grew the soil those carrots grew in!" As a cook, Patty thinks like an Italian. First, do no harm! Stay very close to the integrity of the raw ingredient (which she's raised from a pup). If "hardly touched" is a style, that's how she cooks: just a little garlic, a drop of olive oil, gentle heat.

Here's more wisdom from another of the farmer-poet's Saturday morning letters:

Good morning, dear people.

The summer continues its dreamlike heat wave. Sometimes I stop what I'm doing at the farm and just stand there. I feel the heat bearing down on my body and the blood coursing through my veins. If I'm lucky, I see a pack of dragonflies riding the hot air currents and beautiful birds calling wildly to one another in the tomato patch, signaling which fruit is ripe for the pecking!

Speaking of tomatoes, we are caught in a tidal wave of Juliet. Juliet is a small, red, juicy plum tomato. She is not pasty at all. She is beautiful, yet bold, and yields her fragrant juices through a delicate skin. It's love at first bite! You don't have to beckon in the dark at her window. You don't have to participate in a dangerous family feud to take her home with you. All you have to do is mount your chariot and head down to the farm!

Juliet awaits you! Toss her in a salad. Slather her in olive oil with a touch of salt and some herbs and spoon her on bread. Roast her with fish. Skewer and grill her. Whatever you do, she will enchant you!

In addition to Juliet, you will find . . . baby broccoli rabe (delicious in salad or wilted into pasta!), a spicy salad mix, Little Gem lettuce (grill lightly and dot with goat cheese for a warm salad!), creamy potatoes (boil, butter, eat . . . repeat!!), silky eggplant (broil or grill . . . sure to thrill!!), sweet peppers, chili peppers, cabbage, beets, carrots, leeks, garlic, onions, shallots!! Let's fall in love!!

With bounty as boundless as the sea,
Patty

While spraying the soil off those Juliets, car-wash style, to send to Missy Robbins, chef/owner of the hot Brooklyn restaurants Lilia and Misi, Patty's telling me how Missy (whom Patty cooked with early on in restaurant kitchens) halves these tomatoes; puts them cut side up on a baking sheet; sprinkles them with kosher salt, olive oil, fennel seeds, and cracked coriander seeds; and slow-roasts them in a 275°F oven for 2 hours. "Those tomatoes are heaven over pasta."

BACK HOME, PATTY'S COOKING LUNCH for us in full-on farmer/philosopher mode. "We've come so far in the kitchen from what we once thought we had to do to act like serious cooks. When I cooked professionally, we expended so much effort picking the leaves off thyme stems. When I cook at home, I just toss the thyme in the pan, and if there's a stem or two, well, we'll deal." I agree: picking thyme leaves always represented a level of cheffiness I was never eager to achieve. She slices lovely little black, white, and lavender peppers, plus a colorful French heirloom, Jaune Sucrée (sweet yellow), all of whom she's known since they were seeds. Then she adds more of her progeny, slicing the svelte, tapered, red-violet onions called rossa di Tropea, a breed that originated in Calabria, on the southernmost tip of Italy, just a *bacio* away from Sicily.

Watching Patty, I see not the carefree cook but the conscientious farmer, the one who rises in the chill darkness of 4:00 a.m. to load her truck for deliveries to restaurants in the city; who slogs to work in heavy boots and rain gear to pick three long rows of lettuce before it bolts (or, if it already has, to dispassionately wheelbarrow it straight to the compost); who's resigned to losing an entire crop to invading insects. As she slices Japanese eggplants to add to the pan, I recall her tale of literally nursing rows of sickened eggplants back to health and resolve to never take that vegetable for granted:

In organic farming, where we are working to build healthy soil and refraining from using synthetic nutrients, pesticides, and herbicides, the plants show their true health on their leaves and speak to us that way. They tell you what they need. I often say I wish I had Google Translate for plants so I could know exactly what they are trying to tell me. So, last night at around 3:00 a.m., the nursing continued. I mixed up a warm batch of compost tea with kelp, rock dust, fulvic acid, and trace minerals and fed the eggplants. Miraculously, they are growing. Sure . . . they look a little frayed, and I still wonder if they are going to completely recover from spring and my lack of fluency in their language—but there the plants stand, bearing their little eggplant fruits. . . .

Patty's talking and cooking again. "When I cook eggplant, or peppers, or onions—almost any vegetable, really—I no longer start the garlic first, the way we were taught to do, because I figure all the vegetables cook the same way, together. Now I cook everything in the same pan." On top of the sautéed peppers, onion, and eggplant in that skillet, she slips slim fillets of local flounder, then she opens a jar of the vegan mayo she loves, plops several spoonfuls into a small food processor, adds a handful of basil leaves, whizzes it up, and drops a spoonful on top of the fish. She slips the whole pan—sautéed vegetables, fish, basil mayo, and all—under the broiler for just a minute, and there's lunch.

ONE RAINY DECEMBER MORNING, long after the flush of summer, Patty leads Roger and me into her thirty-by-ninety-six-foot greenhouse, a clean white tube suffused with cool, even light. This structure allows her to plant ninety-foot beds of winter greens (which in the case of kale, translates into four hundred pounds of the stuff) and thus extend her growing season. "It's not heated," she explains, "but it does bring us a few zones south, and I can get almost another season out of the farm." She plants her winter greens—all her vegetables, really—from the organic seed she tenaciously hunts down on long cold nights bent over her computer, scanning the online catalogs of organic seed purveyors (her favorites: Baker Creek, in Missouri; Johnny's, in Maine; and Adaptive Seeds, in Oregon). In the long greenhouse, Patty grows winter greens with poetic names: Red Kitten spinach, with perky red-veined leaves; Barese, a dwarf white-stemmed chard; Spigariello Liscia, a broccoli she prizes for its leaves; and heads of Monte Carlo romaine, each leaf distinct and glossy, with a flavor like lettuce on steroids. She grabs a blue-handled knife in her strong, square hand and, attacking the kale beds, quickly cuts us an armload of the stuff. Patty looks out mischievously over the bounteous leaves, holding the kale up to her smiling face like a bridal bouquet, which she then tosses to me. It feels strange, in winter, to wrap my arms around such fresh, just-harvested leafy bounty.

"I make kale pesto," she says, crouching again in the kale bed. "It's one of my favorite easy dinners: I get the Cuisinart ready on the counter, with garlic and Parmigiano and good olive oil. Then I quickly sauté the kale until it just wilts and transfer it to the Cuisinart and buzz it up. I use this quick pesto immediately on pasta, or I'll smear it on a cauliflower pizza crust and top it with some roasted butternut squash. Or, we'll have kale pesto for breakfast, sautéed quickly with garlic and coconut aminos and a sprinkling of coconut flakes."

Back in New York hours later, as I process Patty's kale into a pesto of my own, about to serve it over pasta, Lincoln drifts through the kitchen. When I offer him some, he declines. "Kale," he proclaims, "tastes like sadness and despair." When I text that to Patty, she immediately shoots back, "Well, if you compare it to Oreo cookies, he might have a point."

EAST HAMPTON SITS GRACEFULLY ON the south shore of the very eastern end of Long Island. It has been an elegant small town ever since the mid-1600s, when it was incorporated, and it is oh so proud of its history. What drew me (and untold throngs of others) was the quality of its light, its proximity to water—not just the Atlantic, but its many bays and harbors, too—its fishing, and its farming. But those defining qualities were becoming subsumed by a flashy social scene of summer people, of celebs and wannabes, of the anything-but-local restaurants, and parties, parties, parties. In *Saveur*, we decided to do a feature, "The Other East Hampton," to focus on the region's early authenticity—a farming family now in its sixth generation; its baymen who fished the netted pound traps on Gardiner's Bay the same way their great-grandfathers and the Native Americans before them did.

Researching the recipes for that story, with the aid of a sympathetic librarian, I foraged deep in the centuries-old files of the East Hampton Library. There I found recipes—some scribbled in pencil in cramped, old-fashioned script on brown paper bags, others in early self-published little books—for the local beach plum jelly, made from the fat purple plums picked in the fall from chubby bushes that grow wild on sandy waterfront paths.

Here was a ritual I could embrace: picking the beach plums as they turned purple with the cooling weather, boiling them down in a huge pot, and hanging the contents of that pot—peels, pits and all—in a double layer of cheesecloth, knotted into a sling, over the pot from a broom handle strategically weighted on the broom end with something heavy: a cement block, or sometimes the base of a blender. After drip, drip, dripping all night, the strained juice (with sugar added) is boiled down into jelly. Beach plums became, for me, a gateway drug for all manner of berry-growing and preserving. I researched recipes for the gooseberries Roger and I eventually grew, each year improving on last year's recipe, carefully noting date, crop size, weather, and yield. First there was Our Gooseberry Jam, inevitably followed by New Gooseberry Jam, then The Perfect Gooseberry Jam, and Yet Another Gooseberry Jam. Currants and raspberries and blackberries and strawberries (bought from a farmer, not grown) followed a similar path. In a profound (and very sweet) way, making jam has always marked the season and connected me to that place.

The deeper I explored those library archives, the more there was to discover. For centuries, locals had wrapped their freshly caught bluefish with bacon before broiling or, more likely, grilling it; of course we did that, too, with excellently smoky results. Clams were a crucial foodstuff in early East Hampton; there were recipes for a dozen kinds of clam chowder, many using a piece of bacon or a hunk of pork to flavor the broth as the early English settlers did. There were recipes for baked clams, and stuffed clams, and clam pie, and clam fritters. Cooks mixed their shell beans with deer fat and onions and baked them in clay pots; they steamed mussels in seaweed, and panfried local blowfish. Early settlers would have celebratory clambakes on wood fires on their beaches. We based the food for *Saveur*'s East Hampton story on those old recipes.

Roger, an avid fisherman of the local waters, bobbed about in boats and walked the fields to photograph the local fishermen and farmers for our story. Christopher shot the food. And somehow, she and I wound up cooking all the recipes for the photographs. (A circumstance that most likely came about because imagining the prospect of a whole day together in the kitchen chatting away deliciously outweighed the support we'd get from bringing in cook helpers.) The main event was a lobster bake on the rocky harbor beach below our house. As the food prep dragged on, taking way longer than we'd imagined, I remember Christopher joking, "Those first settlers must have had a whole lot of time on their hands."

WE PRODUCED THE LOBSTER BAKE in real time. First, we dug a wide, shallow pit in the sand and rimmed it with beach rocks. Then we built a fire from gathered driftwood and balanced a metal grate on the rocks. A giant galvanized washtub was set on the grate, its bottom filled with a few inches of seawater, then lined with more rocks to lift the food above the water as it steamed in the pot over the fire. We collected tons of seaweed—the kind with the little bubbles we'd pop as kids—from the shore, first rinsing away the sand, then layering the seaweed on the rocks in the tub. We added each ingredient separately, topping each with a layer of seaweed. First came quartered chickens, then dozens of whole cherrystone clams, then mussels in their shells (debearded, of course). Then corn on the cob still in its husks, and finally, wriggling lobsters, covered with more seaweed. On that top layer of seaweed, we did what I discovered East Hampton's settlers had done centuries ago: we placed one single raw potato in the center as a cooking timer. We covered the pot with a tarp (though in the magazine's recipe, we wimped out with heavy-duty aluminum foil). When the potato was done, that meant the dinner was cooked.

Somehow, and uncharacteristically, Christopher and I had underestimated the work involved in cooking all the food for this entire story in one day. As everything took twice as long as it was supposed to, and we were losing the magic hour's glorious golden light, and our invited guests began to make ordering-in-pizza jokes, Christopher looked at me and said: "I think I'm having a heart attack!" "So am I!" I answered. "Maybe we'd better sit down."

Over the years, and probably inevitably, showbiz and glamour moved into East Hampton big-time. The quality of our experience changed. Suddenly, rock stars' gold Escalades were creating traffic jams on back country lanes. People were tearing down perfectly fine big houses to build even bigger houses—just because they could. Ladies in full makeup and important jewelry at 9:00 a.m. were standing in line in six-inch heels for donuts at Dreesen's downtown. Suddenly, you could no longer even get downtown.

AT THE SAME TIME AS our small publishing partnership was inventing and launching *Saveur*, we acquired *Garden Design* magazine, a glossy publication that had been the American

Society of Landscape Architects' vehicle to show the work of their members. Our challenge was to break that publication out of its professional constraints, grow its circulation, and turn it into a high-end consumer magazine that appealed to the readers we knew had a passion for the garden but little experience or expertise. To me, that last was an ideal editorial condition for a magazine: enthusiasm without expertise. These readers needed inspired ideas and real information; they needed . . . us! Of course, a high-end design magazine focused on the garden had one thorny problem: advertising. Undaunted, my old friend and our publishing director, Joe Armstrong, embraced the challenge. "I loved *Garden Design* so much," he recalled, "and of the ten magazines I published in my career [including *Rolling Stone* and *New York*], it was *the* hardest to sell to advertisers, because they were doing fine without it and never even thought about reaching readers with those interests." But sell it he did, ringing a cowbell in his office with every success.

It was inevitable that being the editor of *Garden Design* (as well as *Saveur*) would up my game as a gardener, and everything I learned benefited the kitchen, too. But it took a profile we did on John Jeavons (rhymes with heavens), a visionary California organic farmer, to set me seriously straight. Jeavons teaches and practices bio-intensive farming, the art of getting the highest yield from the least—but healthiest—soil. With twinkly eyes and a white beard, he looks the part of a guru, and is given to such weighty pronouncements as "Feed your dreams and your fears will starve." Get the soil right with mindful management, Jeavons counsels, and fertility and yield will follow.

By then, worn down by the three-hour drive every Friday and Sunday night, we had left East Hampton for a house closer to the city, in East Moriches, what I liked to call the "non-trendy pre-Hamptons." Now, with the room for a new garden, and determined to do it properly—albeit still only on weekends—I found a copy of Jeavons's book *How to Grow More Vegetables* and ceremoniously carried it to the oldest library in New York, the hush, lush Society Library on East 79th Street. There, I settled into a comfortable chair, read the Jeavons in one sitting, and had my eureka moment. It took just a few hours to totally shift my gardening mindset. I had believed my garden was about perfect French breakfast radishes and tender mâche, sorrel, hakurei turnips, and Lollo Rossa lettuce. But what really mattered, I discovered, were the tiny living microbes in the very earth those plants grew in. Jeavons taught me to stop obsessing about growing heirloom vegetables and learn, instead, to grow healthy, productive soil.

To accomplish that, I had to master composting. It would not be about those dopey black plastic barrels you crank, or any device at all, really. What I learned from Jeavons was simple: I needed *two* compost sections, one for our daily deposits of vegetative matter, and a second space, right next to it, to do the quiet job of cooking all that nature into soil.

We figured out the simplest of all solutions: two four-foot squares, side by side, fenced with chicken wire, anchored at each corner by metal stakes in the ground. On an old board, I painted the words "This Side" and wired it to the open bin, so that any resident of our house knew precisely where to deposit that day's detritus. That way, one side would receive a summer season's worth of gleanings while the other side was left to process its contents—becoming a microbe factory, breaking down all that good stuff until it became earth itself: alive, fresh-smelling, soft and loose, and just waiting for its life in next year's garden bed. ("Put me in, Coach!")

The summer evening's walk by moonlight to the southeast corner of the yard, carrying the day's contribution to the compost—bare feet in sandals, damp grass and fireflies, the air sweet with its faint scent of honeysuckle or wild roses or wood smoke, and even the kinda spooky solitary darkness—made for the loveliest kind of taking out the garbage ritual. Each trip was a fresh offering to the garden gods.

For the spring season, Roger made me an inspired compost strainer. Simple enough, this was a rectangular wooden frame about three by five feet, built from one-by-three-inch boards with a screen of half-inch metal hardware cloth tacked onto the bottom. Two dowels attached to each side of the frame held the strainer in place when it was set over our trusty big-wheeled green garden cart. Those side dowels gave us something to hold on to as we used a hand trowel to jiggle shovelfuls of last season's contributions, now broken down, through the screen, where the stuff sifted easily through the holes. Stick and stones were removed and discarded. And in that way, the compost turned into healthy garden soil. It celebrated the circle of life, growing things and preparing them and sending them on to their next life where they would . . . grow things.

Come spring, no matter how careful we were, when we set out to process the cooked side, we'd find all manner of unintentional objects in the siftings: table forks and wooden spoons and paring knives and stubbornly unbroken-down avocado pits and bits of eggshell and the chomped ends of corncobs, and those nasty little oval fruit stickers that do not disintegrate, ever. The odd bit of foil, tough wads of newspaper, ornery walnut shells, a supermarket's worth of plastic ties, mesh bags that once held lemons, and peach pits, polished by the winter. All these accidental ingredients appeared, no matter how well we tried to separate them out.

What did we intentionally compost? Tea bags and coffee grounds; butt ends of bread. Never meat. Two flats' worth of strawberry stems left over from June's preserve-making frenzy. I'd feel less guilty paring away the root ends of Patty's greens, knowing they'd feed next year's tomatoes. Rose prunings, witch hazel fronds long past their wan yellow bloom, bracts of smoke bush, spent lilac blossoms, and the daffodils that didn't make it through the week. Cardboard egg cartons, raked leaves, the occasional grass clippings. Never weeds. Blossom ends from the bushel of red peppers that went into relish. And potash-rich ashes from a season of hardwood charcoal grilling. Earthworms, dug from other garden beds, were carefully moved, pet-like, to do their good work in the cooking compost. Lemon peels and corn husks and pea pods and nibbled rinds of watermelon. Never thick branches. End-of-season Cherokee Purple and Black Krim and Green Zebra tomato plants, their seductive promise now reduced to spent vines and roots, to which dirt clung still (earth to earth), and frost-killed yellow crookneck squashes and cucumbers, all furled leaves and snaky vines, back to the soil from which they grew. Clumps of Mulch Master, the seedless straw mulch that worked only sometimes. Clipped stems of woody herbs like rosemary and pineapple sage. And sorrel and lemon verbena leaves left too long on the plant, victims of an early frost. Never cooked food. This was not, after all, a garbage pail, but a living salad, and the parings of hundreds of meals and the end of the garden. Left there to cook all winter, compost is probably the best stew I've ever made.

TO MAKE THE ACTUAL GARDEN to hold that compost, I dove into garden history, spending hours researching in the library at the Hort (the Horticultural Society of New York). After publishing stories about some of the best gardens in the world (not the most grand but the best thought-out), I knew needed a plan. As I wrote in a *Garden Design* editor's page, "I've learned the hard way that no matter how many glorious specimens you plunge into the ground, you will never have anything that looks like a garden until you design something that looks like a garden." I knew the limitations of my space. I was, for once, determined to be realistic about weekend time constraints. I knew what I loved to grow, and I had an idea in my mind about the way I wanted the garden to look. Poring over lush pages of garden books from around the world, my heart was stopped, frequently, by the small, overflowing French *jardins de curé*, the little curate's garden plots beside small country churches. They seemed to have everything I wanted: a tumbled combination of vegetables and herbs, tamed by geometric structure and modest size.

On graph paper (the Octagon still in my mind), I drew a plan for the Brick Garden: sixteen feet square, with four corner beds delineated by the same old bricks from the Octagon; a center rectangular plot just big enough for six ten-foot bamboo poles tied at the top like a teepee, and underplanted with nasturtiums. On that teepee, I'd grow the decorative scarlet runner beans I'd seen at Thomas Jefferson's Virginia plantation, Monticello. We enclosed the garden with four-foot-high green wire fencing, stapled to cedar posts. We searched on-line for an unprepossessing gate and found a waist-high gal-vanized metal number with a playful fifties curlicue on top. Made in Indiana, it looks just like the kind of gate you'd forget to close in your grandmother's garden, if you had a grand-mother with a garden. Or a gate.

The triumph of hope over experience is my perpetual definition of gardening, and the Brick Garden was no differ-ent. Seeds poked into warming ground in early spring could be terminally snowed on before the week was out. Tender plants were at the mercy of rabbits and groundhogs; that is, until we peeled back the lawn three feet on each side and laid down gnaw-proof chicken wire attached to the surrounding fence so critters couldn't dig under it (an exercise that took about 100,000 times longer than writing this sentence). After the tomato plants were installed on their loopy but effective circular wire frames, in would go a flat of basil plants and another of the old-fashioned Queen Sophia marigolds, prized for their intense jewel-like color and bug-repellant qualities. I unwisely tried cardoons (they're thugs), had a fling with exotic pepper plants (it took the whole summer to produce a scant handful), and loved growing small eggplants, and okra plants with their bashful yellow flowers with deep-set smoky eyes. Exotic Cavaillon melons were a bust. I grew the herbs that you never see in those expensive plastic super-market coffins, like savory and lovage and bronze fennel and angelica.

As delusional as it was, for decades, I was a weekend gar-dener, every Friday night grabbing a flashlight and heading out into the gardens to check on the changes that week had inevitably brought. Whole chapters could (and did) happen in the five days a week I spent in the city, pushing words and pictures around on pages.

One of the first things I planted in the new garden were fava beans for Anita Lo. I filled a whole quadrant with the Windsor seeds I tried to remember to order from Johnny's in late winter so I could get them in the ground when the weather was still cool enough and in time for a July Fourth harvest—before it became so hot for those super-tall, small-leaved plants that they, too, would become compost. When the seeds arrived, I'd dutifully soak them overnight in the inoculant I ordered to encourage the growth of beneficial nitrogen nodules on their roots.

Before then, the only favas I knew were the broad beans served at Ruth Rogers's dreamlike River Café in London, on the rare occasion Christopher and Colman and I could slip into town on the way to or from producing a story. There, favas were mashed on good toast with sea salt, or, shucked, barely steamed, and twice-peeled, bright green and precious, scattered on a salad with shaved Parmigiano and green olive oil. Anita showed us another way with favas that avoided the tedious double peeling of those little beans; she'd brush the whole pods with olive oil and throw them on the grill till they were suitably blackened. We popped open the pods with our teeth and teased out the warmed beans—the perfect companions to a chilled glass of wine. Then she gave me another reason to grow those majestically tall, ant-covered plants. Turns out Anita loves the *leaves* of fava bean plants, first sautéing a bit of garlic and anchovy in oil in a skillet and then quickly tossing in the fava leaves. Delish!

I LOOK AT THE BUNDLE of leek sets I hold in my hand—maybe
sixty teeny plants—with a combination of marvel and doubt;
incredulous that these miniature versions of themselves, these
spaghetti-thin plants with fronds as slim as chives and delicate threadlike roots, these tender little green-and-white leek-
lings, would ever, could ever grow a hundred times their size
in just 150 days.

I'd search the seed catalogs for leek sets (there's never time
enough for seeds), which had to be of the French variety, Bleu
de Solaize (sometimes Solaise), whose origins I trace to a town
on the Rhône, south of Lyon, along the Autoroute du Soleil.
Solaize is not far from the garden my stepdaughter Sandrine's
grandmother Mamie Mimi and her husband, Georges, grew
there. I once photographed Georges, tanned in a white-ribbed
undershirt, triumphantly waving over his head a humongous
ur-leek, fronds unfurled and dirt still clinging to its roots. It's
not easy to get an image like that out of your head.

Solaize takes its leeks seriously. Its brotherhood (which in-
cludes women, too), the Confrérie du Bleu de Solaize—a leek
lay clergy, really—wears leek-green capes over full-length
leek-white robes. Members are inducted into the society by a
ceremonial tap on the left shoulder with a four-foot leek scep-
ter. Holding high their leek-emblazoned crests, the Confrérie
marches in an annual leek parade, with green-and-white ribbons around their necks dangling fat leek-embossed medals
that bounce on their chests as they walk.

As soon as my leek sets arrive, with no bouncy medal or green capelet, I take my leeks just as seriously, poking holes with a pencil to plant the most fragile sets, using a dibble for the sturdier ones. Carefully placing one set in each hole, then sprinkling fine soil in after it, I gently water the plants. And pray. But these French leeks always surprise me with their tenacity, eventually growing into their full and majestic blue-green height on pure white columns. They are among the proudest of my garden accomplishments.

Until I grew them, I never knew why David Tanis was always so finicky about washing leeks; then I discovered how much of the soil they grow in takes up residence within their fronds. So wash them well I do. David showed me to make an elegant, super-green leek soup: a rich puree of a half dozen leeks, whites and pale greens wilted in butter, then cooked down with rice and good chicken broth and, when cooled, pureed with—and this is genius—raw spinach leaves. A fine way to properly honor those leeks. I always make sure to leave enough leeks in the ground long past frost to make, for Thanksgiving, the poireaux vinaigrette Sandrine loves, hoping she'll notice them.

WE MAY HAVE BEEN A bit guilty of taking this living-off-the-land thing a tad close to insufferable with a summer dinner we made for our friends who'd come from East Hampton. They never let us forget that dinner, kept asking how we managed to keep all the cows in our backyard to make the cheese, and where, in fact, were the grapes we grew for the wine?

ALL-EMO DINNER FOR FRIENDS

❧

Mojitos (with spearmint underplanting the apple tree)

Fried Zucchini Squash Blossoms (ours)

Lincoln's Gougères

Grilled Red Pepper Purée

❧

Mussels Hand-Gathered from Moriches Bay, Steamed

Moriches Bay Bluefish Wrapped in Fig Leaves (ours)

❧

Sliced Heirloom Tomatoes with Thyme

Steamed Russian Banana Peppers

Hakurei Turnips with Their Greens

❧

French Cheeses with House-Made Gooseberry Preserves
and Currant Jelly

Our Backyard Pears Poached with Lemon Verbena

A Handful of Raspberries and the Occasional Blackberry

❧

I'd get these swoony, teenage crushes on fruit trees. I had
an intense, but sadly brief, flirtation with a pair of dwarf nec-
tarines, and two irresistible mirabelle plum trees, but nothing
came close to the drama of the quince tree. I caught my first
glimpse of *Cydonia oblonga* in the medieval garden at the Met
Cloisters in northern Manhattan's Fort Tryon Park. There's
something about the scale of a quince—it is voluptuous yet

contained, not too tall, wide where a tree should be wide, all graceful arms and a lovely slim trunk. At the Cloisters, four such trees, each in the center of its own quarter of the garden, are underplanted with a rich carpet of herbs so lush it might have leapt from one of the seven Unicorn Tapestries that hang on the museum's walls just inside.

Having a quince tree of my own became a bit of an obsession. Unlike most obsessions, this was neither expensive nor, as it turned out, too difficult to satisfy. In fact, one of the premier fruit tree growers on Long Island, and among the country's best practitioners of the art of espalier, that elegant pruning of branches that turns fruit trees into prolific producers—and elegant sculpture—lived just at the end of our road. You can keep your diamonds; espaliered fruit trees are the jewels I crave. When a chef friend gave me a taste of his Alabama grandfather's quince preserves—just peeled and quartered fruit gently cooked down in sugar syrup—that was all it took. Quince preserves became a fall compulsion, a Thanksgiving necessity. I made my own from farmers' market fruit before I grew quince, always trying to recapture the flavor and texture of that first taste. The tree was beautifully planted, and for a year, maybe two, there was fruit. Not a lot, but enough for a couple of jars. That was before the dread cedar-apple rust set in. A fungus that, as its name implies, thrives when those trees (or their near relations) live in close proximity, cedar-apple rust has a sinister way of attacking the leaves and turning them brown, stunting the fruit and rendering it inedible. As with many things in life, I got to have my tree, but not eat from it.

CHAPTER 10

THE IMMIGRANTS' PANTRY

WHAT IF THE EIGHTEEN-YEAR-OLD MIKE Solomonov, walking dejectedly down Weizmann Street in K'far Saba, a suburb north of Tel Aviv where his American mother lived and taught English, still pissed off after yet another battle with his Israeli dad, and desperate for a job, and instead of stumbling into a bakery—and after an eternity of scrubbing baking trays (his first Hebrew words were "sheet pan") and painfully learning to make the tricky, layered, puff pastry–like boreka dough to wrap around a filling of potatoes, or mushrooms, or cheese (in the process reigniting his memory of making borekas with his Bulgarian grandmother, his Savta Mati), and through borekas finding a way into the cooking of Israel, then taking that passion to Philadelphia, where he would meet his business partner, Steven Cook, and thereby share his love of Israeli food with America—what if Mike had instead continued down the block past that bakery and happened upon, say, an auto repair shop, where they agreed to take him on?

Surely he would have mastered the subtleties of stripping down the engine of a Škoda, the boxy, cheap Czech can opener of a car that everyone in Israel drove in those days, rebuilding and souping it up instead of mastering the subtleties of flaky pastry dough. Maybe, if Mike had walked on past that bakery, instead of wrapping our minds around borekas and perfecting our own personal versions of 5-Minute Hummus, we'd all be driving hot Czechoslovakian muscle cars.

This is what I'm thinking as Roger and I sit in Merkaz, one of Mike and Steve's eight distinct Philadelphia-based CookNSolo restaurant brands (including a bakery/restaurant called K'Far, which means "village," that makes, yes, killer borekas). Merkaz, meaning "center," is a deceptively simple neighborhood sandwich shop in a classy, glassy space in Center City. Like the best kinds of simplicity, there's a world in the sandwich I'm eating. It's called sabich, and it's a purse, really—a hollow round of pita, charred in spots, and sliced open only at the top. Stuffed and still warm in my hands, it feels like a living thing. Peeking inside, I see crisp shards of purple cabbage, cubes of green cucumber, and red tomato chunks, nuzzled against rounds of browned, fried eggplant. Nibbling, I discover slices of hard-boiled egg, and that the whole is held together by thick, tangy tahini and something oozy and golden that can only be amba, the pickled mango sauce whose flavor—piquant and mellow at the same time—I have come to revere.

As I catch myself in this meditation on a rainy Sunday in a sandwich shop in Philadelphia, I realize that before I met Mike and Steve, I would have had no bloody idea what I held in my hand—this stuffed pita, its exquisite combination of crunch and creaminess. Much as I might, as a casual customer, admire this sandwich, I could never have identified it as sabich. Nor could I have easily named its signature ingredients, or confidently traced its Iraqi origins. I could never have appreciated its journey—how sabich became incontrovertibly Israeli, or even how it came to be a sandwich at all.

I NEVER WANTED TO GO to Israel. There was that long-vanished maternal grandmother; there was the government's position on Palestine; there was the way ultra-Orthodox Jews treat women. Send me anywhere in Europe instead. Then, our friend Joan Nathan, the distinguished cookbook writer (anthropologist, really), invited Roger, as a documentary filmmaker, to join her on a food tour of Israel. Never having been, he was curious—and returned smitten, with the country, its emerging food scene, the energy of its agriculture, the freshness and variety of its ingredients. He was surprised to find a range of culinary influences from across the Middle East and North Africa; he was taken with the warmth and worldly charisma of Israel's chefs, who were turning to their ethnic heritage (and not just Europe) for their inspiration. He decided to make a film, *In Search of Israeli Cuisine.* When he announced that intention to American audiences, he'd get a laugh; people pictured their grandparents' bad Ashkenazi cooking (chicken boiled to within an inch of its life, gluey kugel, leaden challah). He took that laughter as a good sign: here was a fresh story to tell. I was still lukewarm. Anxious, I googled Iron Dome, the vaunted Israeli air defense system.

After more research and preliminary filming, Roger decided he needed an American personality who knew both countries to help focus the film. He asked around, and when he got to Lior Lev Sercarz, the Israeli-born, French-trained spice blender to the stars (chefs), Lior advised: "If you want the best Israeli food in America, you've got to go to Philadelphia, to Zahav, and meet Mike Solomonov."

I still have the menu from that January dinner, where I scribbled Mike's name with two *f*s instead of the one *v*—the last time I made that mistake (though others habitually and maddeningly persist in mispronouncing his name, even from the awards stage!). That night, in meeting Mike and hearing his story, Roger found the core to build his film around. Something quite different happened to me in Philly, and I remember it almost like a dream. Out of a bitter cold night, we walk into the warm world of Zahav. Angels might as well have been singing. The restaurant is a vast, windowed room on a hill, bustling kitchen life just visible behind glass panes, its floor paved with dappled stones that glow golden, like those in the courtyards of Jerusalem's Old City; golden like the meaning of the very word *zahav*. We walk into candlelight that made everything instantly feel, well, chosen. We are seated, and immediately a plate of creamy hummus arrives, a familiar food with an unfamiliar lush texture and depth of flavor. This hummus—chickpeas mellowed by their partnership with an exemplary tahini that makes all the difference, I come to learn—is warm-ish, served on a plate with Mike's signature swoosh, a central well made with the back of a big spoon, all the better to cradle its toppings (in the book *Israeli Soul*, we showed twenty-four of them). To "wipe" the hummus, as they do in Israel, we are offered hot laffa, a crisp and pocketless flatbread, its surface charred and bubbled from the heat of the live fire in the restaurant's taboon oven, manned by Mike.

From that first dish, there is generosity on that table. With the hummus comes salatim—four examples of the infinite number of salads the Middle East is known for: charred, mashed eggplant; pan-roasted green beans with Aleppo pepper; kale tabbouleh with lots of mint; and cumin-scented Moroccan carrots. I experience a different flavor with every bite. We choose small plates from the mezze that follow: sweetbreads with passion-fruit amba; grilled duck hearts with date tahini; and a surprising inch-thick slab of browned challah with a fried egg in the middle, topped with house-smoked sable. And these are not even the main courses. For those, as in every grill restaurant in Israel, you choose a dish cooked over charcoal: merguez—ground lamb sausage with sour cherry preserves, or spiced eggplant with harissa, or salmon shashlik on couscous, or chicken wings with Moroccan-spiced chermoula sauce.

How does one chef master such a vast range of ingredients? I ask Mike when, eventually, he sits down with us. "You came during restaurant week!" he laughs, suggesting that we ain't tasted nothing yet. Surprisingly young, with a salt-and-pepper crew cut, he calls us "Bro," interchangeably. Far from my mind that night were thoughts of ever cooking this food—its flavors so mysterious, its ingredients so worldly. Skipping the chitchat, Mike turns instantly serious, telling us how, as a young chef in Philadelphia, working in the kitchens of the best restaurants, mastering fine Italian and French cooking, he found his mission to reinvent Israeli food for America when his younger brother, David, was killed by Hezbollah snipers on the Lebanese border, on Yom Kippur, on his last night of duty in the Israeli army. Mike's eyes grow dark with memories, then brighten with excitement as he describes how food in Israel today is alive with old ingredients and new flavors, deep history and cutting-edge agronomy. He tells us that every day, he finds new inspiration to cook this food.

Mike gets up from the table and returns to the taboon—that iconic oven, fired by compressed hardwood, whose chimney is part of the architecture of the dining room and opens into it, is strategically placed at the end of the kitchen next to the stone pass, where the chef can stay in touch with his cooks, kibitz with his servers, hug his guests, and still keep his hands on the laffa dough, flattening slabs and flinging them against the fiery taboon's inside walls. And even all these years later, with eight restaurant brands and every award the industry can bestow, standing behind that counter making laffa at Zahav remains Mike's happy place. After Mike left, Roger looked up from his plate and said, "I think I've found my guy!"

EVENTUALLY, OF COURSE, I DID go to Israel. The first time it was with Roger to scout locations for his film, the kind of traveling I like best, moving fast with an agenda, like doing a *Saveur* story, hitting dozens of potential places each day, covering the length of a country the size of New Jersey. One evening at sunset, we were in the north, driving through gentle hills of ancient olive groves to the Druze hill town Daliyat al-Karmel. "Stop!" I cried, jumping out into the wild landscape and wrapping my arms around the expressive trunk of one of those venerable olive trees. "I have to apologize to Israel," I told Roger. "All these years, I've romanticized olive trees in the south of Italy, or France, or Spain. Where did I think they came from? *They came from here!* These are the original olive trees; biblical olive trees. From Palestine. These trees have witnessed civilizations."

Sometime during the production of the film, Mike came to New York to work with Roger and stuck his head in my office: "How'd you like to produce a book with Steve and me? Steve's a great writer." My heart rose and sank at the same time. As an editor, I have learned that exactly nobody's business partner is a great writer, especially an investment banker with a degree from Wharton. But I did recognize the potential of a definitive cookbook about Zahav's contemporary Israeli food. "Great," I managed. "Send me some samples." (I'll use this parenthetical aside to explain that Steve had graduated from the French Culinary Institute *while* he was working in finance in New York, then returned to Philadelphia to open his own restaurant, Marigold Kitchen, where he eventually hired Mike as chef. It didn't hurt that Steve's wife, Shira, knew Mike; his mother had been her English teacher growing up in Pittsburgh's Squirrel Hill neighborhood.)

A manuscript arrived from Steve that chronicled the trip he and Mike had taken to Israel with their six-cook team on the eve of opening Zahav. It was called *Johnny Borekas*, the fond nickname the multiethnic kitchen workers gave Mike in that K'far Saba bakery, and it was written in Mike's voice. "By this point in the day, my staff is practically begging for mercy. It's true we haven't slept for over twenty-four hours, but you know who else didn't sleep much? My grandmother, my Savta Mati, on the boat from Bulgaria in 1948, that's who!" The only explanation for why Steve turned out to be such a heartfelt, elegant writer is the obvious one: he thinks heartfelt and elegant thoughts. And, as it happens, he can cook, too. Just as Mike has whip-smart business instincts, Steve has his moves in a restaurant kitchen. Partnership!

Once, while Mike and Steve and I were meeting with a prospective publisher about the Zahav book, she asked them each to name a quality that best described his partner. Steve immediately nailed Mike: "Generosity!" After years of observing Mike interact with people, *disarming* is the word I'd choose. Humor is his first instinct—his opening move disarms a stranger by relaxing them into laughter, putting them instantly at ease. In this way Mike, an utterly soulful and serious man, passes through his days with laughter, managing his increasingly higher profile with grace.

YOU KNOW HOW IT IS when the cool kids use a word you don't know. You hear it without understanding it and try not to feel dumb. Then, gradually, as you make connections, a sense of its meaning dawns on you. Hesitatingly, you begin use it, too, and eventually and after a while, you come to own it. It was like that with harif, and schug, and amba, and harissa, and tehina. For me, these were musical sounds that didn't become foodstuffs until I understood how they were used. As soon as I'd tasted them, I learned them. My respect for Mike and Steve grew as we worked together—and gratitude not just for what they've brought into my life but also for what they've brought into my kitchen.

It is touching to sift through file boxes and remember that only a few years ago, when I began research for *Zahav* (and despite the popularity of Yotam Ottolenghi's bestselling

Jerusalem), tahini, to most people, was that oily, sticky sludge in a can in the back of the refrigerator that you bought once for a recipe that time forgot. Anything but fresh. Anything but food. Hummus, too, was insipid, an overly garlicky (and often rancid), peanut butter–like dip, sealed in plastic tubs and sold in supermarkets. This was deracinated food, as disconnected from its origins as it was from the true flavors of its ingredients. When *Zahav* was published, its hummus recipe became instantly famous. "The secret to creamy hummus is overcooked chickpeas," the book proclaimed. Everybody was madly soaking dried chickpeas overnight with a bit of baking soda, then cooking them for hours before blending them with tahini. I used to think hummus was all about the chickpeas. Wrong! It's good tahini that makes good hummus.

Producing *Zahav* meant learning so much more than new flavor profiles. I believed we had to present Mike's food in a way that paid homage to its roots but made it accessible to modern cooks. I'd like to be able to say that I always knew how important this book would be, but the truth is that, like my appreciation for Israel itself, it took some time. In order to be definitive, the book had to demystify unfamiliar spices and herbs and sauces and show how they deliver authenticity to a dish; how these new/old substances could be the foundation of a whole other way to cook——one whose flavors are so old they seem familiar. The book had to engage and stimulate readers, not confuse them with head-spinningly strange ingredients. First, I had to convince myself, which meant getting into learning mode, figuring out how to present the singular ingredients and flavors in a way that would encourage readers to adopt them and take them home.

The list was long. I kept reminding myself that in my

early cooking days, I had to learn rosemary, and thyme, and tarragon—all the herbs, really, that today I reach for automatically. Sesame seeds are the new thyme (or more accurately, the old one). It was not enough to concentrate on tahini (or tehina, in Hebrew), the ubiquitous sesame paste made from those seeds that's a foundation of both savory and sweet Israeli cooking. I had to take a step farther back. "Where do sesame seeds come from?" I asked friends who should know. "How do they grow?" I got blank looks. For *Zahav* to be a definitive book, we had to demystify sesame seeds; they had to be understood as more than sprinkles on a bagel or a hamburger bun. We devoted a two-page spread to photos of the graceful, tall, leafy plants and their pods that, when dried, pop open to reveal neat rows of tiny seeds (hence "Open sesame!"). Sesame seeds come in white and black; it's the white ones that are pressed into tahini.

The best sesame seeds, those that make the finest tehina in Israel, I learned on a shoot with Roger at the Al Arz plant in Nazareth, are called humira, and are trucked overland from Ethiopia in burlap sacks as heavy as a man. The tahini I used to know in all its oily permutations was most likely made from inferior seeds from India or China; I never appreciated just how much its provenance—where those sesame seeds are grown, and how they're handled—matters. Not until I experienced Israeli tehina and discovered its universal power in everything from dressings for salads to lovely, crumbly cookies could I fully appreciate the protean potential of humble sesame seed paste. Now I understand that tahini makes up fully half the content of good hummus, and that the quality of the sesame seeds the tahini is made from determines the lilt of its flavor and freshness.

The tahini that CookNSolo use in all their restaurants is made in Israel from those same Ethiopian humira sesame seeds by an American company called Soom (launched by three delightful sisters from Philadelphia) and sold at soom foods.com. The easy availability of good tahini was crucial to making it feasible to cook Israeli food in American kitchens. By the time we produced the book *Israeli Soul*, Mike and Steve had perfected the recipe for 5-Minute Hummus we live on today: excellent tahini, just a nick of garlic, a pinch of cumin, salt, a squeeze or two of lemon juice, ice water, and two cans of good (read organic) chickpeas. Piece of cake.

WHEN I REFLECT ON HOW my pantry has evolved, what I consider essential today, the cooking me of a decade ago would not even recognize the spices and sauces and condiments I regularly depend on to enliven my meals. Ingredients from the everyday Israeli kitchen are now staples in mine, too. And not only when I'm cooking Israeli food. I turn to labneh, the silky, tart, strained yogurt—with lower fat and better flavor—that comes in a tub, any time I'd use sour cream. Soom's tahini, which of course goes into hummus, I use, too, in salad dressings and sauces for chicken and vegetables, and for making Zahav's Tahini Shortbread Cookies. I use Soom's date molasses, an ancient sweetener called silan, like maple syrup, in baked beans and drizzled on pancakes. And ice cream.

Paula Wolfert turned me on to pomegranate molasses as the secret ingredient in the smoky red pepper and walnut dip muhammara in her book *The Cooking of the Eastern Mediterranean*. (Eastern Mediterranean, I later realized, is a euphemism for the Middle East, with the emphasis on water and diet rather than sand and strife.) Israel, I discovered, is all about pomegranates. Orchards of them roll over hillsides, and if you're lucky enough to be there when the trees are in fruit, there is no lovelier sight. Street corners are crowded with fruit sellers who'll instantly press the red globes into a glass of fresh pomegranate juice. Pomegranate molasses is the secret ingredient in Zahav's iconic lamb shoulder, a dish that helped put the restaurant on the map. Making the lamb shoulder involves brining that important chunk of meat overnight, then smoking it (if feasible), and then braising it in pomegranate molasses and water for up to 5 hours. I keep a bottle of pomegranate molasses in the fridge (the bottle needs a warm bath to soften its flow) and use it in a dressing for citrus salads, a glaze for roasted salmon, and, always, in muhammara. Pomegranate molasses became important as I researched *Israeli Soul*. I learned to pour the bittersweet syrup into dishes like Persian meatballs, and into stuffed grape leaves with pomegranate juice and date molasses.

Baharat was not a spice blend I knew, but when Mike seasoned chicken livers with the warm and fragrant combination of cinnamon, allspice, and nutmeg, I could not believe its depth. Mike likes to call it "the pumpkin pie spice." Now I use baharat in everything from chocolate chip cookies to sautéed rice. And PS: It's the secret ingredient in Federal Donuts' master donut batter! I've long bought za'atar flatbread, but now I'll rub a whole chicken all over with handfuls of that wild, herby oregano, sumac, and sesame seed mix (plus a bit of olive oil) before I roast it, drunk on the fragrance za'atar develops in the oven.

Pickles are essential on the Israeli table, and I love to make the pickled vegetables—cauliflower florets, sliced celery, and carrots—they serve at Zahav. This is a ridiculously simple boil of vegetables in an overnight bath of vinegar, sugar, turmeric, and a shot of schug (that strong, chile pepper–based condiment that tastes like a firecracker and sounds like a sneeze). Schug comes in a bottle and in spice packets. At Zahav, schug is made by processing together two dozen shiny serrano chiles, big bunches of parsley and coriander, garlic, cardamom and coriander seeds, lemon juice and salt.

I could go on about the pickled mango sauce called amba (and already have; *see* sabich). In *Zahav*, Mike showed us another way to use it—as a marinade for grilled chicken. This is a showstopper. Sometimes I make the marinade by pureeing amba (Galil, from a jar) with chopped onions and canola oil; other times I just smear half a jar of Kalustyan's Mango Chile Pickle on the chicken and marinate it overnight. I consider harissa, the North African red pepper sauce, the new ketchup. Fermented or fresh, harissa adds a spicy, red-peppery depth I did not know I craved. Sometimes I make my own from the recipes in *Israeli Soul*; sometimes I buy a jar from the Middle Eastern food purveyor New York Shuk. They also make a version with preserved lemon, another signature condiment I prize, salting and curing Meyer lemons when they're in season. And now I always have harif, the ubiquitous Israeli hot sauce in a bottle, with its peppery sting, on my table.

PRODUCING *ZAHAV* WAS A SPECIAL kind of circus. Figuring out how to make something that looked convincingly like a home kitchen in the vast Zahav restaurant space was its own challenge. The daylight from those huge windows was gorgeous;

the proximity to Zahav's kitchen, crucial. But that dining room looks not remotely like home. For readers to believe they could cook these mostly unfamiliar recipes, we had to make our set itself believable. Our team was small. Mike Persico, a Philadelphia-based photographer whom Mike and Steve had worked with for years, quickly made a partner of Don Morris, our design director. Don and I would take an early train from New York and head to the restaurant, where we'd meet up with Mike and Steve and Mike. Our first act was to lug slabs of super-heavy fire bricks from somewhere in the recesses of the kitchen out into the dining room. Stacking them up to a counter height that looked reasonably home-kitchen-like, we'd lay a tabletop over the bricks, plug in a portable burner, and station Mike behind that faux counter so we could photograph every step of his process as he cooked each recipe.

Our plates and other props were stashed between shoots deep in a cupboard in a back dining room; every day, I'd dig them out and spread them on the surrounding restaurant tables. We photographed each dish from the ingredients up, figuring out its signature flavors and methods, recording the meaning and construction of each recipe, step by intriguing step, learning them just the way our readers would. Then, around 3:00 p.m., as soon as the clink of glasses signaled the setting up of Zahav's bar, we'd make the set disappear and be out of the restaurant just in time for it to turn back into a dining room bustling with prep for the evening service.

PRODUCING ZAHAV WAS A GRADUATE course in Israeli cooking. Eggplant? I thought I knew eggplant. For decades, I've made the Provençal specialty petits farcis, diminutive vegetables stuffed with . . . themselves, and other chopped vegetables; I've blackened my share of football-size cudgels on a grill till they almost collapsed and mashed them with tahini and lemon juice for baba ghanoush; I've mastered grilling lovely slim Japanese eggplants and slicking their tops with sweet miso. But Mike taught me that just when I thought my eggplant was cooked was when I needed to cook it even more.

For his twice-cooked eggplant, you cook the slices three times, in fact, if you count the half-hour salting and the subsequent draining on paper towel stage as the first one. Mike fries the slices till they're almost black in a skillet with lots of olive oil, giving the eggplant a "rich, deep, almost chocolaty flavor," then removes them from the pan. Next, adding more olive oil to the skillet, he cooks down chopped red pepper, onion, coriander, and paprika until they're soft, then returns the cooked eggplant to the pan with 1/2 cup of sherry vinegar and mashes it all together. This now-chunky puree is removed to a plate, squirted with lemon juice, and sprinkled with parsley. That, my friends, is eggplant cooked Solomonov-style. Nobody said flavor came easy.

Even better than Mike's twice-cooked eggplant is his whole eggplant grilled over coals. Of course, the wood's fragrant smoke matters—that flavor is inseparable from Israeli cooking. Mike equates beach barbecues, on those little portable grills you can buy at gas stations everywhere, and the browning that results from the intense heat of their charcoal fires with a near spiritual Israeli flavor. Which is exactly what's missing from the now-ubiquitous gas-powered grills, which, with the bling of their heavy metal chassis and the spin of a tricky valve, seem to signify power at your fingertips. Heat? Sure! Flavor, not so much.

Brining helps; slitting the whole eggplant to let salted water soak into its flesh, even as long as overnight. Drained, the eggplant is set over the coals for a half hour until it becomes soft and creamy. It's a good idea to grill some cherry tomatoes alongside. And then. And then! The grilled eggplant, skin side down, is opened on a plate. Labneh is spooned over the top, followed by those grilled tomatoes, some basil, maybe a few pine nuts. You can keep your boneless rib-eyes.

Even more about eggplant: Mike advises peeling the whole vegetable in alternating stripes before slicing it, especially for the crispy cornstarch-coated slices you need to make sabich. Besides looking cool, the striping leaves just enough of the skin to hold the slice together without the skin slipping off like a shoelace into the pan.

COMING DOWN FROM THE MOUNTAINTOP that was *Zahav*, we careened into its polar opposite, *Federal Donuts: The (Partially) True Spectacular Story*, a slim and whimsical volume that told the story of the boys' improbable and groundbreaking entry into the donut business. For the Fed Nuts book, we (okay, they) figured out how to make every one of their donuts (and their Korean fried chicken recipe) at home. To show how to make the donuts, I acquired the famous KitchenAid stand mixer. Full disclosure: I have not made donuts since. But you can. Really! I did learn, however, the secret to the incomparably crispy Korean chicken (fry it twice!). Federal Donuts now has nine locations, including one at the Phillies' ballpark.

But Mike was restless. (Mike's resting state is restless.) Yes, *Zahav*, the book, was the definitive guide to his interpretation of American Israeli food, but Mike knew there was more to tell. He wanted to revisit *Israeli* Israeli food—the soulful food he loves—food whose roots go back generations to the ingredients and cooking methods brought to that country by settlers from hundreds of cultures around the world. Understanding Israeli street food, he contended, was essential to understanding the complexity of the country. But people don't want to cook street food, some of us argued. They want *other people* to cook it, and then to be able to eat it at the very instant the aromas catch their nostrils; they want immediate gratification.

Mike persisted. What, he asked, about the unique cooks who perfect just one special thing—say, shawarma, or falafel, or Jerusalem grill, or that sabich with its Iraqi roots, or chirshi (Libyan squash salad), or khachapuri (Georgian cheese-filled bread)? Those cooks have one specialty, Mike insisted. Their *thing*. And through repetition, making that thing and only that, decade after decade, he contends, they achieve perfection. Such cooks influenced Mike and Steve infinitely more than the flashy Israeli chefs who get lots of press. But Steve makes an excellent point in the introduction to *Israeli Soul*, the book devoted to their passion for street food: "This food would remain relevant only as long as it was delicious."

So, after we (and our publisher, the estimable Rux Martin) were convinced of the general rightness of the idea, we took off for Israel to produce *Israeli Soul*. Mike and Steve and Mike Persico, Don Morris, and me, a lean team on a small bus for ten days, traveling in a frenzy of high spirits and frequent nuttiness, stopping at eighty-one (eighty-one!) places: restaurants and roadside kiosks, storefronts and markets. We tasted, we photographed, we interviewed, and we took notes. Occasionally, we disagreed. "You liked that konafi [pastry made with shredded dough]? It was so sweet they served it with two glasses of water!"

With us, too, was Avihai Tsabari, a certified Israeli guide and advisor, wise beyond his years, with deep food and wine expertise, and the owner of his own boutique travel business, Via Sabra. Avihai had played the fixer role on Roger's film and had since become BFFs with Mike (I am no longer surprised by such things when it turns out that Mike's mother had been Avihai's transformative high school English teacher in K'Far Saba). Avihai is kind of an adorable history professor who can and will reveal on demand deep information on every village, building, and palm tree you pass; we quickly learned to be careful what we asked him. On this, my third trip to Israel, I kept feeling the jolt of Israeli tech as it bumps into the ancient past, sometimes on the same block. I am always aware of the sharp contrast between this hyper-wired country and the hole-in-the wall humility of the handmade food we sought.

I CAN STILL TASTE THE complexity of flavor and texture of sabich, that fried eggplant sandwich (my favorite is from Tchernichovsky, a sidewalk shop named for its street in Tel Aviv). It's the sandwich I rediscovered at Merkaz that rainy Sunday in Philly. Producing the recipes for *Israeli Soul*, I learn that the amba sauce that holds the sandwich together doesn't always mean pickled mango. Mike and Steve amplify that Indian-spiced sauce with a version made from apples and served with potato and leek latkes; and another based on strawberries—strawberry amba with deep-fried mushrooms. I prefer amba from a jar, but it comes in powdered form, too.

At home, I've figured out a knockout deconstructed version of sabich and serve it as a first course in wide, shallow bowls. First come a few leaves of crispy chicory, then several spoonfuls of Israeli salad—little cubed cukes and chunks of ripe tomatoes mixed with lots of fresh chopped mint and torn parsley leaves, dressed in olive oil and lemon juice. Leaning against the salad are two dark and crusty slices of crispy cornstarch-dusted and fried eggplant (their skin first peeled in strips). Then comes a neat row of hard-cooked eggs, sliced on an egg slicer, after an overnight in the oven—*hamin*, in Latin—which gives egg whites their signature haminados-style mottled brown color (a color sometimes cheated by hard boiling them in coffee water!). Then come a couple of slim and vinegary Israeli pickles (Galil, from a can), a generous swath of homemade 5-Minute Hummus, and several streaks of amba sauce. I scatter the salad with pomegranate seeds and serve warmed pitas on the side.

OPERA, IN HADERA, TOPS MIKE'S list of favorite places. It's his touchstone for Yemenite cooking. Years ago, he'd met the owner, Rachel Arcovi, already into her eighties, whose children and grandchildren now run the restaurant. The first time Mike tasted the deep flavor of Rachel's Yemenite soup, he begged her to tell him the source of its flavor. Rachel promptly filled a small jar with cumin, turmeric, and black pepper. And that is precisely how Mike literally carried the signature Yemenite spice blend called hawaij back to America.

I picture Rachel and her defining place in Mike's story every time I make Opera's bean soup. It starts and ends humble:

with boiled marrow bones (or chicken, or short ribs, or veal) for depth, fat white beans soaked overnight then cooked in tomato juice and flavored with serrano chiles, pimentón, and those iconic hawaij spices. That soup's aroma is a trip back to the restaurant, where great bowls of the stuff cover every tabletop, and surround a basket of freshly made breads: pita and laffa, the flaky, buttery malawach, and the dimpled Yemenite flat-pancake called lachuch.

I wouldn't exactly call it Yemeni night at our house, but when I do make Yemenite braised short ribs (which Steve describes as "sort of like upside-down Yemenite soup—it's the broth flavoring the meat, rather than the other way around"), I slow-cook the short ribs for a very long time in hawaij-scented broth until it's falling-off-the-bone soft and oh so fragrant. And while the short ribs braise, I make the lachuch batter and let it rise, then pour it into a skillet as if I were making pancakes. Lachuch is a funny bread. You cook it on one side only, till it dimples in the pan like an English muffin. It kind of tastes like one, too.

That packet of spices that Rachel gave Mike—hawaij—is traditionally joined on the Yemenite table by schug, the chile pepper–based condiment, as well as hilbeh, a soup thickener based on fenugreek (a maple syrup–flavored spice so strong that Mike claims he can tell, on a midnight flight home from Tel Aviv, which of his fellow passengers has had Yemenite soup for dinner).

These spice-forward flavors of Yemenite cooking seem inevitable considering that the country of Yemen, on the Arabian Sea, is directly on the spice route from India to the Middle East. Still, Yemen's outsize influence on Israeli cooking mystifies me—the Yemenites' culinary contributions far surpass their numbers, and their political power.

I asked Gil Hovav, a Yemenite-Israeli and well-known authority on Israeli food (and a character in Roger's film), how it is that one of the poorest countries on earth has made such a rich culinary contribution. He credits Yemenites' tenacity. "My family walked all the way from Yemen to Palestine [in the late nineteenth century], and when they finally got to Jerusalem, there was no money left. So poverty was no stranger. This is why Yemenite food is a Middle Eastern version of cucina povera: you make the most of humble ingredients: flour, water, salt, yeast, bones, and spices. For instance, idam—the Yemenite bouillabaisse—is made from heads and bones of fish that you can get for free in the market. There is even a Yemenite version of aspic or p'tcha (called ar'ar), that's made from fish bones, too."

Schug (aka zhoug and s'chug and endless other fanciful spellings) came alive for me in a story Lior Lev Sercarz (the spicemaster, chef, and owner of La Boîte, who turned Roger on to Mike so long ago) told me. "A New York chef asked me: 'What's up with schug?'" Lior begins. "'Well, schug is schug,' I answer. 'But why do you have to make it every day?' he asks. And I say schug is based on fresh ingredients that turn brown after a few days. 'What if we made a schug powder?' he suggests. And I say, 'Let's do it!' And that was the birth of Shabazi, the schug-based spice blend that I made and named for the seventeenth-century Jewish Yemenite poet Shalom Shabazi. But get this! Mike decides to use the Shabazi powder as seasoning for the fried chicken at Federal Donuts. And one Saturday morning, I'm sitting in Fed Nuts with my wife, and two construction workers walk in. One turns to the other and says: 'Dude, the Shabazi chicken is off the hook.' And I look at Lisa and say: 'I think I can retire. My mission on this planet is accomplished!'"

I order Shabazi N.38 from laboiteny.com, and that small container has indeed transformed a labor-intensive condiment into an easy-to-use spice blend I sprinkle on everything from scrambled eggs to the icy rim of a margarita glass.

I'VE ALWAYS BEEN SUSPICIOUS OF shawarma, those piled vertical stacks of sliced meat that turn, turn, turn all day and all night in street restaurant windows all over the world. How long has that meat *been* there? I wonder, instinctively distrusting it. And I am right to do so, I discover, interviewing Arik Rosenthal, chef/owner of HaKosem (the Magician) in Tel Aviv, whose informal restaurant makes arguably the best shawarma in Israel. Like many young chefs, Arik has classic culinary training, but instead of running a fine dining restaurant, he became inspired to take just the kind of street food Mike loves and make it the best it can be. "I would only eat shawarma in a handful of restaurants in Israel," he confides. "The quality is too uneven. Here, I have a guy who comes in at 6:30 a.m. every day to build our shawarma. We only use turkey legs. And then, only the *female* turkey legs—they're so much less muscular and more tender. We layer them with lamb fat, which melts as the meat turns." And shawarma doesn't have to be meat. In *Israeli Soul*'s Shawarma chapter, a whole head of cauliflower is brined in a pot of the book's Shawarma Spice Blend and water for a few hours; then a paste of the spices is rubbed over the head before it's roasted in a hot oven. What an excellent way to reimagine cauliflower and turn it into a meal.

IN HOD HASHARON, A SUBURB of Tel Aviv, Mike takes us to Kaduri, one of his favorite falafel places, a little blue kiosk on the sidewalk. We sample their unusually tiny and flavorful just-fried chickpea balls; they remind me of the falafel at Goldie, the boys' Philadelphia falafel joint. When he hears us speaking English, the owner is so excited, he pulls out a clipping from *New York* magazine naming his place among Israel's best. Mike laughs. Turns out he wrote the story!

Hussein Abbas, a Palestinian chef at El Babour, in Umm al-Famm in the Galilee, teaches us what's become, for me, a favorite summer obsession: forming spice-scented ground lamb (or veal or beef) kebabs around long cinnamon sticks, then laying them over glowing coals to grill. They're so fragrant you could eat the smoke!

Safed (or Tzfat or a dozen other spellings) is a village so old it is said to have been founded by a son of Noah. In this the highest city in the Galilee, snow is no stranger. Safed is the center of Jewish studies—the Kabbalah—so maybe I'm persuaded by its aura. Or perhaps it's the soft wind whispering through tall cedars that makes me light-headed, just the power of suggestion. But there's plenty of loud traffic, too, on the narrow street where we meet Zahava Lagziel in front of her startlingly funky storefront, Fricassee Zahava. (We love to name check the restaurant!) Her improbably tiny place has become known for its couscous, which she rolls by hand from semolina flour in a kitchen barely big enough to turn around in, and the vegetable tagine she serves on top of the couscous, in bowls on two rickety tabletops on the narrow sidewalk in front of her shop.

Zahava, a woman of a certain age in a flowered housedress and a crocheted cap, personifies the spirit of *Israeli Soul*. Her fricassee is not a French chicken stew. Rather, it's her native Tunisian version of salade niçoise on bread: tuna with preserved lemon, harissa, and the squash salad called chirshi. In her little kitchen, in addition to couscous, she even manages to bake the crusty baguette-like roll the sandwich is served on. "It's like a tuna hoagie from the imaginary Wawa on the Barbary Coast," Steve recalls. And as I stand on that sacred street, still heady from the flavors of Zahava's food, I smile at how tricked out Americans think their kitchens must be before they can even make dinner.

MOST OF OUR MEMORABLE PHOTOGRAPHS for *Israeli Soul* were made on location, but now we had to test the recipes against our memories, taste the flavors again, and get real with the finished food. And for that, dear God, we—Mike and Steve, and the whole production team—found ourselves crowding into an apartment (near Zahav, the restaurant), with its Fricasee Zahava–sized kitchen with only a small fridge, a half sink, and a dead-basic stove. Helping in that teeny kitchen was Andrew Henshaw (then executive chef at Zahav, not yet thirty but an old soul, and now head chef at CookNSolo's newest restaurant, Laser Wolf). Since *Israeli Soul* was emphatically *not* about restaurant food, the funky shooting setup worked for us. It made it clear that sure, you can make this food at home.

We used every available surface; production meant constant dishwashing and endless garbage runs. Mike cooked, Steve cooked, Andrew cooked. Caitlin McMillan, former chef at their falafel place, Goldie, and now head of their commissary, demonstrated green falafel—laden with vegetables and herbs—in a home food processor. Yehuda Sichel, then chef at the group's remarkable Abe Fisher, squeezed into that kitchen to make his enlightened versions of Ashkenazi Israeli soul; hello, smoked whitefish salad, silky chicken liver mousse, lithe cured trout, and crusty little rye breads. Watching Yehuda, I keep telling myself, *I can make this!* We photographed helpful preparation steps, demystified unfamiliar ingredients, and, of course, tasted the food—it was a connected loop. Paired with the atmospheric Israeli images we made on location, these finished food shots had the advantage of being true to our recipes. The message: "When you cook this dish at home, this is what it will look like."

MIKE ENTERED COOKING LITERALLY THROUGH the bakery door. It's part of who he is. He's a boxer, too (for exercise, not competition). Boxing is a perfect outlet for his coiled energy, and in baking, the two disciplines meet. Watching him roll dough with one of those long, tapered pins, I observe how he's light and balanced on the balls of his feet, always moving. He leans over the board—all focus, no tension. When he looks up and sees me watching him, he laughs. "It's all in the shoulders!" As he works, an illuminated manuscript's worth of tattoos— mostly food from the Bible—dance decorously up the muscles of both arms; there the pomegranates, there the figs, a tree branch of green olives, a pineapple, a sheaf of wheat, the coiling, sinuous snake. There the elephants. Elephants?

Mike is a gentle baker. As he makes borekas, his fingers are ever so lightly but deliberately on the roller. No tension. All that buttering and flouring; all that rolling and cutting and rolling again. All that kneading of the dough, and spreading of softened butter on the board, and then gentle folding of the dough into something resembling a sleeping bag and sliding it onto a tray and into the freezer. And more rolling and more spreading of butter and more sleeping-bag folds. Five distinct times. At fifteen-minute intervals. Do you know how much patience this takes? Imagine Mike's singular focus—his ability to keep his eyes on the prize of the eventual glorious crispy layers of the baked thing. Mike remembers his Bulgarian grandmother as he moves. "We didn't have a lot going for us; no common language. She made her borekas with margarine. In a toaster oven. It was her way of doing something for me. These borekas smell like her kitchen."

It would be lovely to report that after hours of watching Mike make borekas—preparing an array of their fillings (mushrooms, and greens, and mashed potatoes) and tenderly stuffing them into the pastry—and weeks taking notes and working with Mike Persico to capture the chef's every move, and after tasting the unbelievably flaky results and their always delicious fillings, I came to believe that I could follow his lead, that I could do that boreka thing with the dough. But I would be lying. I cannot. Watching Mike make borekas—and rugelach and challah, for that matter—is proof positive to me that making such dough is not for a girl who cowers before a box of Pepperidge Farm frozen puff pastry sheets. When it comes to being a baker, it turns out, I'd rather see than be one.

STEVE'S WORD *GENEROSITY* LEAPS INTO mind as we experience the bounty of the table at CookNSolo's newest Philly restaurant, Laser Wolf. Named for the butcher (Lazar Wolf) in *Fiddler on the Roof*, this is an American *shipudiya*, a big, informal grill where meats and fish and vegetables are cooked over coals while the exuberant rest of the meal—the hot flatbreads and the vegetable-centric salads, dazzling in their sheer abundance arrives at the table. This presentation is an Israeli tradition, a version of the bounty Roger and I experienced at that first dinner at Zahav, and that our book production group was served at Itzik HaGolol (Big Isaac), in Jaffa, where the pleasure of the table takes on new meaning: the entire tabletop is paved with great charred flatbreads, and platters of fire-roasted eggplant, and tomato-and-cucumber salads, and roasted peppers and hummus, and . . . It's a Persian carpet of vivid color, texture, and flavor. Worlds away from the finicky presentation of one lone white-rimmed oversize dinner plate with one tiny piece of protein, garnished by a lonely sprig of esoteric herb. This communal presentation is heaven for a platterist like me!

Back in Philadelphia, at Laser Wolf, more than a dozen salads appear on the table at once: hummus with fresh pita, kale baba ghanoush, braised fennel with orange, shaved cucumbers with harissa, shaved Brussels sprouts with hazelnuts and amba, Israeli pickles and Castelvetrano olives, eggplant and pepper relishes, white beans with peppers and tomato, sweet potato muhammara, dill and lentil tabbouleh, shipka peppers and pickled long hots, eggplant baba ghanoush, pumpkin chirshi. Then, the skewers you've ordered arrive from the grill: spicy lamb merguez sausages, chicken shaslik in guava marinade, Romanian beef kebabs, Tunisian tuna with harissa glaze, mushrooms with pine nut tahini, and whole branzino stuffed Palestinian-style, with ginger, caraway, and Aleppo pepper.

This is just the way I want to cook; the way I want to serve food to my friends and family. It is uncomplicated food, made delicious by the imagination, the ingredients, the spices, and the preparations I've learned from Mike and Steve. Sumptuous food, but food that comes from a big heart. From two big hearts, in fact—from their idea of sharing the pleasures of the table. This is food as connector, the comradeship of tearing flatbread—blistered and still burning hot from the oven—together and wiping it through fire-roasted eggplant. So much to look at, to breathe in, to eat. So much well-being. Your heart swells and your eyes tear with the splendor of such generosity.

CHAPTER 11

DAUGHTERS & MOTHERS

SHE KNOWS A DOZEN WAYS to tie a scarf. She can wear a hat! She's undaunted by fashion. Every day, in every way, she is put together. Hell, even her eight-year-old son, Aster, is put together, in an appropriately offhand way. In her almost twelve years as director of Gracie Mansion during the Bloomberg administration, she would easily pull off a barbecue for a thousand people on the mayor's lawn for, say, the Parks Department; entertain the likes of Bishop Desmond Tutu; have the city council to breakfast. Yet my forty-something stepdaughter, Sandrine, who grew up in my house since the age of ten, is not at home in the kitchen.

I've kept a paper menu from New York's old Café Un Deux Trois, where I drew for her—with the crayons they scattered on each paper tablecloth—a pictograph of each dish (upside down, as I recall, since she was sitting across from me). She was born in France (she's been here since she was three), but this little French girl didn't know much about food. (Once, as a teenager, she called from Paris complaining that there was no smoked mozzarella or sun-dried tomatoes.) So, I drew the soupe à l'oignon with canary-yellow cheese sizzling in its earthenware marmite; and lipstick-pink slices of pâté maison surrounded by electric-green lettuce; and platters of salade niçoise, with black olives and cherry-red tomato quarters; and parsley-flecked escargots in their brown shells; and the inevitable rosy steak frites. I explained the entire menu in living Crayola so she'd know what to order. So she'd understand what she was eating. I guess explaining matters to me; I'm still doing it.

Shortly after we all moved in together, I cooked a first meal: diminutive Rock Cornish game hens stuffed with wild rice and apricots. I thought it was a pretty adorable choice for a kid. But Sandrine, who may not have thought much about food but by age ten already knew what she liked, announced after one bite, "We French do not like to mix sucré and salé"—sweet and salty. Took my breath away. My appetite, too. When she bit into a slice of the first roast chicken I made for her, Sandrine didn't miss a beat: "Trop sec!" she declared. Too dry! Clearly there was more than just cooking going on in those early eating skirmishes. She was settling in. Settling down. Claiming her territory. Claiming healthy defiance. We laugh about it now.

Decades later, when talking about this book, Sandrine told me, "I want you to be my Kitchen Whisperer. I need you to convince me to stick to cooking and not give in to the easier solution of ordering in. When I'm tired and just getting home from work, I know that cooking for my family is better, and healthier, but I'm not confident about how to pull off quick meals without a recipe. When I discover something I like— say, fennel—I'll make fennel salad every day. Four days in a row. Lewis has to tell me: 'Enough with the fennel salad.'

"I don't like to follow recipes. My brain is not structured

that way. I can't seem to master mise en place. Then I get frustrated and forget what I'm doing. But if I am using a recipe, I do need to know what to substitute when I'm inevitably missing an ingredient. I would love to be able to enjoy cooking more. I like the idea of cozying up to being in the kitchen; I have my music playing. It's warm. I do find some joy there, but I am not like you. Sometimes," she confesses, "I cook just to use up ingredients. And sometimes there's just too much going on in my head to like cooking."

Sandrine is looking for magic-bullet answers, when, like many of us, the only thing she really needs to learn is to slow down. And I am trying to not dwell on why she did not learn to do that hanging out in my kitchen.

ONE AFTERNOON, ALARMINGLY LATE IN my writing process and unannounced, nine pages of text suddenly appear on my phone. Dated more than a decade ago, and just discovered by Sandrine in some random box, the pages, written in my script and complete with my drawings, are cooking lessons from a trip to the supermarket we made where I endeavored to make her lighten up on some basic cooking principles. Sketches of endive and escarole and red buttercrunch lettuce were there, to help with the "lots of crunchy salads" she wanted to make. There was a page called "The Chuka Chuka Lesson—or how to sear a chicken breast and not cook the living daylights out of it." She still mimics my example of a straight hand rotating quickly, and the sound of a chicken breast being quickly sautéed on each side: *chuka chuka.* Under a drawing of a tongue licking a spoon I'd written: "*Tasting.* Gotta figure out how to convince you how important tasting your way as you go is to the process of cooking. You seem freaked out by it, as if tasting is too intimate, or scary, or too much of an intrusion. You learn to taste olive oil [drawing of bottle] for freshness by turning the open bottle onto your palm and licking it." This evidence only proves that our current conversation has been going on for much of her life.

"Did you ever even cook anything from those lessons?" I text her back.

"I may have made the chicken. Chuka chuka."

IF I WERE NOT SO wary of adding to the noise in her head, I'd tell Sandrine, Be calm and *just cook.* You worry about it too much. You think that cooking is a mysterious skill. You fret that you don't know the secrets; you fear that you don't have the elusive 'It.' But you *do* know how you want your food to taste. You have a great palate. Cooking well is just figuring out how to get there. Cooking happens in the doing and in the doing over and over again, until it *becomes* the dance. Repetition makes mastery. *There is no magic involved!* Cooking does not happen without thinking. Thinking hard. Thinking ahead. Imagining ingredients and visualizing how they work together. Remember how you learned to parallel park!

"Recipes can hang you up," I want her to know. "They can make you doubt yourself; interrupt what you value as 'the flow.' Recipes have all the allure of an algebra equation. You think that because they're written with precise measurements, they must have all the answers. They don't. Recipes are only best guesses. Recipes can be false friends, road signs that can wind up pointing you in the wrong direction. They frequently emphasize technique and obscure the goal. Like instructions on a GPS, recipes may do a good job of telling you where you are, but they do not always tell you how to get to . where you want to go. Only experience can do that. A recipe is a road map. Only after you've made the dish, and made it again, does it begin to look like the place itself."

WHEN WE STARTED SAVEUR MAGAZINE, my hope was that we'd write our recipes as long narratives; tell them fully as the stories they are. I wanted our recipes to show readers how to find their way to the heart of a dish. And we did try that, but recipes written that way became mini-novellas—about six times too long to print. Which proves my point, in a way. Recipes are the shorthand version of the journey. CliffsNotes. They lack juice!

I want Sandrine to know that there is no substitute for just doing it. To understand that cooking is cutting your way through the jungle, so that when you pass this way again— and you will—you'll recognize the path and have a much better idea of how to get there. Precise measurements do not really matter (unless, of course, you're baking). I need to reassure her (though I'm loath to lecture) that she will eventually get to a point where she'll see where she's going in her mind, come to feel cooking in her fingertips. She'll actually imagine how that food should taste, and instinctively know what combination of ingredients will get her there. Sandrine gets nervous because she believes she must follow directions, but like the math homework she struggled with in high school, those recipes make sense only in the result.

Sandrine believes good cooks are effortless in the kitchen, but,

I gently remind her, that's because good cooks put themselves totally in the zone. They may look like they're just moving around the room, but their minds are working overtime, always thinking, thinking, thinking. I know this because I've been fortunate enough to work with many of them. Good cooks are considered and focused—each move leads inevitably to the next. That's what they're doing when you watch them: they may look casual, but they're totally in their heads. Super intentional. Always pondering their next steps; always one move ahead. What matters is to keep imagining where you're going. Like driving, it only looks automatic.

Jacques Pépin once made gentle fun of Americans' cooking, telling me, "Today people buy skinless breasts of chicken, toss them in a nonstick pan, add pre-sliced mushrooms and pre-washed spinach from a bag, and say they're cooking from scratch. In my time, cooking from scratch might have started with finding the wood to make a fire to heat the stove. Then managing that heat. Maybe you even had to catch the chicken first, and pluck it, and cook it in a pan where everything stuck. You had to be careful."

I want Sandrine to watch the classic YouTube video of Jacques Pépin making an omelet—four million others have—and listen to his running commentary. "His voice will be familiar; when he speaks English, he sounds just like your uncle Laurent." "But he's a *chef*!" she'll object. "Sure," I'll agree. "But he's an effortless, generous home cook, too. Conversational. Always instructive." Pépin's omelet-making is a perfect example of everything that cooking takes. Watch as he pays careful attention to every single move he makes. Watch the way the pan becomes an extension of his arm. See how he pierces each yolk with a fork, all the better to beat them, and notice that he stirs the eggs in the pan with the same fork he's beaten them with. He's done those moves a thousand times; he has them in his blood. But, and this is key: *He does not wing it.* He gives his cooking the attention it deserves. It is that simple. And that complicated.

LAST NIGHT, HOPING TO ILLUSTRATE for Sandrine my cooking-is-thinking theory, I decided to write down everything that went through my head as I made a simple supper. I was glad my brain was not broadcasting those thoughts, because I sounded like a crazy person. In the freezer, I had some tortelloni, silky rounded domes of handmade (not by me!) pasta filled with lemon ricotta. But what did I need to turn them into dinner? There was fresh spinach in the fridge. And heavy cream. I decided on the torts in a spinach cream sauce. Here's how it went in my mind:

Boil water for pasta in a smallish pot (because the roiling water in a big one could break the torts). How big a skillet do I need for the sauce? Don't want to crowd the delicate torts when I spoon them in. Bigger skillet! Heat it first? Butter or olive oil? Start with which alliums? Scallions? Shallots? Do I have a leek? Wash that fresh spinach really well. So much dirt still on the leaves. Trim off those skinny stems. Any reason to save the stems for stock? Well, I just froze a bunch of veg stock. Bit of guilt, but nope. Toss 'em. Drain spinach but keep a little water on the leaves. How much water? Wait for the pasta water to boil. Remember what Marcella says and don't salt the water until it's boiling. Should I add a bay leaf? Couldn't hurt. Carefully spoon a few tortelloni at a time into the boiling water. Keep the boil gentle; don't want to break up those delicate torts. What's happening in the skillet? I'll add butter to the oil in the pan to mellow the sauce. Then add the spinach. Not all at once, but quickly, careful not to lose that deep green color and texture. Squeeze half a lemon over the spinach. Can't find the lemon. Okay, got it. Roll it. Slice it. Squeeze it. Dig a whole nutmeg out of the jar and grate a few passes over the wilted spinach. Now pour in some heavy cream and swirl it around the skillet. Is that enough cream? A bit more will make it saucier. But not too thick! Keep the heat low. Stir really gently. Can't let the spinach wither away to nothing. Get out some shallow soup bowls. Fish a tort out of the pasta water. Carry it, dripping, to the cutting board. Cut into it to test. Taste. Hot! Is it soft enough? Yup. And it will cook a bit more in the spinach cream. Now, where's that big slotted spoon to transfer the tortelloni into the sauce in the skillet? Only a few at a time. Let a bit of the pasta water cling to the torts to thicken the sauce. Do this gently! Careful not to break those delicate pockets! Add another spoonful of pasta water. Now swirl the skillet, bathing the torts in the spinach and cream mixture. Spoon the spinach sauce over the torts so they get to know each other. Let the sauce cook down a bit. Grate a bit more nutmeg over the pan. And some salt and pepper. Where are those soup bowls? And where's that hunk of Parm to grate?

SANDRINE AND I ATTEMPT AN apple pie with the early McIntoshes we picked from an orchard nearby. Intending to make dessert to bring to a friend's house for dinner, we are both picturing the croustades we've seen Christopher produce as easily as a sneeze, before we'd even unpacked the day's shopping: lovely burnished golden crust flung around those apples like a cashmere shawl; perfectly concentric rows of apple slices—demilunes—their surfaces fairly glowing with caramelized sugar.

That apple tart glistening in the window of a Parisian patisserie is what we have in our heads. Sandrine oversleeps her afternoon nap. I get distracted making a potato salad. Time goes out for a walk. When, an hour before our departure, we finally read the directions on the package of frozen puff pastry sheets, we discover that it should have been thawed overnight. Okay. Plan B. We paw through her crowded freezer and find two frozen pie shells. Good save. They'll defrost in twenty minutes. Companionably, we peel and slice the apples, add butter to a skillet, then the sliced apples, then lemon juice, sugar, and cinnamon.

Giggling, we pile the aromatic softened apple slices high in the now-thawed pie shell. Then, at the same time, we both say, "What about using the other pastry shell to make a lattice?" Great idea. Only problem, the pastry is too thick to weave. Only problem, it breaks. "How do we do this?" she asks. "I dunno!" I cry. "You're the one with three French grandmothers! How can you not know how to make a tarte aux pommes?"

QUARANTINED IN UPSTATE NEW YORK with her husband, and their son, Sandrine has no choice but to cook, and to cook every day. To be careful with the ingredients she can buy and mindful about how to use them. During her first weeks upstate, the texts keep coming:

"What is almond flour?"

My heart sinks, recognizing online recipe tyranny. Too complicated to even explain. She shouldn't even be messing with that stuff.

"Really finely ground almonds."

"What can I substitute?"

"Flour."

"What do I do with leftover pork roast?"

"Do you have canned beans?"

"Canned beans?"

My heart sinks again.

Then, gradually, as the weeks—and then the months—go by; as the need to cook becomes regular and inevitable, Sandrine begins to lighten up. Just gets on with it. She cooks. Makes meatballs from good ground beef.

"How were the meatballs?"

"So good I had three portions!"

She was liking her own cooking!

More texts: "Why do you coat beef in flour before you make a stew?" instigates our first substantive cooking discussion— about the difference between a braise and a stew and the role liquid plays.

Last night she couldn't stop eating her beef stew as we FaceTimed.

She tells me she imagined, then actually made, a fresh, herby chimichurri sauce in the blender.

"I started with lots of fresh herbs, then added anchovies. I kept going until I got the green tanginess of the sauce that was in my head. I just tasted my way there."

"Quarantine is turning you into a cook."

"I know," she agrees, smiling.

ACKNOWLEDGMENTS

———— ✎ ————

A book like this is nothing without the family, friends, and colleagues I'm so fortunate to be surrounded by. The idea itself was wrestled into reality from my early thoughts by the very tenacious David Black, to whom I am (almost always) grateful. "DK! These people are walking around with secrets!" His quote is stuck to my computer. Next, it took an editor who really connected with the message, and Cassie Jones, with her heartfelt, gentle guidance and positive spirit, proved the perfect partner. I'm grateful to Danny Meyer for his lightning-fast understanding of the subject and for his graceful foreword. And to Christopher Hirsheimer for the radiant cover image.

Then the Whisperers, the unwitting subjects of this book: those no longer among us, Gil Kalins, Lola Mae Autry, and Marcella Hazan. And those vivid friends whose generosity and talent I celebrate: Colman Andrews, Christopher Hirsheimer, David Tanis, Michael Anthony, Anita Lo, Patty Gentry, Mike Solomonov and Steven Cook, and Sandrine Lago. And Melissa Hamilton, Tom McNamee, Miles Chapin, and Lincoln Sherman. And to the authors of the books I've cited in the bibliography, whose particular wisdom is a constant inspiration.

Big thanks to my helpful first readers: the forever clever Stevie Pierson, Jordana Rothman, Pamela Fiori, and Colman

Andrews. And to Don Morris, Maura McEvoy, Joan Nathan, Joe Armstrong, Kathy Brennan. Jim Autry, Martha Lynn Crawford, and Randal Breski.

At William Morrow/HarperCollins, special thanks to the always helpful Jill Zimmerman, designers Mumtaz Mustafa and Bonni Leon-Berman, production manager Andrew DiCecco, production editor Rachel Meyers, and copyeditor Sibylle Kazeroid.

And a worldful of gratitude to Roger Sherman, whose face I studied as he reacted to every word he read, and who, with humor and kindness, lived through a pandemic year and more with me and this manuscript.

BIBLIOGRAPHY

———— ❧ ————

Adler, Tamar. *An Everlasting Meal: Cooking with Economy and Grace.* Scribner. 2011.

Admony, Einat, and Janna Gur. *Shuk: From Market to Table, the Heart of Israeli Home Cooking.* Artisan. 2019.

Andrés, José. *Tapas: A Taste of Spain in America.* Clarkson Potter. 2005.

Andrews, Colman. *Catalan Cuisine: Europe's Last Great Culinary Secret.* Atheneum. 1988.

————. *Everything on the Table: Plain Talk About Food and Wine.* Bantam. 1992.

————. *Flavors of the Riviera: Discovering Real Mediterranean Cuisine.* Bantam. 1996.

————. *The Country Cooking of Ireland.* Chronicle. 2009.

————. *Ferran Adrià: The Inside Story of El Bulli and the Man Who Reinvented Food.* Gotham Books. 2010.

————. *The Country Cooking of Italy.* Chronicle. 2011.

————. *The Taste of America.* Phaidon. 2013.

————. *My Usual Table: A Life in Restaurants.* Ecco. 2014.

————. *The British Table: A New Look at the Traditional Cooking of England, Scotland, and Wales.* Abrams. 2016.

Anthony, Michael, with a history by Danny Meyer. *The Gramercy Tavern Cookbook.* Clarkson Potter. 2013.

————. with Dorothy Kalins. *V is for Vegetables.* Little, Brown. 2015.

Attlee, Helena. *The Land Where Lemons Grow: The Story of Italy and Its Citrus Fruit.* The Countryman Press. 2015.

Autry, Ewart A. and Lola M. *Don't Look Back Mama.* Maverick. 1979.

Autry, James A. *Nights Under a Tin Roof: Recollections of a Southern Boyhood*. Yoknapatawpha Press. 1983.

Autry, Lola Mae. *Please, God, I'm a City Girl. What Am I Doing in the Country?* Xulon. 2004.

Bailey, Freddie. *Aunt Freddie's Pantry: Southern-Style Preserves, Jellies, Chutneys, Conserves, Pickles, Relishes, Sauces . . . and What Goes with Them*. Clarkson Potter. 1984.

Bailey, Lee. *The Way I Cook*. Clarkson Potter. 1996.

Brillat-Savarin, Jean Anthelme, trans. Fisher, M. F. K. *The Physiology of Taste*. Alfred A. Knopf. 1971.

Bruni, Frank, and Jennifer Steinhauer. *A Meatloaf in Every Oven: Two Chatty Cooks, One Iconic Dish and Dozens of Recipes—from Mom's to Mario Batali's*. Grand Central. 2017.

Buford, Bill. *Heat: An Amateur's Adventures as a Kitchen Slave, Line Cook, Pasta-Maker, and Apprentice to a Dante-Quoting Butcher in Tuscany*. Alfred A. Knopf. 2006.

———. *Dirt: Adventures in Lyon as a Chef in Training, Father, and Sleuth Looking for the Secret of French Cooking*. Alfred A. Knopf. 2020.

Cardoz, Floyd. *One Spice, Two Spice: American Food, Indian Flavors*. William Morrow. 2006.

———. *Floyd Cardoz: Flavorwalla*. Artisan. 2016.

Carey, Benedict. *How We Learn: The Surprising Truth About When, Where, and Why It Happens*. Random House. 2014.

Child, Julia, Louisette Bertholle, and Simone Beck. *Mastering the Art of French Cooking*, Volume One. Alfred A Knopf. 1961.

Child, Julia, and Simone Beck. *Mastering the Art of French Cooking*, Volume Two. Alfred A. Knopf. 1968.

Claiborne, Craig. *A Feast Made for Laughter*. Doubleday. 1982.

Clark, Eleanor. *The Oysters of Locmariaquer*. Pantheon Books. 1965.

Cunningham, Marion. *The Fannie Farmer Cookbook*, 12th edition, revised by Marion Cunningham, Alfred A. Knopf. 1984.

———. *Lost Recipes: Meals to Share with Friends and Family*. Alfred A. Knopf. 2003.

Donovan, Lisa. *Our Lady of Perpetual Hunger*. Penguin Press. 2020.

Edge, John T. *The Potlikker Papers: A Food History of the Modern South*. Penguin. 2017.

Garutti, Randy, and Mark Rosati. *Shake Shack: Recipes & Stories.* Clarkson Potter. 2017.

Gordinier, Jeff. *Hungry: Eating, Road-Tripping, and Risking It All with the Greatest Chef in the World.* Tim Duggan Books. 2019.

Gray, Rose, and Ruth Rogers. *River Café Cook Book Green.* Ebury Press. 2000.

Greenberg, Paul. *Four Fish: The Future of the Last Wild Food.* Penguin. 2010.

Harris, Jessica B. *Beyond Gumbo: Creole Fusion Food from the Atlantic Rim.* Simon & Schuster. 2003.

———. *My Soul Looks Back.* Scribner. 2017.

Hazan, Marcella. *The Classic Italian Cook Book: The Art of Italian Cooking and the Italian Art of Eating.* Alfred A. Knopf. 1973.

———. *More Classic Italian Cooking.* Alfred A. Knopf. 1978

———. *Marcella's Italian Kitchen.* Alfred A. Knopf. 1995.

———. *Marcella Cucina.* HarperCollins. 1997.

———. *Marcella Says . . . : Italian Cooking Wisdom from the Legendary Teacher's Master Classes, with 120 of Her Irresistible New Recipes.* HarperCollins. 2004.

———. *Amarcord: Marcella Remembers.* Gotham. 2008

———. *Essentials of Classic Italian Cooking.* Alfred A. Knopf. 2012.

Hazan, Marcella, and Victor Hazan. *Ingredienti: Marcella's Guide to the Market.* Scribner. 2016.

Hirsheimer, Christopher, and Melissa Hamilton. *Canal House Cooking,* Volume No 7, *La Dolce Vita.* Canal House. 2011.

———. *Canal House Cooks Every Day.* Andrews, McMeel. 2012.

———. *Canal House Cooking,* Volume No 8, *Pronto!* Canal House. 2013.

———. *Cook Something: Recipes to Rely On.* Voracious, Little Brown. 2019.

Hovav, Gil. *Candies from Heaven.* Toad Publishing. 2017.

Jenkins, Allan. *Plot 29.* 4th Estate. 2017.

Kander, Mrs. Simon, and Mrs. Henry Schoenfeld. *The Settlement Cook Book.* The Settlement Cook Book Co. 1951.

Kennedy, Diana. *The Art of Mexican Cooking.* Clarkson Potter. 1989.

Kurlansky, Mark. *Cod: A Biography of the Fish That Changed the World*. Penguin. 1998.

———. *The Basque History of the World*. Penguin. 2000.

Ladies Village Improvement Society of East Hampton. *The East Hampton Cookbook of Menus and Recipes*. 1975.

———. *A Full Century of Tip of the Island Cooking Wisdom, 1896 to 1996*. 1996.

Lo, Anita. *Cooking Without Borders*. Stewart, Tabori & Chang. 2011.

———. *Solo: A Modern Cookbook for a Party of One*. Alfred A. Knopf. 2018.

Marks, Gil. *Encyclopedia of Jewish Food*. John Wiley & Sons. 2010.

McNamee, Thomas. *Alice Waters and Chez Panisse: The Romantic, Impractical, Often Eccentric, Ultimately Brilliant Making of a Food Revolution*. Penguin. 2007.

———. *The Man Who Changed the Way We Eat: Craig Claiborne and the American Food Renaissance*. Free Press. 2012.

Meyer, Danny. *Setting the Table: The Transforming Power of Hospitality in Business*. HarperCollins. 2006.

Nathan, Joan. *Jewish Cooking in America*, expanded edition. Alfred A. Knopf. 2006.

———. *The Foods of Israel Today*. Alfred A. Knopf. 2010.

———. *King Solomon's Table: A Culinary Exploration of Jewish Cooking from Around the World*. Alfred A. Knopf. 2017.

Pierson, Stephanie. *The Brisket Book*. Andrews McMeel. 2011.

Raviv, Yael. *Falafel Nation: Cuisine and the Making of National Identity in Israel*. University of Nebraska Press. 2015.

Robbins, Missy. *Breakfast, Lunch, Dinner . . . Life: Recipes and Adventures from My Home Kitchen*. Rizzoli. 2017.

Rosso, Julee, and Sheila Lukins. *The Silver Palate Cookbook*. Workman. 1979.

———. *Silver Palate Cookbook, 25th Anniversary Edition*. Workman. 2007.

By the Editors of *Saveur* Magazine:

Saveur Cooks Authentic American. Chronicle. 1998.

Saveur Cooks Authentic French. Chronicle. 1999.

Saveur Cooks Authentic Italian. Chronicle. 2001.

Schank, Roger C. *The Connoisseur's Guide to the Mind: How We Think, How We Learn, and What It Means to Be Intelligent.* Summit Books. 1991.

Sercarz, Lior Lev. *The Art of Blending.* Lior Lev Sersarz & Ma'amoul Shop. 2012.

———. *The Spice Companion: A Guide to the World of Spices.* Clarkson Potter. 2016.

———. *Mastering Spice: Recipes and Techniques to Transform Your Everyday Cooking.* Clarkson Potter. 2019.

Severson, Kim. *Spoon Fed: How Eight Cooks Saved My Life.* Riverhead Books. 2010.

Solomonov, Michael, and Steven Cook. *Zahav: A World of Israeli Cooking.* Houghton Mifflin. 2015.

———. *Federal Donuts: The (Partially) True Spectacular Story.* Houghton Mifflin. 2017.

———. *Israeli Soul.* Houghton Mifflin. 2018.

Stitt, Frank. *Frank Stitt's Southern Table.* Artisan. 2004.

Sussman, Adeena. *Sababa.* Avery. 2019.

Stupak, Alex, and Jordana Rothman. *Tacos: Recipes and Provocations.* Clarkson Potter. 2015.

Tanis, David. *A Platter of Figs.* Artisan. 2008.

———. *Heart of the Artichoke.* Artisan. 2012.

———. *One Good Dish.* Artisan. 2013.

———. *David Tanis Market Cooking.* Artisan. 2017.

Thelin, Emily Kaiser. *Unforgettable: The Bold Flavors of Paula Wolfert's Renegade Life.* Mortar & Pestle. 2017.

Truong, Monique. *The Sweetest Fruits.* Viking. 2019.

Wechsberg, Joseph. *Blue Trout and Black Truffles: The Peregrinations of an Epicure.* Alfred A. Knopf. 1966.

Walls, Jeannette. *The Glass Castle.* Scribner. 2005.

Wells, Patricia, and Joël Robuchon. *Simply French.* William Morrow. 1991.

Wolfert, Paula. *Couscous and Other Good Food from Morocco.* Harper & Row. 1973.

————. *The Cooking of the Eastern Mediterranean*. HarperCollins. 1994.

————. *The Food of Morocco*. HarperCollins. 2011.

Women's Service Club. *The Neighborhood House Cookbook Food, Friends, and Neighbors*. East Hampton Neighborhood House. 1920–1922.